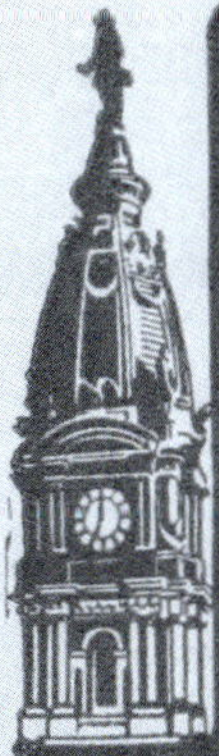

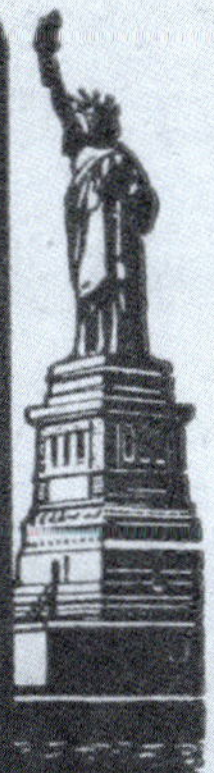

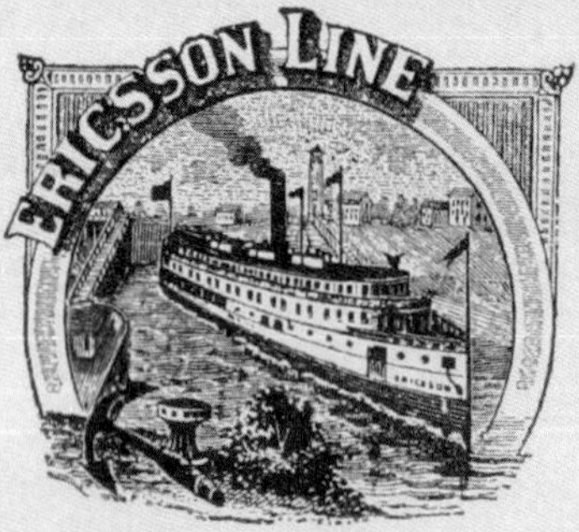

Excursion Tickets to Baltimore or Philadelphia, cabin, $2.50

Philadelphia to Betterton, $2.00

GOOD FOR FIFTEEN DAYS

NIGHT BOATS LEAVE PHILADELPHIA AND BALTIMORE EVERY DAY AT 5.00 P. M.

(Except Sundays, New Year's Day, Fourth of July, Thanksgiving, and Christmas.)

Arriving at each port early following morning. Weather permitting, landings will be made at Betterton (both ways) daily, and on Mondays and Wednesdays from Philadelphia, and Saturdays, Mondays, Thursdays, and Fridays from Baltimore, at Reybold's Wharf and Town Point Wharf.

Through tickets to Norfolk and Richmond, Va., also Washington, D. C., with privilege to return via boat or rail from Washington, D. C.

RATES OF FARE ONE WAY:

Cabin Tickets, $2.00 Deck Tickets, $1.50

State Rooms Extra

MEALS, 50 CENTS EACH.

Excursion tickets to and from all way landings for sale on steamers. All way freight must be prepaid. For special excursion rates for parties, clubs, etc., apply at office.

Additional Charges for Berths on all Excursion Tickets.

DAY BOAT

Fare, $1.50

Leave both Philadelphia and Baltimore at 7.30 a.m. daily, Sunday included, during June, July, August and September.

Excursion tickets to and from all way landings for sale on steamers.

For special excursion rates for parties, clubs, etc., apply at

Pier 3
South Delaware Ave.,
Philadelphia,

or 204 Light Street,
Baltimore.

PRICE 25 Cts

RAND, McNALLY & Co's

HANDY GUIDE TO

PHILADELPHIA

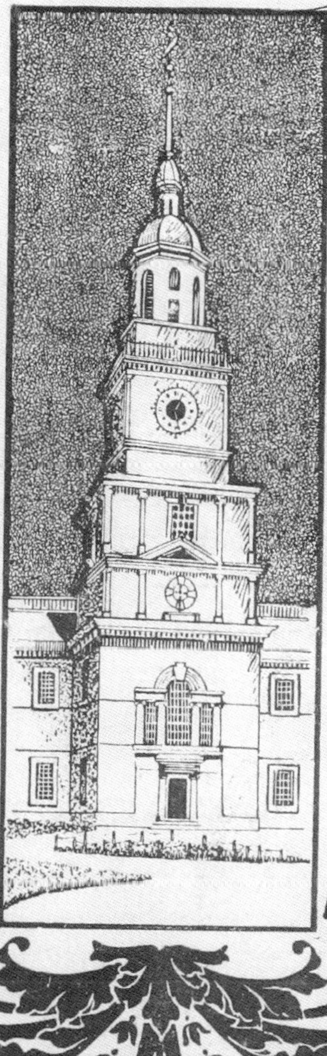

ATLANTIC CITY AND CAPE MAY

RAND. McNALLY & CO. PUBLISHERS.

Marula

An imprint of Arcadia Publishing

Rand, McNally & Co.'s Handy Guide to Philadelphia and Environs, Including Atlantic City and Cape May

A Marula Historical Reprint
Originally published in 1905

Published by Arcadia Publishing
Charleston SC

ISBN 978-0-7385-9478-1

Printed in the United States of America

For all general information contact Arcadia Publishing at:
Telephone 843-853-2070
Fax 843-853-0044
E-mail sales@arcadiapublishing.com
For customer service and orders:
Toll-Free 1-888-313-2665

Visit us on the Internet at www.arcadiapublishing.com

THE FREDONIA

FIRST-CLASS FAMILY HOTEL.

AMERICAN PLAN

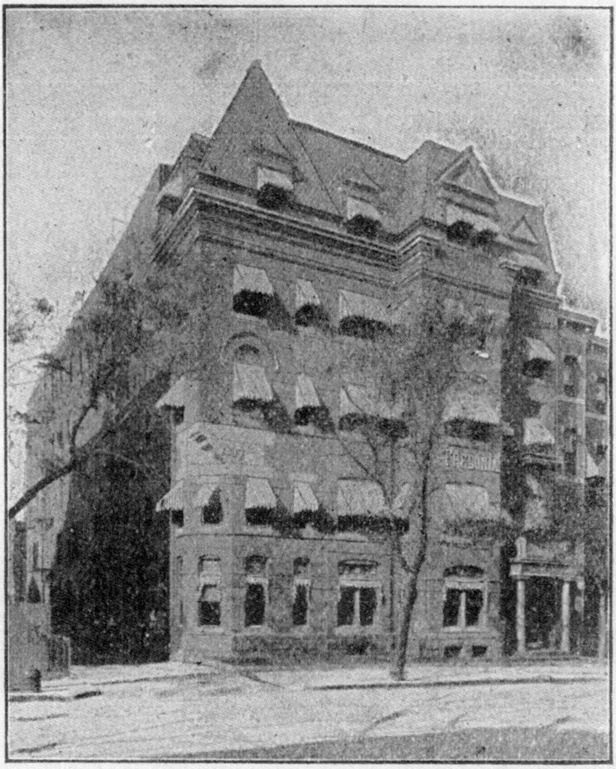

EUROPEAN PLAN

1321-1323 H Street, Northwest, WASHINGTON, D. C.

"THE FREDONIA HOTEL, A MODERN HOTEL HOME."

"The man without a home of his own will find this Hotel of 100 rooms the next best thing to it. It is **centrally located, thoroughly equipped with every modern appliance,** both for comfort and safety, **newly furnished throughout** from top to bottom, **convenient to all lines of cars,** and is in the **midst of many** of the city's most **prominent points of interest.** It is conducted upon both the **American and European** Plans and has a **cuisine not excelled** by any hostelry **in the city.**"

RATES.

American: **One person, $2.00** per day, **$12** per week, **$40** per month and upward. **Two persons, $3.50** per day, **$20** per week, **$75** per month and upward.

European: Rooms, **one person, $1** per day and upward. **Two persons, $1.50** per day and upward.

Special Excursion Rates will be quoted to parties of twenty or more upon application to

WM. W. DANENHOWER, Proprietor.

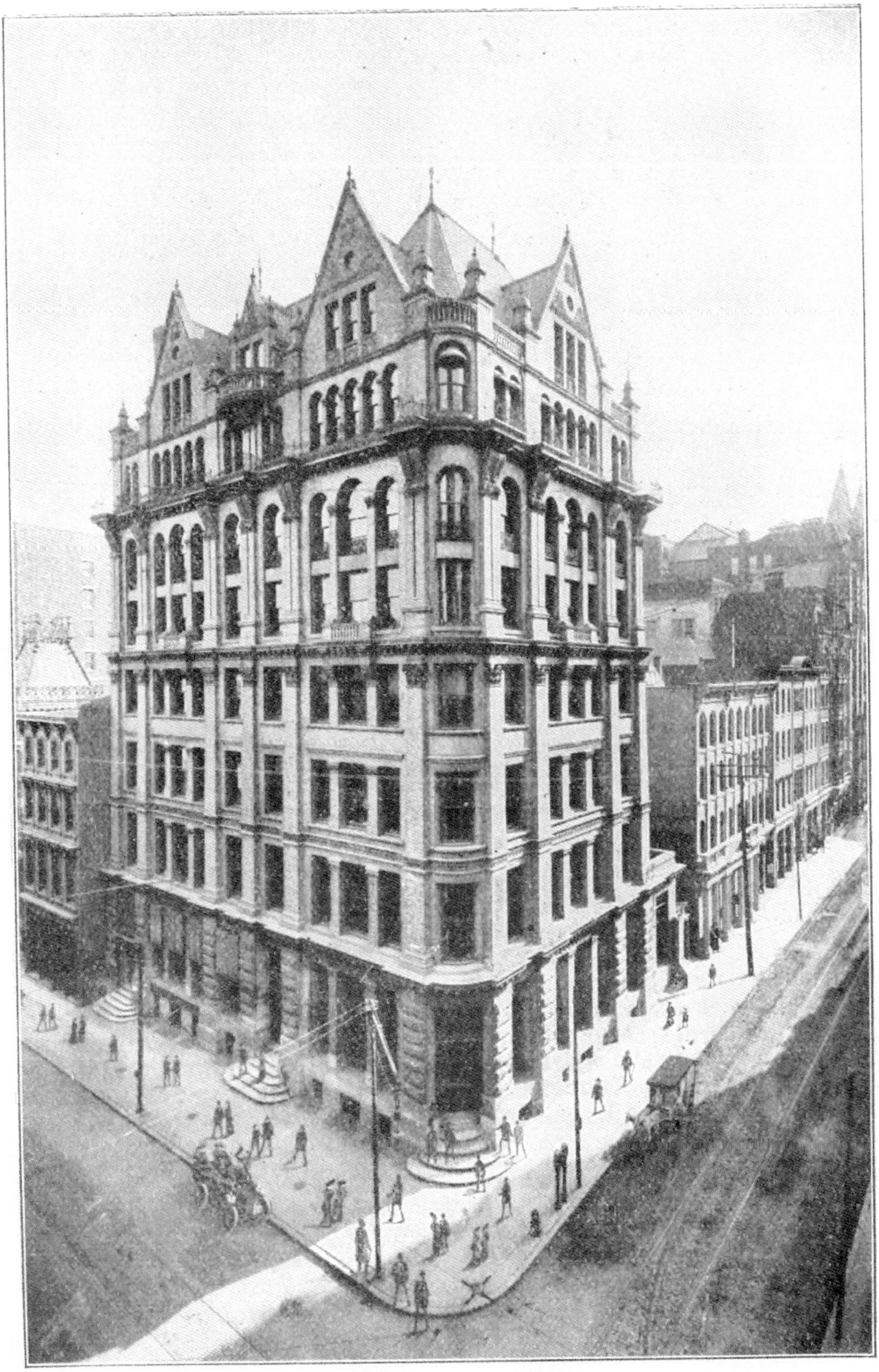

BROWN BROTHERS' BUILDING — Southwest Corner Fourth and Chestnut Streets.

RAND, McNALLY & CO.'S

HANDY GUIDE

TO

PHILADELPHIA

AND ENVIRONS

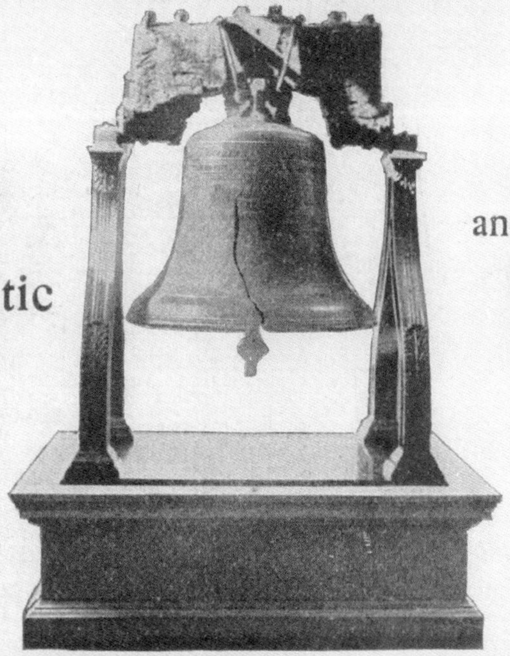

Including Atlantic City and Cape May

FOURTEENTH EDITION.

With Maps and Illustrations

CHICAGO AND NEW YORK:
RAND, McNALLY & CO., PUBLISHERS
1905

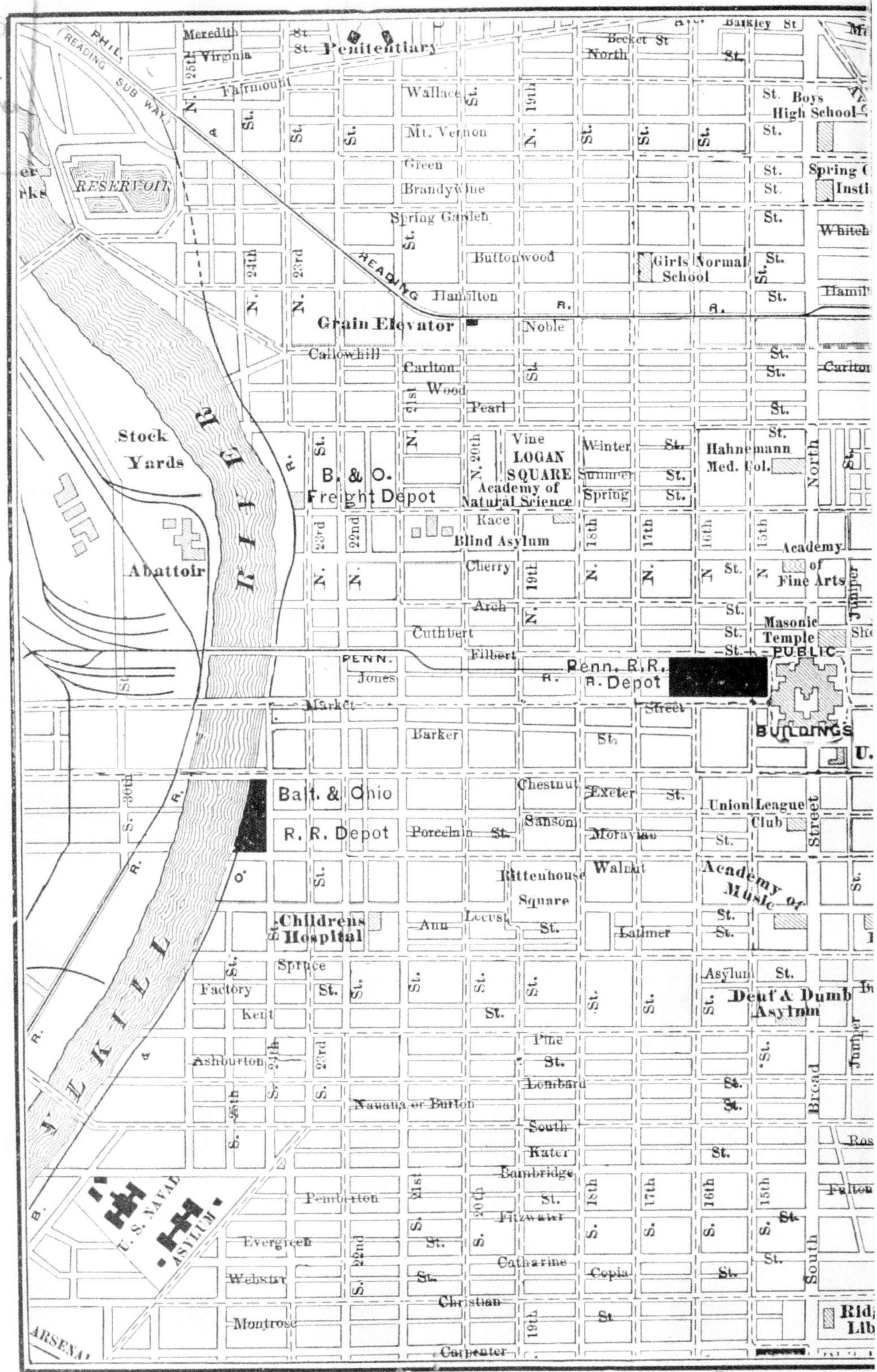
Penitentiary
Meredith
Virginia
Fairmount
Wallace
Mt. Vernon
Green
Brandywine
Spring Garden
Buttonwood
Hamilton
Noble
Callowhill
Carlton
Wood
Pearl
Vine
Winter
Summer
Spring
Race
Cherry
Arch
Cuthbert
Filbert
Jones
Market
Street
Barker
Chestnut
Exeter
Sansom
Moravian
Porcelain
Walnut
Locust
Ann
Latimer
Spruce
Factory
Kent
Pine
Ashburton
Lombard
Nanana or Burton
South
Kater
Bainbridge
Pemberton
Fitzwater
Evergreen
Catharine
Webster
Copia
Christian
Montrose
Carpenter
Becket St
North
Barkley St
Boys High School
Spring Garden Institute
Girls Normal School
RESERVOIR
READING SUB WAY
READING R. R.
Grain Elevator
Stock Yards
Abattoir
RIVER
SCHUYLKILL
B. & O. Freight Depot
LOGAN SQUARE
Academy of Natural Science
Blind Asylum
Hahnemann Med. Col.
Academy of Fine Arts
Masonic Temple
PUBLIC BUILDINGS
Penn. R.R. R. Depot
PENN. R.
Balt. & Ohio R. R. Depot
Union League Club
Rittenhouse Square
Academy of Music
Childrens Hospital
Asylum
Deaf & Dumb Asylum
U. S. NAVAL ASYLUM
ARSENAL
Broad
North
Juniper
South
Ridgway Library

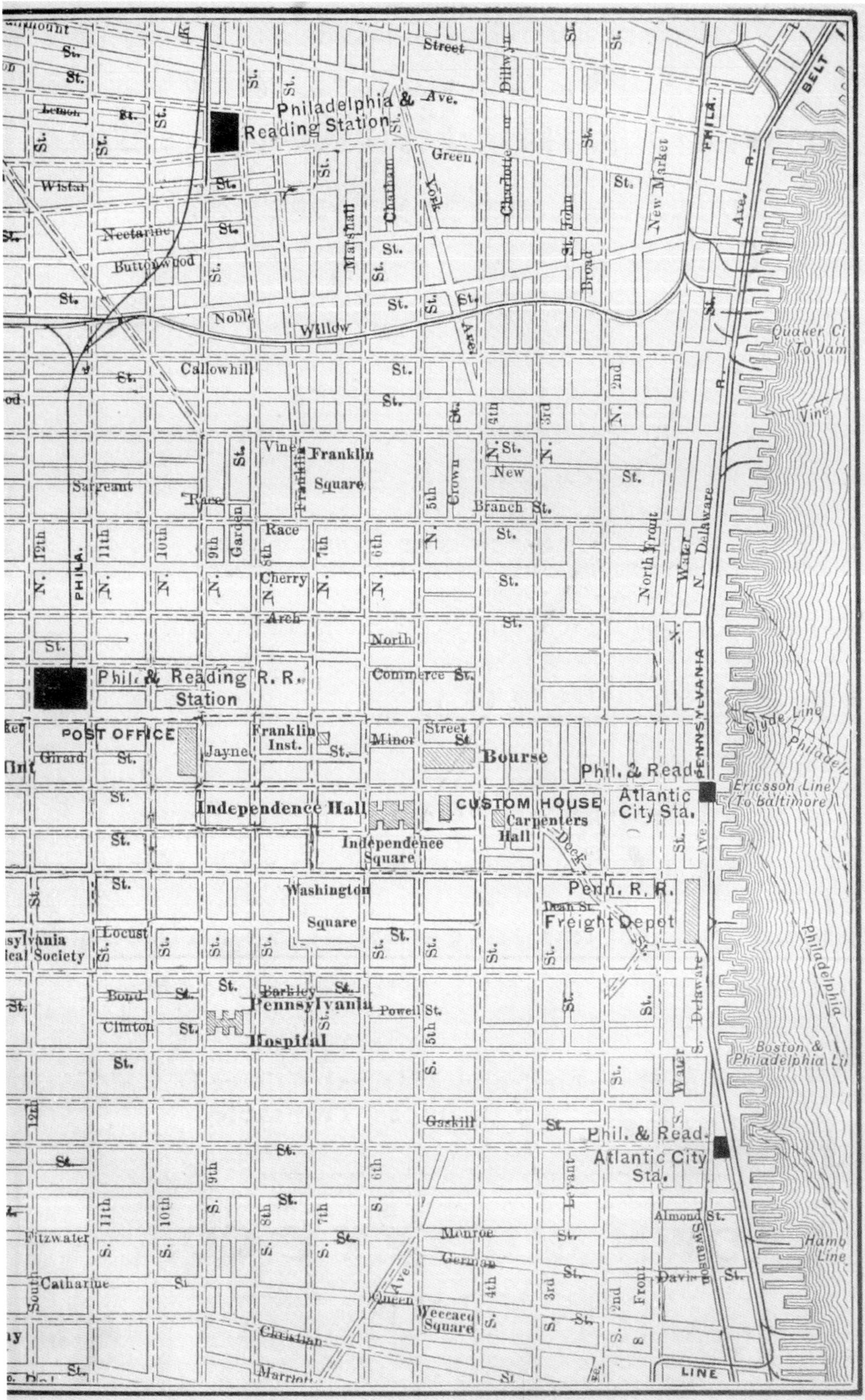
Philadelphia & Reading Station
Phil. & Reading R. R. Station
POST OFFICE
Franklin Square
Franklin Inst.
Bourse
CUSTOM HOUSE
Independence Hall
Independence Square
Carpenters Hall
Washington Square
Pennsylvania Hospital
Phil. & Read. Atlantic City Sta.
Penn. R. R. Freight Depot
Weccacoe Square
PENNSYLVANIA
PHILA.
BELT
LINE
Delaware Ave.
Quaker Ci (To Jam
Vine
Clyde Line
Philadelp
Ericsson Line (To Baltimore)
Philadelphia
Boston & Philadelphia Li
Hamb Line
Callowhill
Willow
Noble
Green
Wistar
Nectarine
Buttonwood
Vine
Race
Cherry
Arch
Sargeant
North
Commerce St.
Jayne
Minor
Girard
Locust
Bond
Clinton
Barkley
Powell St.
Gaskill
Monroe
German
Queen
Christian
Marriott
Fitzwater
Catharine
Almond St.
Davis St.
Swanson
Dock
Dean St.
Branch St.
New
Crown
Marshall
Chatham
York
Charlotte
Dillwyn
St. John
New Market
Broad
Levant
North Front
N. Water
N. Delaware
S. Water
S. Delaware
Mint
Pennsylvania Historical Society

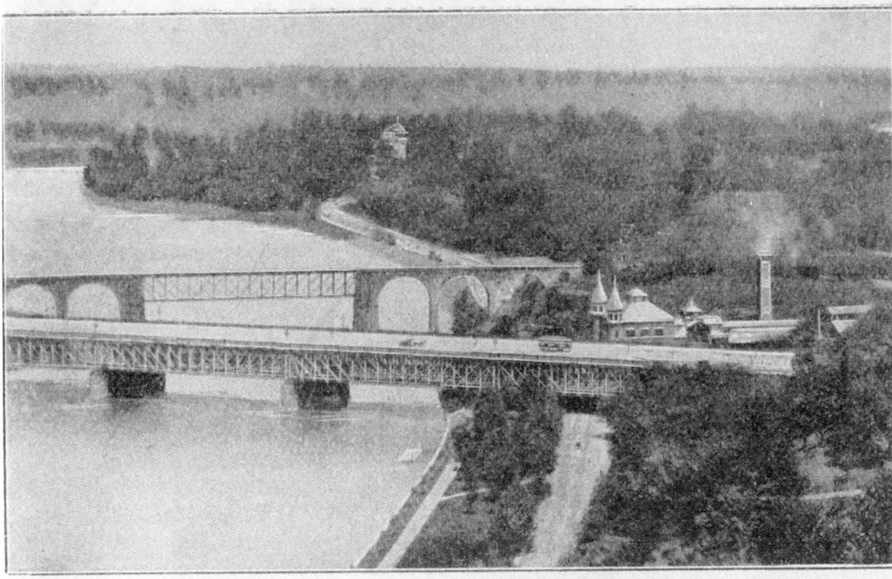

TABLE OF CONTENTS

I.

AN INTRODUCTION TO PHILADELPHIA.

Railroads and Depots.

Four great railroads have direct entrance into Philadelphia — the Pennsylvania, the Philadelphia & Reading, the Baltimore & Ohio, and the Lehigh Valley—which has through car service by the Reading. The three first named have terminals which for magnificence and comfort are unsurpassed in any other city in the country. All are within the heart of the city, and two are but three or four minutes' walk from most of the chief hotels and many of the greatest business houses.

The Pennsylvania Railroad Depot, at Broad and Market streets, is a splendid example of modern Gothic architecture. Directly opposite the new City Hall, its eleven stories of granite and brick, with terra cotta trimmings, add materially to the beauty of Philadelphia's chief public building. The main building of the depot has a frontage of 306 feet on Broad Street, and of 212 on Market. Beneath it runs Fifteenth Street, and on the north side, Filbert.

Trains enter and depart from this station over an elevated viaduct of solid brick arches, reaching nearly five squares west to the steel bridge over the Schuylkill. They run into the largest railroad train-shed in the world, not excepting anything of like construction in this country, or the St. Pancras, or other huge terminals, in London. It covers an area 707 feet long, 307 feet wide, and is 140 feet in height; the main arches have a clear span of 294 feet at track level, and a clear height of 141 feet. The entire structure, with its 60,000,000 pounds of iron, presents the appearance of a gigantic sun parlor, for its extensive roof is largely composed of translucent glass in iron frames. The glass in the roof alone would cover an area of one and three-quarters acres.

This shed is on a level with the second or main floor of the building, which contains all the conveniences looked for in such a place, and some of the most comfortable and attractive waiting-rooms in the country. Two costly works of art in high stucco-relief, by Karl Bitter, enhance its beauty, principally the colossal panel "Transportation," which decorates the wall facing the grand staircase.

The conception as executed by the sculptor is a portrayal of the development of Transportation, in harmony with the purpose of the building. The artist has embodied the spirit or genius of his theme in the form of a female figure seated on a car, forming a part of a triumphal procession This figure is in the act of uniting the two hemispheres,—the East, represented by an Arab, old and infirm, together with a sprightly Japanese girl; the West, by a youth in Puritan garb, typifying the North, and, for the South, a woman in Spanish costume carrying fruit and flowers. The chariot on which the figure representing Transportation is seated is drawn by horses, guided by a young girl in the costume of the present time, symbolizing America. In front of the horses, leading the procession, is a group of children, one carrying the model of a locomotive, another the model of a steamboat, while the youngest child runs ahead with a model of an airship, indicating future methods of transportation. These children are under the watchful guidance of a dignified female figure. Following the North and South is a figure on horseback, in Spanish costume, who holds up a model of the Santa Maria, the first transport that came to this country. Following him, and bringing up the rear of the procession, are the early pioneer and the Indian, together with the emigrant's wagon drawn by oxen and driven by early settlers. A handsome clock surmounts this panel.

A second fine relief decorates the wall of the restaurant next the waiting-room; and another ornamental decoration of the main hall is the immense water-color map which covers the entire north wall.

The upper floors of the building are occupied by the general offices of the Pennsylvania Railroad, and are reached by elevators at the Market Street entrance.

The ground floor of the building contains the ticket offices, baggage-rooms, telegraph offices, etc., and a large covered space where will be found the Company's cabs and messengers.

The Philadelphia & Reading terminal building is at Twelfth and Market streets, and has won the admiration of all who have seen it. It fronts on Market Street 266 feet, and extends northward on Twelfth 107 feet. It is eight stories in height, built of New England granite to the second floor, and above that of pink-tinted brick and white terra cotta. The waiting-rooms are fitted in sumptuous style, and its patrons are provided with a fine restaurant, carriages, and every-

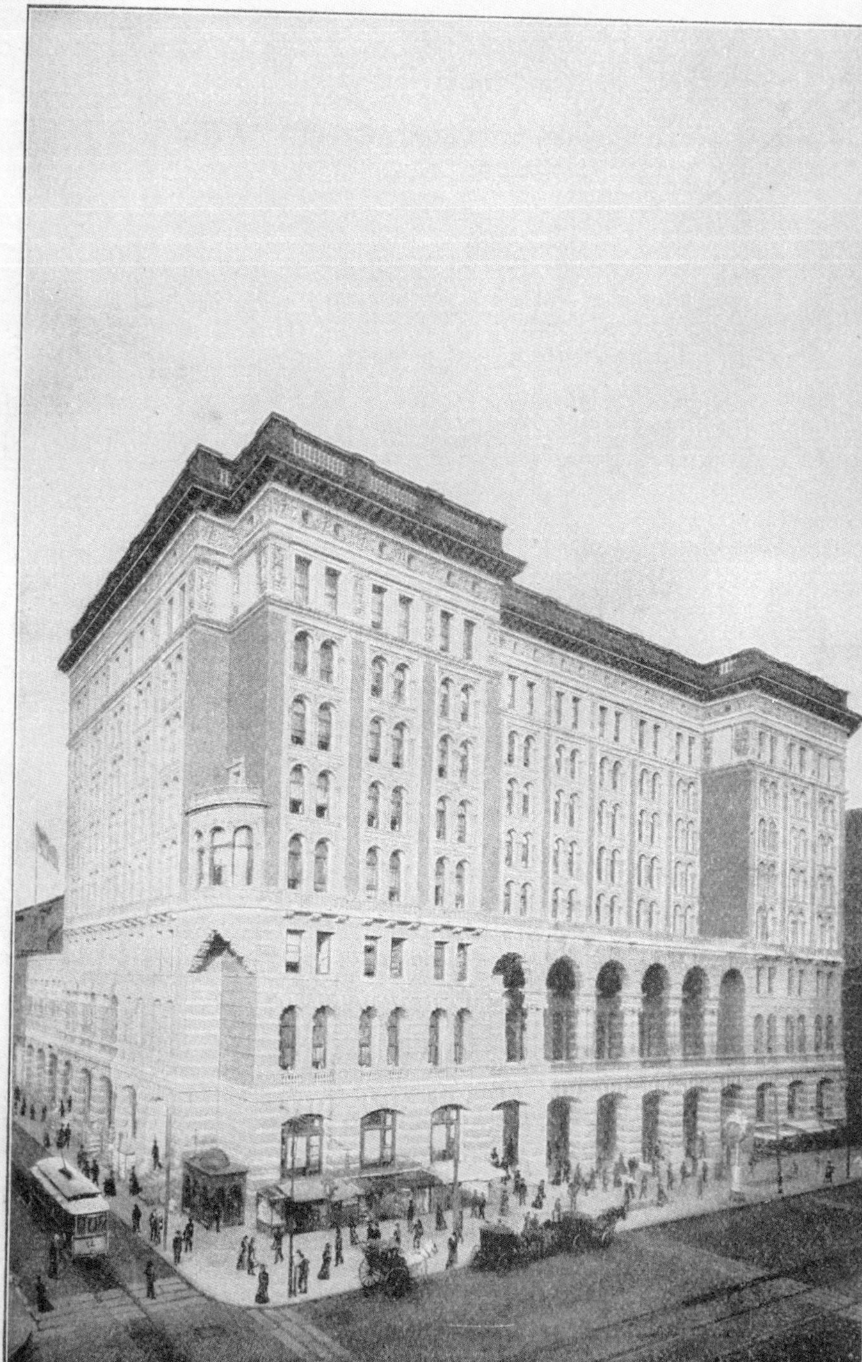

THE PHILADELPHIA & READING TERMINAL — 12th and Market Streets.

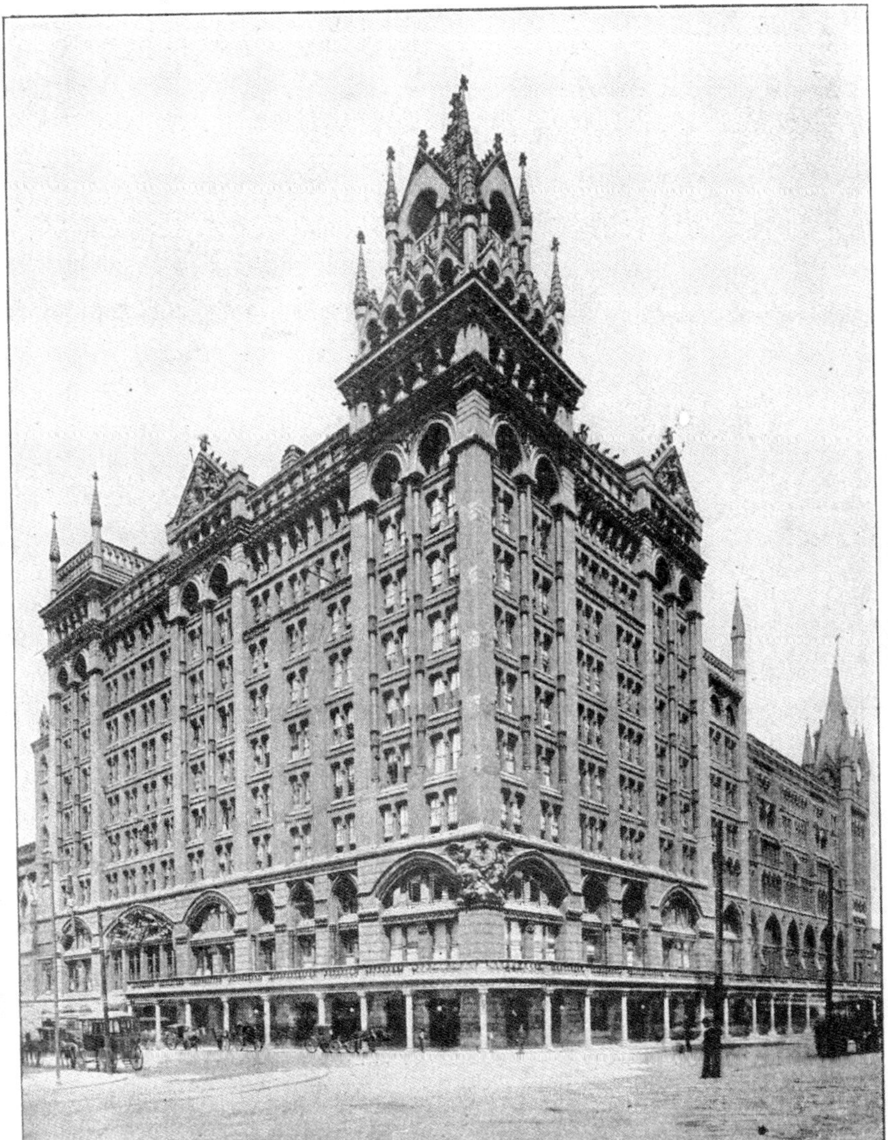

BROAD STREET STATION, PENNSYLVANIA RAILROAD,
Broad, Market, and Filbert Streets.

thing for their comfort and convenience. The train shed is 266 feet wide and 507 feet in length, extending to Arch Street. The great span covers sixteen tracks, besides wide asphalted platforms. A handsomely and solidly built elevated railroad extends northward to Callowhill Street, where it divides into two branches, one running toward Ninth Street, where it reaches the surface at Fairmount Avenue, and the other toward Broad, where at present it touches the ground a little to the east of that thoroughfare, not far north of Callowhill. The city has built a great subway from Broad Street to Fairmount Park, to connect with this branch of the elevated road, in order to do away with grade crossings at Broad Street and those lying to the westward. This branch also leads to the "Reading" main line, and is used also by incoming Baltimore & Ohio Royal Blue Line trains to New York. The Ninth Street Branch, besides being used by trains to Manayunk, Norristown, Germantown, Chestnut Hill, and points on the North Pennsylvania, Bound Brook, Northeast Pennsylvania, Lehigh Valley, and numerous other roads, is made use of by the outgoing trains of the Royal Blue Line to New York, and from that city to Philadelphia.

The Baltimore & Ohio Depot is at the southwest corner of Twenty-fourth and Chestnut streets, a short distance east of the Schuylkill River. A beautiful building in every way, the architects have taken advantage of an unfavorable situation to enhance, if anything, the pleasing effect of the structure. A tall clock tower forms a prominent landmark, and the general architecture harmonizes perfectly with the handsome Chestnut Street bridge, which spans the Schuylkill close by. As the tracks of the Baltimore & Ohio Railroad are depressed at this point, the general waiting-room is in the second story of the depot and on a level with Chestnut Street. The appointments are on a scale scarcely less magnificent than the depots of the Pennsylvania and the Reading railroads.

Lehigh Valley.—Although, theoretically speaking, the Lehigh Valley Railroad has no entrance into Philadelphia, in reality its facilities for taking passengers into the heart of the city are good, as the Lehigh Valley Company uses the station facilities of the Reading Terminal.

Other Depot Entrances.—Besides the three magnificent edifices noted, there are other depots for railroad entrance. Among them are those of the North Pennsylvania Railroad (Philadelphia & Reading System) at Third and Berks streets; Kensington; Market Street ferry for the many New Jersey branches of the Pennsylvania Railroad System, and Chestnut and South Street ferries for the Philadelphia & Reading System. For these, see below. Third and Berks and Kensington depots, however, are but little used, because the major part of the business has been transferred to Twelfth and Market and Broad and Market depots respectively. They are, moreover, remote from the center of the city, and offer few conveniences for travelers.

Baggage and Checks.

A uniformed and accredited solicitor, belonging to a transfer company, boards all incoming trains of the Pennsylvania and Philadelphia & Reading railroads and their interchangeable traffic lines, some distance out of town, and takes orders for the delivery of checked or other baggage. To him may be delivered the checks in exchange for a receipt, and the baggage therefor, or article handled, will be taken quickly to any point within the city limits for a moderate sum, which can be paid on delivery. Travelers going to hotels may also properly deliver their checks to the attendants of the various hotel omnibuses. Package-rooms are provided in every station, where hand luggage may be checked and left, at the rate of 10 cents a day for each piece for a limited number of days.

Outgoing Baggage.—When a person is ready to depart there are many baggage and express companies with call stations all over the city, who will come for the baggage and deliver it to any station desired for a small charge. If the person has purchased a railroad ticket, before the call is made, the expressman will furnish checks for the baggage, thus saving trouble or delay at the depot.

Ferries.

Directly opposite Philadelphia on the Delaware River, is Camden, N. J., connected with the city by several ferries, as follows:

Camden Ferries, from Market Street to Federal, and to Market Street, Camden, and to the Camden station of the West Jersey (Pennsylvania) Railroad.

Kaighn's Point Ferries, from Chestnut and from South Street to Kaighn's Point, Camden, and the station of the Atlantic City (Philadelphia & Reading) Railroad.

Vine Street Ferry, from Vine Street to Vine Street, Camden, and the station of the Camden & Atlantic (Pennsylvania) Railroad to Atlantic City.

Shackamaxon Street Ferry, from Shackamaxon Street to Vine Street, Camden, as above described.

Gloucester Ferry, from Arch Street and from South Street to Gloucester, N. J., (three miles).

Steamship Lines.

The owners of shipping in Philadelphia devote themselves chiefly to the transportation of freight, in which they do an enormous business with other countries and sister cities along the Atlantic and Pacific coasts. The list of transatlantic passenger lines follows:

Allan Line.—Pier 24, North Wharves, foot of Callowhill Street. Office, 421 Chestnut Street. To Glasgow, touching on western voyage at Liverpool, St. Johns, and Halifax.

American Line.—Piers 53 and 54, South Wharves, below Washington Avenue. Office, 305 Walnut Street. To Southampton from New York. Passengers from Philadelphia are given tickets to New York and embark there. The vessels of the American Line plying between Philadelphia and Liverpool carry second cabin passengers only, but these have the good fortune to be berthed in the first-cabin state-rooms, and have the use of accommodations usually accorded to tourists paying first-class fare; and embark and are landed at the company's piers as if they were first-class passengers.

Atlantic Transport.—Piers 41 and 43, South Wharves, foot of Washington Avenue. Office, 303 Walnut Street. To London and Swansea.

Hamburg-American.—Piers 41 and 44. Office, 425 Chestnut Street. To Hamburg, occasionally carrying passengers.

Red Star.—Pier 55, South Wharves, below Washington Avenue. Office, 305 and 307 Walnut Street. The Red Star Line steamers of the International Navigation Company, which leave this port fortnightly for Antwerp, also carry second-class and steerage passengers only, and, as on the American Line boats, the former are given nearly all the accommodations of first-class passengers. This line books first-cabin tourists for their vessels which sail every Wednesday from Pier 14, North River, New York, furnishing free transportation from Philadelphia to New York.

COASTWISE STEAMSHIPS.

Boston and Philadelphia.—Pier 20, South Wharves, Pine Street. Office, 338 S. Delaware Avenue. To Boston and Providence.

Clyde Line.—Pier 22, South Wharves, Pine Street. Office, 12 South Delaware Avenue. To Charleston and Jacksonville. This is the same company whose steamers are so well known as passenger boats between New York and the South, but passengers are not taken on the Philadelphia boats.

Ericsson Line.—Pier 3, foot of Chestnut Street. Office on the Pier. To Baltimore. The steamers of this popular line pass through Delaware & Chesapeake Canal, and during the summer months a day-boat is run, leaving Philadelphia at 7:30 a. m. The fare is low, the boats good, and the trip furnishes an interesting experience. The regular night-line, daily except Sunday, leaves each terminus at 5 p. m.

United Fruit Co. Line.—Pier 5, North Arch Street. Office on Pier. To Jamaica and West Indies. One of the new and well appointed steamers of this line sails every Thursday at 9 a. m., for Port Antonio, Jamaica, direct. The voyage covers about four and one-half days, and is a popular tourist trip to the West Indies.

Railroad Cabs and Vehicles.

The railroads have provided vehicles for those who prefer them to omnibuses or trolley cars. These hansoms and cabs are leased to the driver in charge, and are always to be had at the stands in or by the depots, and may be ordered by telephone to any point desired; they are intended for local city travel, and can not be hired for pleasure driving. A strict schedule of charges is arranged by the hour or by the mile, and it is highly important that this question be settled by the patron before starting, since if no agreement is made beforehand, the driver is privileged to charge either by the trip or by the mile, as suits him best.

To avoid disputes with the drivers, passengers should compute the whole distance traveled in squares—allowing ten squares to the mile—and multiply by the rate per mile for the services rendered, being careful to consider the number of addresses served. Patrons who order vehicles to call at their addresses will be required to pay one-half rates for the calls and full rates for the services—except within a radius of four squares from the Broad Street Station, in which case no charge will be made for calls. In ordering by telephone or messenger, patrons should state whether they desire the service by the hour or trip. If by the trip, and driver is kept waiting fifteen minutes at the address called to, he will charge at the hour rates.

The head of the cab service suggests that in case of controversy between patron and driver, and to save time and trouble, the passenger take the number of the vehicle and hour of the day; also, pay the charges as computed by the driver, and forward statement of the facts to Superintendent of Cab Service, who will give the complaint proper attention.

The limit of this handy railroad cab-service north is Cambria Street; south, Snyder Avenue; east, the Delaware River; and west, Fiftieth Street. In case of an emergency, when a passenger is desirous of using one of the vehicles of this service to go to a point beyond the limits (provided said point is not a cemetery, Fairmount Park, or outside of the city limits), he should give notice of such intention or desire to the Superintendent of Cab Service, at the Broad Street or Reading Station, who will direct the driver accordingly. The extra rate to be charged for service to be performed beyond the regular limits will be upon the basis of double the amount for like service in the regular limits.

Charges.—The rates charged are as follows:

Hansoms.—*By the Trip.*—One mile and one-half or less, to one address, one or two persons, 25 cents; one mile and one-half or less, to two addresses, one or two persons, 50 cents; each additional mile or fraction thereof, 15 cents. *By the Hour.*—For the first hour or fraction thereof, one or two persons, 65 cents; for each additional hour, one or two persons, 65 cents; for each additional quarter hour or less, one or two persons, 20 cents.

Trunks are not carried on hansoms.

Four-Wheel Cabs.—*By the Trip.*—One mile and one-half or less, to one address, one or two persons, 40 cents; one mile and one-half or less, to two addresses, one or two persons, 70 cents; each additional passenger, 10 cents; each additional mile or fraction thereof, one or four persons, 20 cents. *By the Hour.*—For the first hour or fraction thereof, one or four persons, 75 cents; for each additional hour, one or four persons, 75 cents; for each additional quarter hour or less, one or four persons, 20 cents.

For each trunk carried on a cab there is a charge of 25 cents. On every valise carried on top the cab a charge of 10 cents is made. Valises taken inside the vehicle are carried free. Only two trunks are allowed on a four-wheel cab.

Other Cabs and Carriages may be had by application to the American District Telegraph Companies, for which regular scheduled rates are charged. There are also public hack-stands at most of the large hotels. But wherever a public conveyance is hired it is essential, in order to avoid any possible unpleasant controversy with the driver, to have beforehand a clear understanding as to the amount to be paid. This is quite as necessary a caution to those who use these vehicles during the day as to those who employ them at night.

Hotels.

Because of the practical centralization of business in Philadelphia, the most important hotels are grouped within a comparatively restricted area. As in most other large cities, the hotels are run on three plans: American, European, and Combination.

The American Plan.—At these hotels, rooms, meals at stated hours, and attendance are furnished at rates varying from $1.50 to $5 a day. Unless understood at time of registering, the charge begins with the meal supposed to be spread at the time. Thus an arrival at 9 o'clock at night is charged for supper, unless, when the name is placed on the book, the clerk is instructed to note lodging instead. The same rule holds good for departing guests, so that if a traveler does not intend to remain until supper the clerk must be notified to close accounts immediately after dinner. The principal hotels in Philadelphia on the American plan, with the rates charged, are as follows:

Continental, Chestnut and Ninth streets — $2.50 to $4.50 per day.

St. Elmo Hotel, 319 Arch Street — $2 per day.

Hotel Hanover, Twelfth and Arch streets — $2 per day.

Hotel Lorraine, corner North Broad Street and Fairmount Avenue — $3.50 per day.

The Linden, Main and Coulter streets, Germantown — $2 to $3 per day.

European Plan.—The hotels on the European plan are usually patronized by those whose business or inclination keeps them away the whole or the greater part of the day. Hotels on the European plan provide rooms ranging from 50 cents to $3 or more a day, according to the location or the manner in which they are fitted up. The most noteworthy of this class of hotels are:

Aberdeen, 40 North Broad Street, above Filbert Street — $1 a day and upward.

Bellevue-Stratford, northwest corner Broad and Walnut streets — $2.50 up.

Bingham House, Market and Eleventh streets — $1 a day and upward.

Dooner's, 23 South Tenth Street — $1 to $2 per day. Ladies not received, even when attended by husbands or relatives.

Green's, Chestnut and Eighth streets — $1 to $1.50 per day.

Hotel Walton, Broad and Locust streets—$1.50 a day and upward.

Hotel Flanders, Fifteenth and Walnut streets — $3 a day and upward.

Imperial, Eleventh and Filbert streets — $1 a day and upward.

New Lafayette Hotel, Tenth Street, below Chestnut Street— $1 a day and upward. For gentlemen only.

Stenton, Broad and Spruce streets — $1.50 a day and upward.

Vendig, Twelfth and Market streets — $1 to $2.50 a day. Gentlemen only.

Combination Plan.— Hotels run on the combination plan furnish either rooms without meals or give service on the American plan, according to the expressed desire of the guest on registering. The chief hotels in Philadelphia operated in this manner are the

Aldine, 1914 Chestnut Street — American plan, $3.50 per day and upward; European plan, $1 per day and upward.

Normandie, Chestnut and Thirty-sixth streets—American plan, $3.50 per day and upward.

Bornot, Tenth Street, below Chestnut Street.—American plan, $2.50 per day and upward; European plan, $1 per day and upward.

Colonnade, Chestnut and Fifteenth streets.—American plan, $3.50 per day and upward; European plan, $1 per day and upward.

Rittenhouse, Twenty-second and Chestnut streets.—American plan, $3.50 per day and upward; European plan, $1 to $5 per day.

Windsor, 1217 Filbert Street.—American plan, $2 per day and upward; European plan, $1 per day and upward.

Some of the More Prominent Hotels.

For the better information of visitors the following additional information is given regarding some of the more prominent hotels:

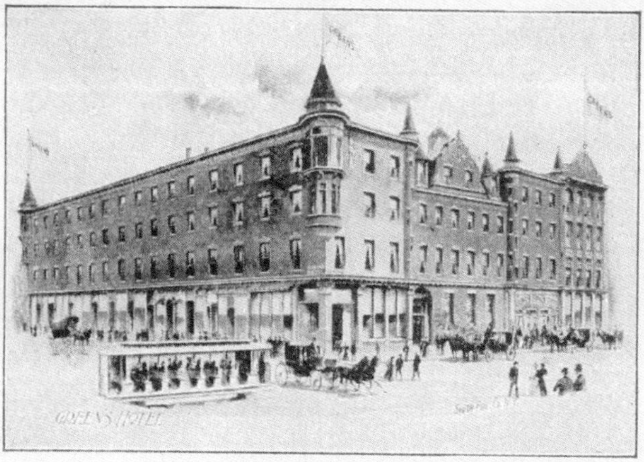

Green's Hotel.

Green's Hotel.

This hotel is at Chestnut and Eighth streets, and is patronized by business men and tourists. It has a central situation, convenient to both the wholesale and retail shopping districts, and contains no less than 315 rooms. Some of the principal theaters are near by. There are elegant restaurants for ladies and for gentlemen attached to this hotel.

The Aldine.—This great hotel, which began by occupying, upon its present site, the house of Dr. John Rush, the founder of the Ridgway Library, now enjoys possession of a fire-proof steel structure on Chestnut Street, just above Nineteenth, which extends back to Sansom Street. It contains all the modern appliances for comfort, and is furnished in a most luxurious manner.

The Colonnade derives its name from Colonnade Row, a series of dwellings which occupied this site many years ago, and which were remodeled, giving a curious and unique appearance.

The Continental has long been one of the famous hotels in the country. It has sheltered many great Americans, among them several presidents and statesmen; in addition, numerous distinguished foreigners have entertained here.

The **Hotel Lorraine** is on the corner of North Broad Street and Fairmount Avenue. It is a new ten-story building, with all modern improvements and is fireproof. The situation is one of the best in the city.

The Bellevue-Stratford—opened September 20, 1904, is the newest and largest hotel in Philadelphia. The rooms are the most comfortable. Prices range from $2.50 upward, but satisfactory rates may be made for all. It is under the same management as the Waldorf-Astoria, New York.

Hotel Walton.—This place of entertainment at Broad and Locust streets is the finest addition to Philadelphia's hotels, was opened in February, 1896, and ranks among the most palatial hotels in the world. It is of pleasing architecture, fireproof, and contains all structural and sanitary improvements, while its furnishing, table, and service are of the highest order. It has the finest roof-garden possessed by any hotel in America. European plan, $1.50 a day.

Bingham House.—During the year of 1904 there has been expended upon this famous hostelry $200,000, thereby making it one of the most modern in the country. Among the many improvements was the addition of a spacious roof-garden, the handsomest in the United States, and a favorite spot for the hotel guests.

Hotel Stenton.—A new hotel at Broad and Spruce streets, run on the European plan. It is an entirely fireproof building and possesses elegantly furnished rooms.

Hotel Hanover.—This is a large and well-appointed hotel, at Twelfth and Arch streets and is conducted on the American plan. Although but recently opened, it is already widely known for the excellence of its table and the comfort of the rooms. Rate, $2.

Restaurants.

Philadelphia is well supplied with restaurants, and they are so widely scattered over the whole city that no one need go hungry more than a few minutes before finding a comfortable place in which to satisfy his appetite. Restaurants are most numerous and of the best quality within a short radius of the City Hall. Most of the hotels, in that neighborhood, especially the Lafayette, Walton, Stenton, and Bellevue, provide for a restaurant custom; the restaurants of both the Broad Street Station and the Reading Terminal are very excellent, and not extravagant in price; and the Raths Kellar, Kugler's Chophouse, Wanamaker's (particularly designed for ladies' lunches) and many lesser and cheaper places exist in this neighborhood. Somewhat farther down, the restaurants of the Bingham House and Green's Hotel are conspicuous in contrast to the cheap restaurants, dairies, lunch-counters and ice-cream saloons, which abound all along the shopping streets. In the business quarter Green's probably takes precedence; and the café in the Bourse is a good example of another class. Of the French and Italian table d'hote restaurants, so common in New York, Philadelphia has few or none; and it may be said, in general, that evening dinner is provided for in few places, where light "supper" fare is expected to be called for at that time. A few restaurants may be more particularly noted:

Soula's Raths Kellar.—This locally celebrated place occupies the basement floors of the Betz building, at Broad and Chestnut, and is an excellent imitation of one of the old beer-drinking halls of Germany. It includes a handsome ladies' restaurant; a reading-room, where, after dining, men may smoke and read any of many European as well as American newspapers kept on file; and the Raths Kellar. This is mainly a large room in the sub-basement, furnished and decorated to resemble such a place in Munich or Dresden. Paintings of scenes from German legends and myths are spread upon the walls, which are further adorned with old-text mottoes: tables of old oak, and grotesquely carved chairs are scattered about: the chandeliers are of deer antlers, and other ornaments in keeping.

Green's Restaurant is an attachment of long-established reputation to Green's Hotel, on Chestnut Street, between Seventh and Eighth streets. It has for many years been a favorite place for the *bon vivants* among business men, lawyers, etc., and has constantly enlarged its facilities.

Boldt's Restaurant occupies the whole of the eighth floor of the Bullitt Building, 133-143 South Fourth Street. A notable feature of this restaurant is the Grill Room.

The New Bingham Café occupies the ground floor of the Bingham Hotel at Market and Eleventh streets, and is one of the finest cafés in Philadelphia. It is patronized by the best people of the city.

Boothby's, on Chestnut Street, near Thirteenth, is another high-class restaurant. It occupies two floors, the second being used for ladies and gentlemen, and the first for the latter only. Boothby's is famous for the manner in which oysters are cooked and served.

Boarding Houses and Furnished Rooms.

Among the names which have been applied to Philadelphia, is the one of "City of Homes." This is due in a great measure to the fact that a large proportion of the families constituting the population of Philadelphia, instead of living in flats or hotels, occupy, each, dwellings owned or rented by them. This domestic character imparts to the Philadelphia boarding-house a feeling of home comfort that is rarely felt in other cities. Such boarding-houses are numerous. The business directory contains more than 600 of them, and a little search will develop what is wanted in the way of accommodations. From $5 to $10 a week will provide good average accommodations. In beginning the search for boarding places, and particularly for furnished rooms, it would be advisable to scan carefully the advertising columns of the newspapers, especially the *Public Ledger*. For those who wish to be installed in the center of the city, and can afford to pay a fair price, most of the establishments on Arch, Chestnut, Spruce, and Pine streets are reliable. Where distance is no objection, West Philadelphia, Germantown, or Chestnut Hill will be found particularly desirable situations in which to locate. The two last named are particularly attractive places, and the facilities for rapid transit are abundant and comfortable. One-half hour by steam and one hour and twenty minutes by trolleys are the times to Chestnut Hill. Nearly every proprietor of a first-class boarding-house will require references. This is an essential protection, not only for the proprietors, but the applicants as well, and therefore no offense ought to be taken.

Furnished Rooms.— Many persons prefer to rent furnished rooms in a lodging-house and take their meals at a restaurant, rather than secure quarters in a regular boarding-house. Such opportunities are numerous, but it is well to caution strangers, particularly ladies, to exercise the utmost caution in regard to this matter, and under no circumstances to close an argeement with the person renting until full inquiry has been made regarding the character of the place. Furnished rooms can be had from $1 to $10 per week. A handsome and well-appointed apartment, with bath privileges, can be had for from $4 to $5 per week. In most of the lodging-houses the rented rooms are cared for by the keeper.

Apartment Houses are uncommon in this city, as yet, the principal ones being the Colonial, at Eleventh and Spruce, and the Gladstone, at Eleventh and Pine streets.

II.

GETTING ABOUT PHILADELPHIA.

Although Philadelphia is twenty-two miles long and nearly six miles wide, it is comparatively an easy matter for strangers to go from point to point without danger of being lost. This is largely due to the simple plan on which the streets generally are mapped out and the houses numbered. With the exception of one or two districts of small area away from the center of the city, and Kensington, Philadelphia is laid out like a chess-board, with the streets extending north and south from Market Street, and from the Delaware River westwardly at almost equal distances apart. Those running north and south are numbered, and those extending west are named. The numbered streets begin on the east, or Delaware River side, and in only two instances are the numerical titles dropped for named ones — Front for First Street, and Broad for Fourteenth.

As Market Street, one of the westward running, is, theoretically speaking, considered the center of the city, that part of the town lying above it is termed North Philadelphia, and that below it South Philadelphia. Thus the buildings fronting on the numerically named streets are numbered in a rising scale, both north and south from Market, and the corresponding figures in the north and south are maintained at almost equal distances apart. Thus, No. 400 north and No. 400 south would be four squares, or about half a mile, above or below Market Street. The blocks between the main intersecting streets are called squares, and are nearly, though not quite, square, as each northward or southward extending line is a little longer than the one running westward. As a result, in reckoning distances by squares, about eight in traveling along the numerically named streets constitute a mile, and ten along the named thoroughfares. Each square is supposed to contain 100 buildings; thus, whether or not this is the case, every new square begins with another hundred, the odd numbers being placed on the north side and the even ones on the

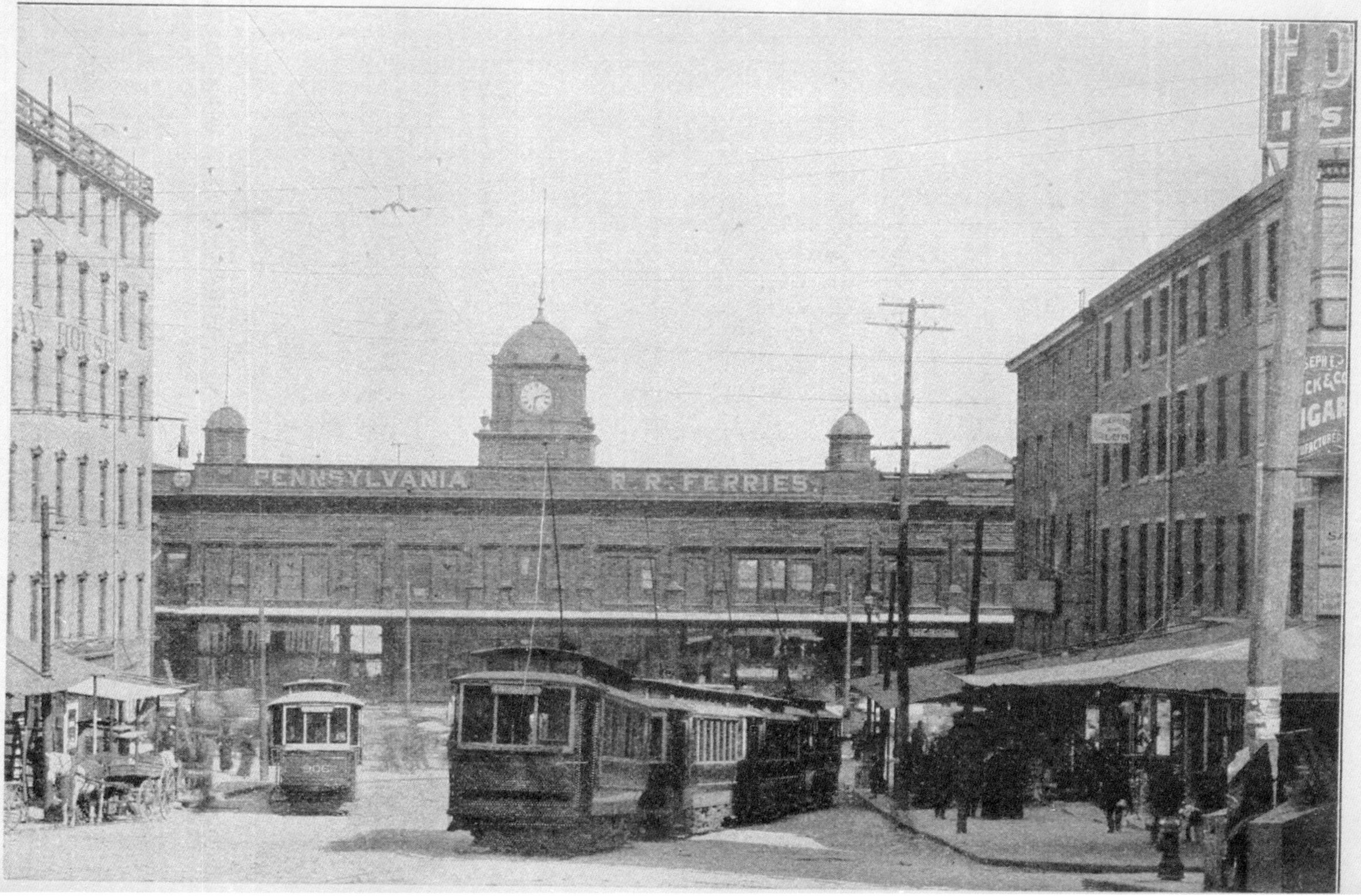
PENNSYLVANIA R.R. FERRIES

south side of named streets, and along the numerically named streets on the east and west sides respectively. Thus, no matter where a person may be on a named street running from the Delaware to and beyond the Schuylkill, the numbers on the houses will give instant and accurate information as to his whereabouts. For instance, 1014 Chestnut Street would be between Tenth and Eleventh; or, to explain in another manner, if a person on Chestnut, or any of the streets running parallel with it, wished to go to Tenth Street, and saw that the numbers were in the thirteen hundreds, he would have to walk between two and three squares with the descending numbers, until number 1000 was reached. Or, supposing him in the same spot, with a desire to go to Twenty-first Street, he would only have to follow the ascending scale of numbers eight squares, where the house numbers show the completion of the twenty hundreds.

In going north or south, along the numerically named streets, while each square is numbered in the same manner, memory or a table must be brought into play. For those who wish to go only four or five squares north or south, the following old rhyme will be found convenient to commit to memory:

"Market, Arch, Race, and Vine,
Chestnut, Walnut, Spruce, and Pine."

The first line of the couplet indicates the first four main westward streets north, and the second those south, of Market.

Street Numbers.

The street numbers north and south are located as follows:

NORTH OF MARKET.

1—Market, Filbert, Commerce, Church.
100—Arch, Cherry.
200—Race, New, Branch.
300—Vine, Wood.
400—Callowhill, Willow, Noble, Hamilton.
500—Buttonwood, Spring Garden.
600—Green, Mt. Vernon, Wallace, Mellon.

SOUTH OF MARKET.

1—Market, Jayne, Merchant, Ludlow.
100—Chestnut, Sansom, Dock.
200—Walnut, Locust.
300—Spruce, De Lancey.
400—Pine.
500—Lombard, Gaskill.
600—South, Kater.
700—Bainbridge, Monroe, Fitzwater.

NORTH OF MARKET—CONT.

700—Fairmount Avenue, Olive.
800—Brown, Parrish, Ogden.
900—Poplar, Laurel, George.
1200—Girard Avenue, Stiles.
1300—Thompson, Seybert.
1400—Master, Sharswood.
1500—Jefferson.
1600—Oxford.
1700—Columbia Avenue.
1800—Montgomery Avenue.
1900—Berks.
2000—Norris.
2100—Diamond.
2200—Susquehanna Avenue.
2300—Dauphin.
2400—York.
2500—Cumberland.
2600—Huntingdon.
2700—Lehigh Avenue.
2800—Somerset.
2900—Cambria.
3000—Indiana.
3100—Clearfield.
3200—Allegheny Avenue.
3300—Westmoreland.
3400—Ontario.
3500—Tioga.
3600—Venango.
3700—Erie Avenue.
3800—Butler.
3900—Pike.
4000—Luzerne.
4100—Roxborough.
4200—Juniata.
4300—Bristol.
4400—Cayuga.
4500—Wingohocking.
4600—Courtland.
4700—Wyoming Avenue.
4800—London.
4900—Rockland.
5000—Ruscomb.
5100—Lindley, Wynne.

SOUTH OF MARKET—CONT.

800—Catharine.
900—Christian.
1000—Carpenter.
1100—Washington Avenue, Ellsworth.
1200—Federal.
1300—Wharton.
1400—Reed.
1500—Dickinson, Greenwich.
1600—Tasker.
1700—Morris, Watkins.
1800—Moore, Siegel.
1900—Mifflin.
2000—McKean.
2100—Snyder Avenue.
2200—Jackson.
2300—Wolf.
2400—Ritner.
2500—Porter.
2600—Shunk.
2700—Oregon Avenue.
2800—Johnston.
2900—Bigler.
3000—Pollock.
3100—Packer.
3200—Curtin.
3300—Geary.
3400—Hartranft.
3500—Hoyt.
3600—Pattison.
3700—Beaver.
3800—Hastings.
3900—Avenue 39 South.
4000—Avenue 40 South.
4100—Avenue 41 South.
4200—Avenue 42 South.
4300—Avenue 43 South.
4400—Avenue 44 South.
4500—Avenue 45 South.
—Government Avenue.
—Schuylkill Avenue.
—League Island.

Between Poplar and Girard avenues there is a gap of three squares, in which there are no main avenues leading from the Delaware to the Schuylkill. The distance, as may be seen by subtracting between 900 Poplar and 1200 Girard Avenue, is about three-eighths of a mile.

Street Car Lines.

The street railway lines, though vast in extent, are yet so simple in plan that their many ramifications are easily explained and soon understood. A passenger can ride to almost any part of the city for 5 cents, or, at most, under an exchange arrangement, for 8 cents. All the lines are now united under the management of the Union Traction Company, whose headquarters is at Eighth and Dauphin streets, where also is the Lost Property Office. With few exceptions, the cars run north and south, east and west on alternate streets. Tabulated, the directions follow:

NORTHWARD BOUND.—On Third, Fifth, Eighth, Ninth, Eleventh, Thirteenth, on far North Broad, Sixteenth, Eighteenth, Nineteenth, Twentieth, Twenty-third, Thirty-third, Thirty-eighth, and Forty-first streets.

SOUTHWARD BOUND.—On Second, Fourth, Sixth, Seventh, Tenth, Twelfth, far South and North Broad, Fifteenth, Seventeenth, Nineteenth, Twentieth, Twenty-second, Thirty-third, Thirty-sixth, and Fortieth.

EASTWARD BOUND.—On Dauphin, Lehigh Avenue, Norris, Columbia Avenue, Jefferson, Girard Avenue, Wallace, Green, Spring Garden, Callowhill, Race, Arch, Filbert, Market, Chestnut, Spruce, Lombard, Bainbridge, Christian, and Morris.

WESTWARD BOUND.—On York, Lehigh Avenue, Susquehanna Avenue, Columbia Avenue, Master, Girard Avenue, Poplar, Fairmount Avenue, Spring Garden, Callowhill, Vine, Arch, Market, Sansom, Walnut, Pine, South, Catharine, Ellsworth, and Tasker.

Several of these lines connect, at their outward termini, with suburban electric lines, which reach far out into the State. The Traction Company prints and will give to enquirers a detailed account of all the city and suburban lines, with a note of the transfer or exchange privileges each offers, but a few questions now and then will enable the stranger in town to obtain all the information he needs as to this matter. An *exchange ticket* bought from the conductor, for eight cents, pays your fare on the first line, and entitles you to a ride upon the exchanging line, saving you two cents of the second fare.

Camden has a system of electric street cars which reaches all parts of that city from the ferries, and also extends to Gloucester and Woodbury.

Suburban Lines extend from the termini of several of the city lines far into the country, reaching Chester, Media, Doylestown, Bristol, and other distant points, and these are constantly extending, and afford the means of delightful excursions. Following is a list of

SUBURBAN POINTS AND HOW TO REACH THEM.

NOTE.—Where a place is on a line which does not start in town, the connecting line is shown first.

PLACES.	LINES.
Abington	Eighth or Thirteenth.
Adele	Market—Philadelphia & West Chester Traction Company.
Angora	Walnut or South.
Ashbourne	Eighth or Thirteenth.
Barren Hill	Ridge Avenue or Eighth—Rox., Chestnut Hill & Nor. Railway.
Boone	Walnut—Chester Traction Company.
Branchtown	Eighth or Thirteenth.
Bridesburg	Third.
"	Third or Fifth—Holmesburg, Tacony & Frankford Railway.
Broomall	Market—Philadelphia & West Chester Traction Company.
Burmont	Walnut—Delaware County & Philadelphia Railway.
Chestnut Hill	Eighth.
"	Ridge Avenue—Rox., Chestnut Hill & Nor. Railway.
Chester	Walnut—Chester Traction Company.
Clifton	Walnut—Delaware County & Philadelphia Railway.
Collegeville	Third or Fifth—Holmesburg, Tacony & Frankford Railway.
Collingdale	Walnut—Chester Traction Company.
Crescentville	Fifth.
Crum Lynne	Walnut—Chester Traction Company.
Darby	Walnut.
Doylestown	Eighth or Thirteenth to Willow Grove—Doylestown Trol'y Line.
Eddystone	Walnut—Chester Traction Company.
Essington	Walnut—Chester Traction Company.
Falls of Schuylkill	Ridge Avenue.
Feltonville	Fifth.
Fernwood	Walnut—Delaware County & Philadelphia Railway.
Five Points	Fifth.
Fitlers	Third or Fifth—Holmesburg, Tacony & Frankford Railway.
Folcroft	Walnut—Chester Traction Company.
Forty-ninth Street	Walnut.
Fox Chase	Fifth.
Franklinville	Fifth.
Frankford	Third or Fifth.
Germantown	Eighth or Thirteenth.
Glenolden	Walnut—Chester Traction Company.
Gloucester	Trolley from Camden, or by Ferry.
Haddington	Arch or Market.
Hestonville	Arch or Vine.
Holmesburg	Third or Fifth—Holmesburg, Tacony & Frankford Railway.
Holmesburg Junc.	Third or Fifth—Holmesburg, Tacony & Frankford Railway.
Jenkintown	Eighth or Thirteenth.
Llanerch	Market—Philadelphia & West Chester Traction Company.
Lawndale	Fifth.
Lansdowne	Walnut—Delaware County & Philadelphia Railway.
Laurel Hill	Ridge Avenue or Lehigh Avenue.
Lazaretto	Walnut—Chester Traction Company.
League Island	Twelfth or Fifteenth—League Island Branch.
Logan	Eighth or Thirteenth.

SUBURBAN POINTS AND HOW TO REACH THEM—Continued.

PLACES.	LINES.
Manayunk	Ridge Avenue or Rox.; Chestnut Hill & Nor. Railway.
Manoa	Market—Philadelphia & West Chester Traction Company.
Marcus Hook	Walnut—Chester Traction Company
Media	Walnut—Delaware County & Philadelphia Railway.
"	Walnut—Chester Traction Company.
Melrose	Eighth or Thirteenth.
Milestown	Eighth or Thirteenth.
Moore	Walnut—Chester Traction Company.
Mooretown	Eighth or Thirteenth.
Morton	Walnut—Delaware County & Philadelphia Railway.
Mt. Aira	Eighth.
Mt. Moriah	Walnut.
Navy Yard	Twelfth or Fifteenth—League Island Branch.
Newtown Square	Market—Philadelphia & West Chester Traction Company.
Nicetown	Eighth or Thirteenth.
Noble	Eighth or Thirteenth.
Norristown	Ridge Avenue or Eighth—Rox., Chest. Hill & Nor. Railway.
Norwood	Walnut—Chester Traction Company.
Oak Lane	Eighth or Thirteenth.
Olney	Fifth.
Overbrook	Arch.
Ogontz	Eighth or Thirteenth.
Oxford Church	Fifth.
Paschall	Walnut.
Pelham	Eighth.
Plymouth	Ridge Avenue or Eighth—Rox., Chestnut Hill & Nor. Railway.
Point Preeze	Tasker or Passyunk Avenue.
Primos	Walnut—Delaware County & Philadelphia Railway.
Ridley Park	Walnut—Chester Traction Company.
Rising Sun	Eighth.
Rockledge	Fifth.
Roxborough	Ridge Avenue or Eighth—Rox., Chestnut Hill & Nor. Railway.
Secane	Walnut—Delaware County & Philadelphia Railway.
Sharon Hill	Walnut—Chester Traction Company.
Swarthmore	Walnut—Delaware County & Philadelphia Railway.
Tabor	Eighth or Thirteenth.
Tacony	Third or Fifth—Holmesburg, Tacony & Frankford Railway.
Tioga	Eighth, Thirteenth or Eighteenth.
Torresdale	Third or Fifth—Holmesburg, Tacony & Frankford Railway.
Trainer	Walnut—Chester Traction Company.
Upland	Walnut—Chester Traction Company.
Upper Darby	Market—Philadelphia & West Chester Traction Company.
Wallingford	Walnut—Delaware County & Philadelphia Railway.
"	Walnut—Chester Traction Company.
West Philadelphia	Arch, Walnut, Girard Avenue, South, Market, or Vine.
Willow Grove	Eighth or Thirteenth.
Wissahickon	Ridge Avenue.
Wissinoming	Third or Fifth—Holmesburg, Tacony & Frankford Railway.
Woodbury	Line from Camden.

III.

THEATERS AND OTHER PLACES OF AMUSEMENT.

Theaters.—When night approaches, one of the first thoughts of most visitors to the city is to attend some place of amusement. In this particular, Philadelphia is well provided. There are over twenty theaters, including the famous Academy of Music, besides numerous halls for concerts, lectures, and miscellaneous entertainments. The theaters of Philadelphia compare favorably with those of any city in the Union, and their stage room is usually much greater. The municipal laws governing the safety of audiences in these places of amusement are very stringent, and generally observed scrupulously by the proprietors. All the houses have asbestos curtains, many fire escapes, and abundant fire-extinguishing apparatus. All the new theaters are built as nearly fireproof as human ingenuity can make them, and, in case a conflagration should occur, every theater has provided for it so many exits that there is probably not one that can not be emptied inside of five minutes from gallery to parquet. The rates charged at the theaters giving regular dramatic performances are rather lower than in New York, the most fashionable charging $1.50 for a seat in the orchestra or parquet. Naturally, since the great mass of the floating population centers between Broad and Seventh and Spruce and Arch, the greater number of the large and finest theaters are located within this area. These are: The Academy of Music, Broad Street Theater, Chestnut Street Theater, Chestnut Street Opera House, and the Walnut Street Theater. There are other first-class theaters scattered in the northern part of the city at which a high grade of dramatic performances are given. Chief among these are: The Park, the Grand Opera House, and the Girard Avenue Theater, the last mentioned of which has long supported a stock company. In the neighborhood of North Eighth and

along Arch will be found several "continuous performances" and cheap-seat houses of respectability; while variety shows frequented by men alone cluster farther north in the doubtful region of lower Race and Vine streets. A list of theaters and prominent houses of amusement follows:

Academy of Music.—Broad and Locust streets. This is an old and famous house, seating nearly three thousand persons, where are heard not only the most important operas and superior dramas, but which has been the scene of some of the most important public meetings, conventions, balls, etc., in the recent history of the city.

Arch Street Theater.—Arch Street, between Sixth and Seventh streets. Vaudeville.

Broad Street Theater.—225 South Broad Street. Melodrama and other performances.

Chestnut Street Opera House.—This is one of the important theaters, where light opera and legitimate dramas are seen.

Chestnut Street Theater.—1211 Chestnut Street. This is one of the oldest and best known of the city's playhouses, and has exhibited its share of the best drama witnessed in Philadelphia during the past half-century.

Eleventh Street Opera House.—19 South Eleventh Street. Minstrelsy and vaudeville.

Dime Museum.—Arch and Ninth streets. Living curiosities and variety performances.

Forepaugh's Theater.—225 North Eighth Street. Dramatic performances.

Garrick Theater.—Chestnut, below Broad Street (new).

Gilmore's Auditorium.—Walnut, above Eighth. Variety performances, frequented mainly by men.

Girard Avenue Theater.—Girard Avenue, near Seventh Street. Drama.

Grand Opera House.—Broad Street and Montgomery Avenue. Vaudeville.

Horticultural Hall.—South Broad Street, next to the Academy of Music. Concerts, lectures, fairs, etc., and two flower-shows annually.

Kensington Theater.—East Norris Street and Frankford Avenue. Drama.

Keith's Theaters.—215 North Eighth Street, and Chestnut Street near Eleventh Street (new). Continuous vaudeville performances.

Lyceum Theater.—729 Vine Street. Minor drama and burlesque.

Musical Fund Hall.—806 Locust Street. Concerts, lectures, etc.

National Theater.—Ridge Avenue and Tenth Street. Drama.

Oriental Theater.—532 North Third Street. Performance in Jewish language.

Park Theater.—Broad Street and Fairmount Avenue. Drama.

People's Theater.—Kensington Avenue and Cumberland Street. Drama.

Standard Theater.—1126 South Street. Drama.

Star Theater.—Eighth Street, above Race. Burlesque.

Walnut Street Theater.—Walnut and Ninth streets. One of the oldest and best houses in Philadelphia, and identified with the growth of the drama in the United States. Every great artist has been heard here.

Zoölogical Garden.

Among the attractions of the city is the *Zoölogical Garden.* It is situated in Fairmount Park, on the west side of the Schuylkill, and fronts on Girard Avenue, close beside the bridge. It is reached by all street car lines connecting with Girard Avenue line. The "Zoo" occupies a once famous tract known as "Solitude," the country seat of John Penn, a grandson of William Penn, the founder of Philadelphia. The old house in which Penn lived still stands on the grounds. The property is part of Fairmount Park, but is leased to the Zoölogical Society of Philadelphia, for the purposes for which it is used. Thirty-three acres are contained in the garden, and there are housed in tasteful and picturesque buildings an extensive and educational assemblage of animals from all parts of the world, which, in some respects, is better than anything else of the kind in America. A large herd of the almost extinct American bison; a herd of elk and other American deers; several grizzly and other bears, in well-built pits, and many representatives of our lesser mammals, birds, and reptiles exhibit the fauna of the United States. Notable foreign mammals include elephants, and a remarkably large collection of the greater beasts of prey; an Asiatic rhinoceros, a tapir, the wart-hog, several African and Asiatic antelopes, an interesting series of monkeys and lemurs; several species of kangaroo, and other marsupials, and a fine lot of sea-lions and seals, which are happy in large open-air tanks. The aviary of living foreign and domestic birds is well filled; and the collection of living reptiles is perhaps the best in the world. In addition, there is usually some special object of zoölogical interest shown, and, on the whole, the "Zoo" is one of the things every visitor ought to see. The grounds are beautifully laid out, planted with trees, and well kept. The Garden is open every day in the week, including Sunday, and is an interesting and instructive place to visit.

Lectures and Miscellaneous Exhibitions.

Lectures form an important feature of Philadelphia life, and many are constantly being given in different parts of the city. They are heard at the Academy of Music, Horticultural, and at the Y. M. C. A. Halls, both in the center of the city and in Germantown, but by far the greater number are given under the auspices of church and other organizations. To find where and when these lectures are held, those interested should look for the advertisements in the morning newspapers, particularly the *Public Ledger* and the *Record.* During the autumn, winter, and spring, the Academy of Natural Sciences, at Nineteenth and Race streets, gives almost a continuous course of afternoon and evening lectures on popular scientific subjects, the cost of admission to which is little more than nominal. Information regarding these lectures can be had from the Secretary of the Academy, an institution well worth visiting.

Balls and Masquerades.

At the Academy of Music, two balls are given annually by the elite of the city. These are called the Assemblies. Money can not purchase entrance to them, and a card may be had only after the applicant's name has been duly passed upon by two boards—one of ladies and one of gentlemen. The first Assembly is extraordinarily exclusive, far more so than the most exclusive social circles in any other city in the Union. The second is more liberal, many guests being invited annually from other cities. Besides this, several other large and fashionable balls are given in the Academy of Music annually, exclusively by invitation card. While the public is not admitted to any of these, there are numbers of other balls given at this great place of amusement which people may attend by the paying of a certain sum. Among these are the functions given by the Order of Elks, the Hebrew Charity Ball, the Philopatrian, and several masquerade assemblies.

Suburban Pleasure Parks.

Within a few years there has grown up in the neighborhood of Philadelphia a series of out-door pleasure-grounds, where music, refreshments, and varied amusements combine to furnish recreation in summer to all classes of the population, who can choose among them what is to its taste. They were organized and are promoted by the Traction Company, for the most part, and are free to all, the management reaping its profits from the sale of refreshments and the patronage given to the shows and various more or less catch-penny devices that flourish in each place. The most elegant and important of these is that at

Willow Grove.—This is a lovely spot, twenty-three miles north of City Hall, on York Road, the ancient turnpike which continues North Broad Street into the country. It is reached by a line of electric cars, and is also a station on the Philadelphia & Reading Railway, which runs frequent trains from its terminal, most of which make the trip in thirty-five minutes. One, therefore, has the choice of two routes; and the visitor is recommended to start about 4 P. M., go by trolley (1½ hours), dine at the Grove, and return by steam train. The trolley fare is 15 cents; the railroad fare, one way, 20 cents; excursion, 35 cents.

The trolley ride to Willow Grove is of itself an extremely interesting experience. Through open cars may be taken on Thirteenth Street, or Eighth Street, or elsewhere, and these, beyond Columbia Avenue, run along North Broad Street, showing many of the beauties of that new and wealthy part of the city. Gradually, the city is left behind, and the cars run along the old turnpike, which becomes more and more rural and inviting. Grand trees shade the ancient highway, which winds through pleasant dells and over hills that give wide views across a most charming country. Few cities in the country can show environs so beautiful; and the companionship of a person versed in the local history would be highly entertaining, since every mile is replete with interesting reminiscences. Fine country-seats, some of them going back to colonial times, border the road, and here and there quaint old stone houses abut upon it, and speak of the peaceful and prosperous past. Logan Station, Oak Lane, and Ashbourne are passed. Then the Chelten Hills come into view at the left, and beyond are the pretty scattered streets of Jenkintown, one of the pleasantest and most historic of Philadelphia's suburbs, near where Washington's repulsed, but not defeated, army made a fortified stand after the disastrous battle of Germantown. Beyond this is the more rural region about Huntingdon, and then Willow Grove appears in the distance, upon an eminence separating the Wissahickon from Pennypack Creek. At its gates is an old-fashioned roadside inn, near a long-famous mineral spring, and having a grove with seats and tables, where one may sit and drink beer if he wishes—a privilege denied the visitor within the park.

Willow Grove itself is an extensive area, combining open lawns, orchards, woodlands, lakes, and streams, all elaborately beautified by the landscape artist, and provided with various buildings of Colonial style, nowhere crowded, and harmonizing into a picturesque whole. The electric cars enter and encircle the park, landing one where he will, but not obtruding upon its beauty. A large lake is provided with boats, and has in the center an electric fountain. Upon its shore is a grove devoted to luncheon parties and picnickers. Further along, a scenic railway sends its cars winding through the tree-tops of another forest open to picnic parties. Near there is a merry-go-round, and a large kiosk for the sale of ice-cream, soda-water, etc.; no alcoholic drinks whatever are dispensed on the grounds. A pretty theater exhibits kinetoscope pictures and gives popular entertainments of a high class. Farther on is a "shoot-the-chutes" arrangement, where the boats are hoisted by an elevator and descend into a miniature lake open to the general view. The central hillock is occupied by a beautiful Colonial casino, where meals are served *à la carte* at prices within the reach of the average excursionist; and near it, beneath a grove of great oaks on the border of the lake, is a music stand where afternoon and evening concerts are given by an excellent band, and occasional special entertainments are seen. There are said to be free seats for 30,000 persons beneath these trees; and three times each evening, within view of the listening audience, the electric fountain is splendidly illuminated. These arrangements are all directed toward quiet, restful, rational enjoyment; and the best people of the city go to enjoy them in a quiet and elegant manner. This recreation ground is one of the most admirable things of its kind in the world. It is now in its third season.

Woodside is a smaller and much more lively place at the northern end of Fairmount Park, and hence within the city limits. It is reached by the Park trolley-line (see elsewhere), and several other lines of cars, is crowded full of restaurants, merry-go-rounds, dancing pavilions, chutes, and all sorts of amusements for children, and is resorted to by crowds, notwithstanding its lack of breeze and coolness. It is an orderly place, however, and no intoxicating beverages are sold there.

Chestnut Hill Park is a newer and more lively resort, opened by the Traction Company in the northern outskirts of the city, about a long-familiar resort and roadhouse known as the Wheel Pump. It is reached by the Eighth Street and contributory lines of trolley cars, is something over an hour's distance from Market Street, and the fare is only five cents. Here, within a comparatively small space, are packed every sort of amusement customary at such parks, and in the evening great crowds assemble and enjoy them. Music is provided by a large band in a free amphitheater, and beer and light wines may be bought. Though always lively and noisy, the place is orderly, and is frequented by all sorts of respectable people.

Washington Park is an older resort four miles down the Delaware, on the New Jersey side, near Gloucester. It is reached by steamboats from the foot of Arch Street, running every half-hour; fare, 20 cents for the round trip. All the usual amusements are provided, but liquor is sold and the patrons of this resort are largely of the less orderly class. The police provisions here, however, are too strict for the really "tough" element, which takes its outing amid the unrestrained delights of Gloucester.

Roof-Gardens and similar out-door places of entertainment, such as exist in New York, are unknown in Philadelphia.

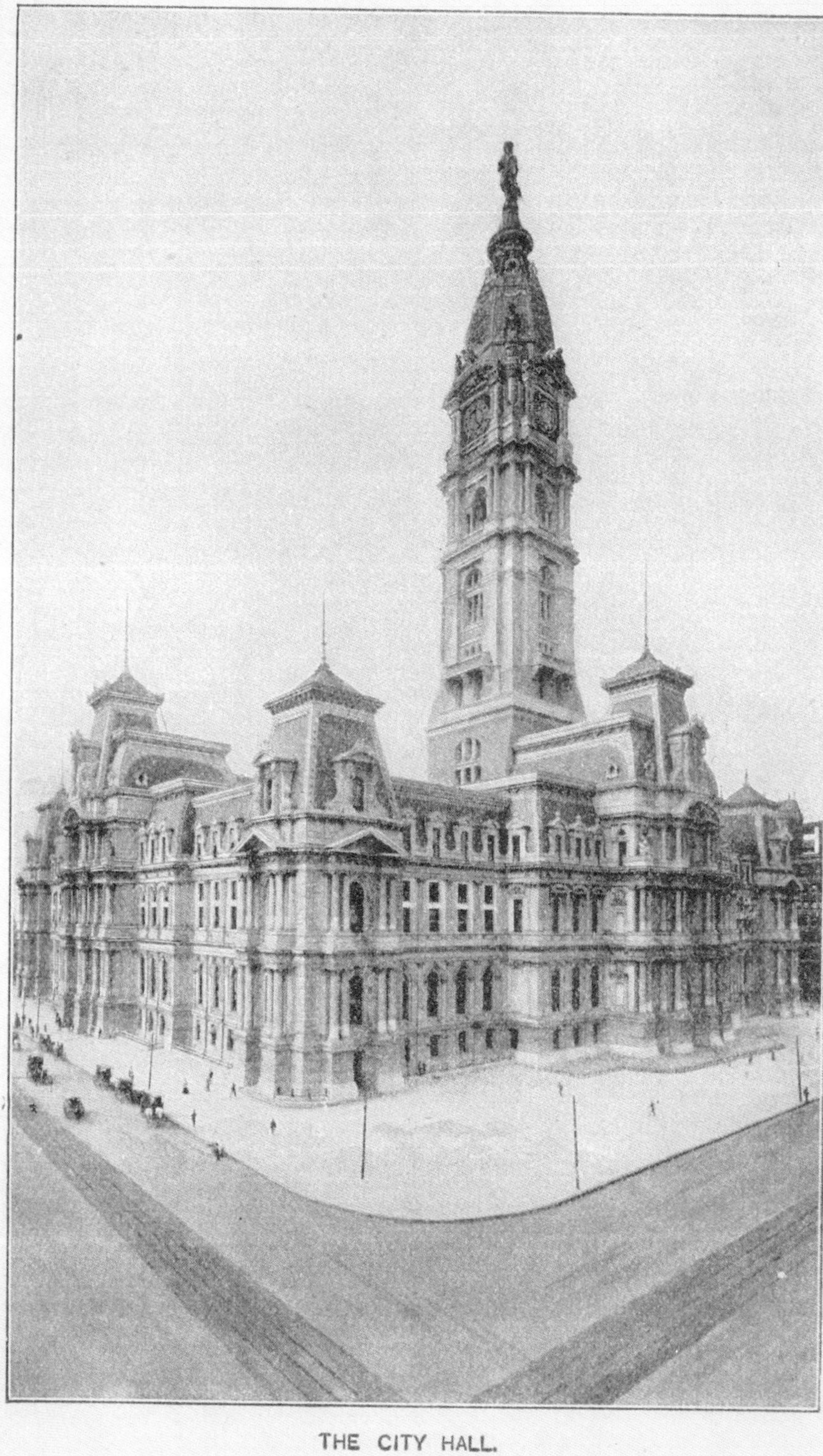

THE CITY HALL.

IV.

A TOUR OF THE CITY.

Philadelphia is so large, and there is so much of interest to see, that unless the visitor intends making a protracted stay, it is simply out of the question to visit a tenth part of what is to be seen. A few brief suggestions are therefore here given, by which a fair amount of pleasure may be gathered in a short space of time. The most convenient point of reference in starting is City Hall,* which is the actual center of the city, though Girard College is nearer its geographical center.

The City Hall is a structure of immense size and prominence, but one that is severely condemned by architects and persons of good taste. It covers 4½ acres, exclusive of the central court. Its cost, including the furnishing, is a matter of wide dispute, but $20,000,000 would perhaps be a fair estimate, and it is not yet finished, although begun in 1871. The basement is granite, and the superstructure of Massachusetts marble. It occupies what, in the early days of Philadelphia, was known as Center Square, and later as Penn Square, where was situated the first water works. Intersecting Broad and Market streets, this great pile of marble and granite, surmounted by its lofty tower, with its statue of William Penn for a finish, is one of the first striking objects to visitors arriving by railroad. It is built in the form of a hollow square, with passageways connecting both

---

*It is a local peculiarity to say City Hall, instead of *the* City Hall; and Councils instead of *the* City Councils, referring to the representative boards in the municipal government. These are two, 1. *Select Council*, an "upper house" composed of one representative from each of the thirty-eight wards (of which in 1897 only three were Democratic); 2. *Common Council*, a "lower house" composed at present of 135 representatives of the wards, elected in varying numbers according to population, only seven of which, in 1897, were Democratic. The administration of the Ordinances of Councils, as the municipal laws are termed, is in the hands of the Mayor, whose cabinet consists of a City Treasurer, City Solicitor, Receiver of Taxes, Director of Public Safety (controlling the Police, Fire, Inspection and Health bureaus); Director of Public Works; and a board of five Directors of Charities and Correction. Several minor Boards, Departments and Trusts are outside of these and have independent functions.

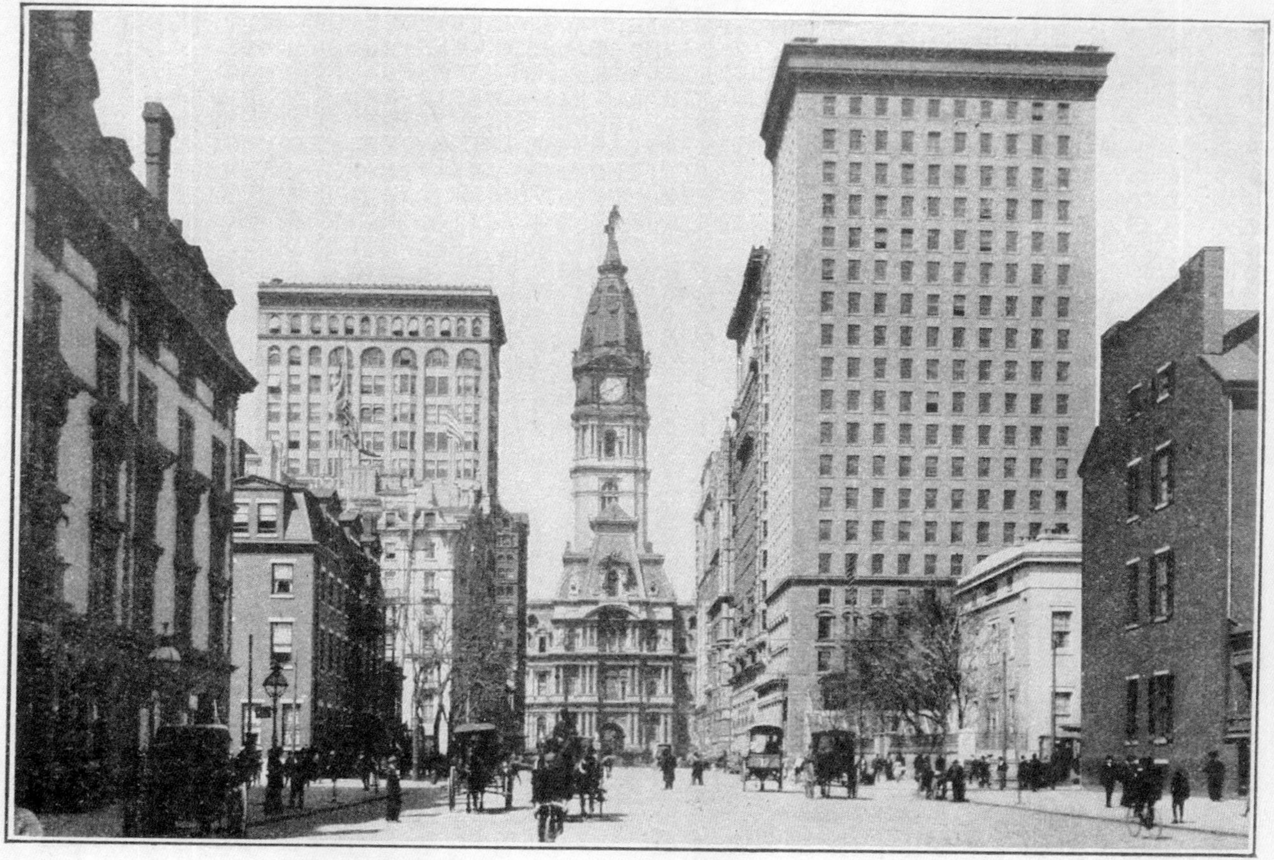

BROAD STREET, LOOKING NORTH FROM WALNUT STREET.

Broad and Market streets. It is four stories high in theory, but actually has eight floors, each of which contain a multitude of rooms of more than ordinary loftiness. The tower at the north extremity of the building is 550 feet high, and, excepting the Washington Monument, is the highest building in the world, overtopping the tallest spire of Cologne Cathedral by thirty-seven feet. The circle of electric lamps about the head of the Penn statue is visible over thirty miles at night. Besides, there are center and corner pavilions with attic stories, and occupied by hanging staircases, of polished granite, projecting from the side walls and having no outside support. The rooms are numbered, 100 numbers to a floor, from the ground floor upward, beginning at the north, or tower side, and running eastwardly around the building. Elevators are running constantly, and all the more public rooms are usually open to view.

The interior of the City Hall will not long detain the average stranger. After noting the ornate entrances, especially that upon the north (the carvings half-hidden in the dark passages), and the pit of the corner-stone at the northwest corner of the tower-foundation, he may glance at the hanging staircase in one of the corner pavilions, and then ascend in an elevator to the office of the Commissioners of Public Buildings (No. 453, fourth floor), where a guide will be furnished him without charge, if he chooses to ask for it; this is, however, scarcely worth the trouble. Only a few apartments are interesting to look at. The Mayor's office, on the second floor (No. 202), is a spacious hall, finished in dark reds, with a gray-green carpet and leathern furniture, and a handsome ceiling panelled in cream and blue, touched with gilt; the inner private office is beyond it. Rooms of several of the eight parts of the Court of Common Pleas and department offices occupy the remainder of this floor and also a part of the third floor. On the fourth floor will be found the richly decorated room of the Supreme and the Superior courts of the State, furnished in a scheme of crimson, olive-green, and gilt, with a magnificent judicial bench of onyx and bronze, old bronze chandeliers and carved mahogany woodwork; it is on the south side of the building, No. 454. On the fifth floor are the halls of the two Councils, each of which has a public gallery, and are fine apartments, the larger, that of the Common Council, being decorated after Pompeiian designs. The blue and white flags here are the city's colors. The sixth floor contains the Law Library, a very complete and valuable collection open to all members of the Pennsylvania bar, and the court-room of the Criminal Courts, which, in its arrangement and subdued color, is, perhaps, the most impressive and admirable of all in the building.

The wide esplanade surrounding the City Hall is intended to be adorned with statues, of which only two have yet been provided,—an equestrian statue of Major-General John F. Reynolds, killed at Gettysburg, which stands at the northern entrance, and a statue of Gen. Geo. B. McClellan, not yet displayed. The sculptor of the Reynolds statue was Rogers, whose plaster "statuettes" are familiar all over the country.

Broad Street.—Broad Street (fourteenth of the numbered streets) is the great north-and-south thoroughfare, extending from the northern Suburbs south to League Island. It is 120 feet wide, is paved with asphalt, and forms the "grand avenue" of the town. No railways are permitted upon it, except at its outer extremities; and, as the omnibuses no longer run, the only way a visitor can view its many architectural ornaments is either to hire a public conveyance or to walk. The latter method is not beyond average strength, since the most that is attractive is within half a mile south and a mile or so north of City Hall.

North Broad Street, starting at City Hall, is a region first of fine public buildings, and then of Philadelphia's handsomest residences. First, at the right, stands the *Masonic Temple*, and next to it the Arch Street Methodist Church. On the west side is the fine edifice of the Evangelical Lutheran Church, and beyond that the lofty and handsome offices of the Fidelity Mutual Life Association (the top floor devoted to artists' studios), adjoining which, on the corner of Cherry Street, is the *Academy of Fine Arts*, a building in Venetian style, having above its entrance a mutilated statue of the Goddess Ceres, exhumed at Megara, Greece, many years ago. Opposite it stands the *Odd Fellows' Temple*, one of the best structures owned by that organization in this country, and a good example of Italian renaissance. Between Race and Spring Garden streets are several large and striking buildings of a public or semi-public character. The first of these is the Gothic edifice of the *Hahnemann Medical College* on the west side, above Race. A short distance up Race, west of Fifteenth Street, are the interesting grounds, meeting-houses, schools, and an ancient cemetery, belonging to the Friends (Quakers). Industrial Hall, used for fairs and the like, and the great jewelry factory in the Muhr Building, are near by. The next structure of interest stands at the northeast corner of Broad and Vine streets. It is a stately pile of marble and granite, and is the *Catholic High School*. Beyond, on the southwest corner of Callow-

4

hill Street, is the attractive armory of the *First Regiment*, or "State Fencibles." Here is a fine bridge erected over the Reading Subway, just finished. This subway was built so that the Philadelphia & Reading trains could reach the terminal without crossing streets at grade, and is about two miles long. From Pennsylvania Avenue, on the west side, to Spring Garden Street, are the famous *Baldwin Locomotive Works*, giving out deafening sounds from the multitude of steam and hand hammers. Spring Garden Street, at the point where it intersects with Broad, is an attractive thoroughfare of unusual width. It is lined with neat buildings, and through the center extends grass-plats, planted with trees and dotted with fountains and flower-beds. At the northeast corner stands the *Spring Garden Institute*, and on the opposite or west side the new *Philadelphia High School* has lately been erected. At this point we come upon another group of fine church edifices, prominent among which, on the east side, is the architecturally unique *Jewish Tabernacle*.

Shortly after passing this group of churches Fairmount Avenue is reached. Here also Ridge Avenue, starting at Ninth and Vine streets, a thoroughfare running diagonally in a northwest direction, intersects. Between Chestnut Street and this point there are little else than public institutions and business houses, but, beginning with Fairmount Avenue, residences begin to appear, though occasionally a large and interesting public or semi-public building is found. At the corner of Fairmount Avenue is the very lofty *Lorraine Hotel*, a handsome ten-story building, one of the few structures of the kind in Philadelphia. Across the street is the neat edifice known as the *Park Theater*. The residences which are now come upon are at first of the old-fashioned type, so much affected in the city half a century ago, of pressed brick, with arched doorways, and steps of white marble, but as one proceeds northward more modern and palatial homes are met with. The first of these is at the southwest corner of Broad and Poplar streets. It is a handsome white marble building set well within spacious grounds surrounded by fine trees and shrubbery. Here the late Charles J. Harrah, who was one of the great street railway magnates, lived and dispensed princely hospitality. From Girard Avenue to Berks Street there is almost an unbroken succession of palatial residences. Beginning at Girard Avenue, a pair of huge brown stone houses have broad and gracefully sweeping steps leading to the entrances. The corner one is the former residence of P. A. B. Widener, donated by him to the city for a free library. Opposite is the residence of Wm. L. Elkins. These gentlemen are widely known from the great railway properties they control. On Broad Street, but above Jefferson, is the *New Mercantile Club*, one of the most striking buildings on North Broad Street. Near by, on the same side, is the beautiful city home of the late Joseph Singerley, proprietor of the *Record*, and nearly opposite is the lovely residence of Mrs. Hamilton Disston, marked by the fountain on the lawn. The *Columbia Club* is at the corner of Oxford Street, and the *Grand Opera House* at the corner of Montgomery; and near them are several handsome churches, conspicuous among which, at the corner of Berks, is the *Temple Baptist Church*. Opposite is *Monument Cemetery*, one of the prettiest of the many cities of the dead in Philadelphia. Unless the visitor has an abundance of time on hand, it is not advisable to proceed north on Broad Street farther than Berks, for, although there are numerous buildings of interest above, the main features have been reached and passed. By retracing the steps to Columbia Avenue, if the visitor desires it, a car can be taken westward to East Fairmount Park, or back to City Hall.

South Broad Street.—Broad Street, south of Chestnut, does not contain as many magnificent residences as are found on North Broad, but has many devoted to public or semi-public purposes. The corner of South Penn Square, immediately opposite City Hall, is the site of the thirteen-story Romanesque Betz Building, "a peculiar feature of the ornamentation being a bronze cornice above the second-story windows, in which are the heads of all the Presidents of the United States from Washington to Harrison, the terms of each being indicated in the frieze." Three of the four corners of Chestnut and Broad streets are occupied by tall and very modern office-buildings—on the northeast the Romanesque home of the Girard Life & Trust Company. Facing it, on the southeast corner, stands the very lofty and beautiful structure of *The Real Estate Trust Company*, completed in 1898; and opposite, on the southwest corner, is a worthy rival in the building of the *Land Title Trust Company*. Next to this is the handsome Lafayette Hotel, filling the block to Sansom Street, beyond which, on the same side, the next short block is filled by the stately home of the *Union League Club*. Opposite is the colonial residence of the late Mrs. Joshua Lippincott. The

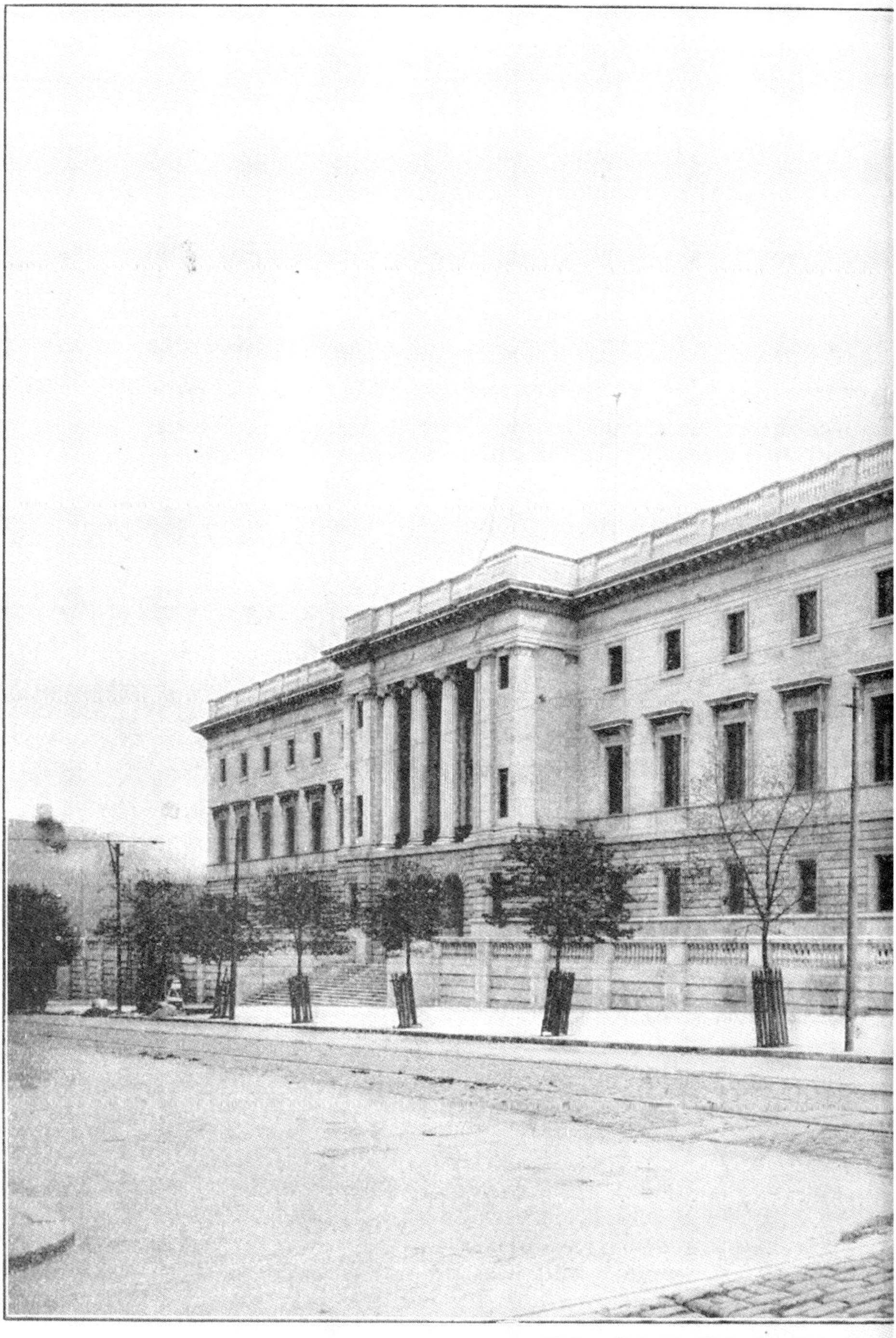

THE NEW UNITED STATES MINT

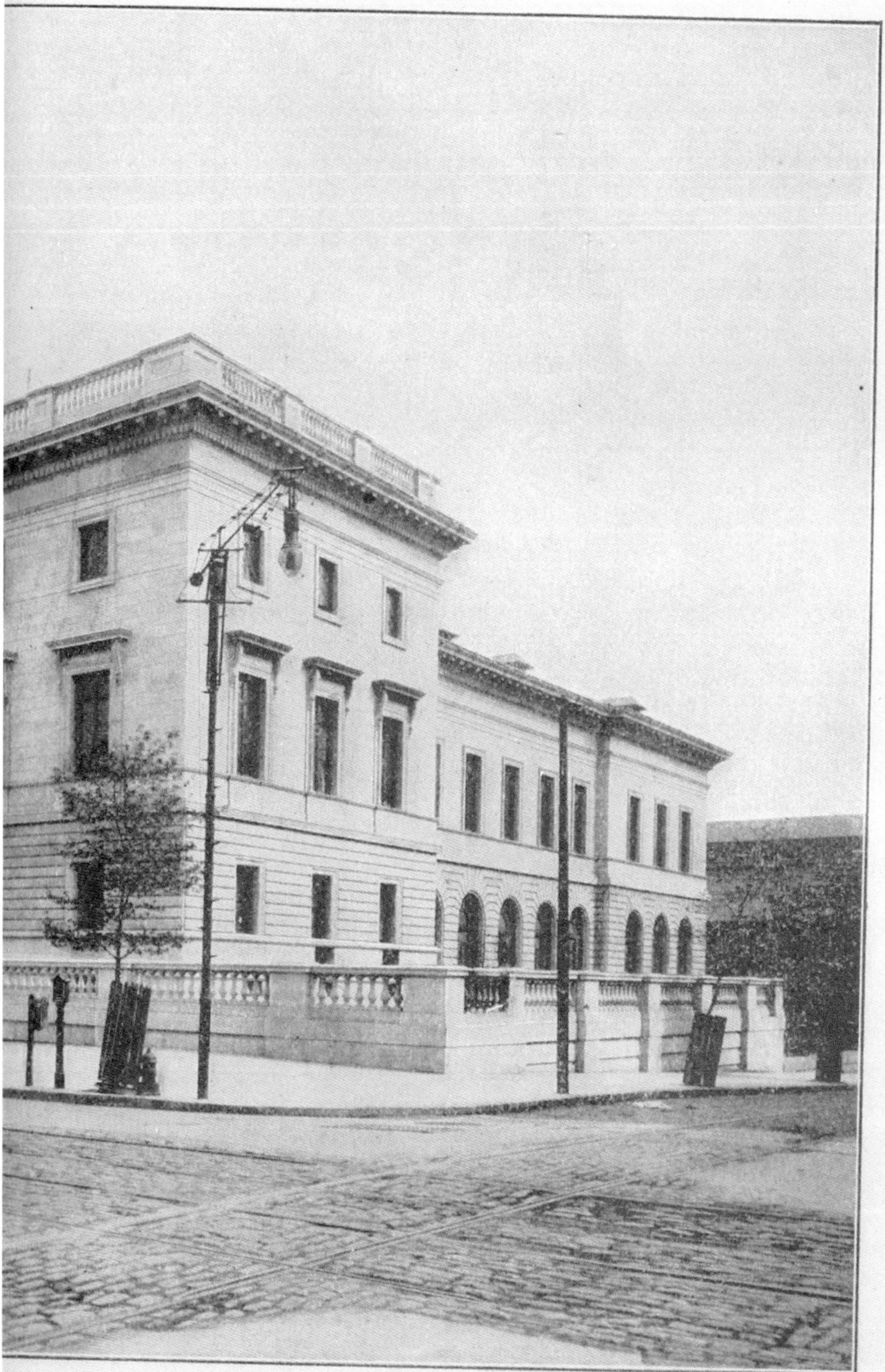

nth and Spring Garden Streets.

elegant homestead fronts on Walnut Street, and the grounds extend clear to Sansom Street. It is unfortunate that a high brick wall shuts out the view of the well-kept grounds, but a few trees, rising above it, hint at the beauty hidden there. Three of these trees have a national reputation. One, at the north end of the grounds, is a fine Southern magnolia, almost the only large specimen of this tropical tree north of the Mason and Dixon's line; on the west side of the house and overhanging the sidewalk is a hawthorn tree, the largest specimen in America; on the east side is a huge elm, the branches of which reach nearly across Walnut Street, and all three have interesting histories. The massive Witherspoon Building towers above this domestic relic, dwarfing and spoiling its effect. Crossing Walnut Street, the Bellevue and Stratford hotels come first on the right, then the elegant Florentine house of the *Art Club*, followed by the *Academy of Music* and *Horticultural Hall*. On the left are the Broad Street Theater, the lofty Hotel Walton, and the more modest but pretty Stenton Hotel, at the corner of Spruce. Little else attracts attention until we reach Pine Street and the Industrial School in the building formerly used as a deaf-mute asylum. Five squares beyond this, at Christian Street, stands the stately "Doric Temple" of the Ridgway Library, completing the list of public edifices of interest in this direction, but many handsome residences may be seen along South Broad Street, as far as Jackson Street, where are the handsome *Methodist Hospitals*.

West Walnut Street and Vicinity.—It has been jokingly said of Philadelphia that all those with newly acquired riches have their fine residences on North Broad Street and the thoroughfares running parallel with or at right angles to it, while all the old-time wealthy families congregated on West Walnut Street and vicinity. While this is not altogether true, it is certain that a large number of those with well-filled purses, who date their ancestry long before Colonial times, do live west of Broad Street, between Arch and Pine, though quite as many more are to be found scattered all over the south-eastern part of Philadelphia, some of the residences even being surrounded by slum districts.

In making a tour of what may be termed West Walnut Street and vicinity, the visitor had better start afoot on Chestnut Street in a westerly direction. For the first square or two, stores and dwellings are found intermingled, the former predominating. At the corner of

Nineteenth and Chestnut streets is the first striking residence, a large, square, white marble building, with extensive side and front lawn. This is the home of Mrs. Jayne, widow of the late Dr. David Jayne, whose "Expectorant" is so widely famous. Close beside is the house occupied by the late Marcellus McDowell, at one time a great tobacco man. It is one of the most striking places on West Chestnut Street. At one corner of Aspen, between Twenty-first and Twenty-second streets, is the quaint and beautiful *First Unitarian Church,* of which the much-beloved and venerable Rev. Doctor Furness is pastor emeritus, and on the other corner is the handsome *St. Paul Reformed Church,* having Bishop Nicholson in charge. Nearly opposite is the *Rittenhouse Hotel*, formerly the Rittenhouse Apartments. Close by is the *Church of the New Jerusalem.*

Passing down Twenty-second Street to Walnut, the northwest corner is occupied by the *Church of St. James.* Diagonally across, at the southeast corner, is a fine, large, white marble pile. It was here that the late George W. Childs lived and died. The residences in this portion of Walnut Street are mostly large and elegant brown-stone structures, all pretty much alike and occupied by some of Philadelphia's most exclusive members of society. At Nineteenth and Walnut is the *Wilstach House,* wherein for many years was the superb collection of paintings which have now become the property of the city through the will of Mrs. Wilstach. Opposite this house is the *Church of the Holy Trinity*, the most fashionable in Philadelphia, at the northwest corner of Rittenhouse Square.

Rittenhouse Square is one of the four squares set apart by William Penn in the original city plot, but remained a neglected lot until 1825. It is now a pretty tree-grown place, adorned by a bronze group by Barye,—the Lion and the Serpent. "On its four sides are the favored sites of the town, and the park lies just in the center of 'old Philadelphia.' It is here that the young mothers wheel their first-born in blue-ribboned carriages, or send them with their nurses. It is here that the Biddles and Cadwalladers, and all the rest, have skipped rope and ridden three-wheeled velocipedes. . . . It is here that the fair young women of Philadelphia may be seen any bright afternoon talking among themselves, or to young men who come over from the Rittenhouse Club, which is just across the way. . . . Rittenhouse Square is a stage on which nearly all of the old Philadelphians have played some of their most important parts. . . . At noon on Sunday morning, the services in the various churches about the square are ended, and the congregations, with one accord, direct their steps to Walnut Street. The parade is confined to the south pavement, and extends from Fourteenth Street to Nineteenth. In these four short blocks the conservative society of old Philadelphia puts itself in evidence. It comes prepared to see and be seen, and it makes up with much care for the spectacle. It jostles and crowds itself up and down the narrow pavement in a very solemn and dignified manner, as befits its high social standing and the day. . . . It is a very fine and a very beautiful crowd to see, and its equal probably only exists in Hyde Park on a warm July afternoon. But this gathering is interesting not only collectively but individually, for every one in it knows every one else. It is composed practically of one class of society, and a fairly well-known man could walk the entire five blocks without having an opportunity of putting his hat on his head."

Many notable people live about this Square. The antique mansion and its two grand new neighbors on the three corners of Seventeenth and Walnut streets are homes of related members of the Drexel family. At another corner lives Dr. J. M. Da Costa, "Philadelphia's greatest physician"; and a near neighbor is another great physician and widely-known novelist,—Dr. S. Weir Mitchell. At Nineteenth Street is a large Colonial house, the residence of Mrs. Joseph Harrison, and close by is the handsome home of C. C. Harrison, Provost of the University of Pennsylvania. A long list, not only of the social *elite*, but of persons of real eminence and far-reaching reputations, might be made among the residents of the surrounding streets. At 1520 Spruce Street dwells Ferdinand J. Dreer, who had a personal acquaintance with Lafayette and other Revolutionary heroes, and whose collection of autographs is celebrated. At the south corner of Eighteenth and Locust streets is the new residence of Mr. George W. Childs Drexel, the publisher of the *Ledger*. This structure is one of the handsomest in that section, and may be considered one of its chief landmarks. Of the whole of Locust Street, the most attractive part is that known as the *Harrison Block*, which extends from Seventeenth to Eighteenth streets. There is probably no other row of houses in Philadelphia so unique or handsome, or which approaches it in appearance. The houses themselves are odd and of the kind of architecture affected half a century ago, with area gardens in front and high steps extending to the doorways. But the striking feature is the gardens, or rather the garden, in the rear of the block. In the whole square there is rot a dividing fence or line of any description. It is one pretty park or lawn, with flower-beds, fountains, shrubbery, and other features to delight the eye. Stand ng on Seventeenth Street, the visitor has an unobstructed view over his plot to Eighteenth Street. Locust Street is locally known as "Bride's Row." We are told that from two to three years is the usually allotted time in which a girl plays an active part in Philadelphia society. "Then she generally has a very expensive wedding, and retires to an inexpensive married existence in Locust Street."

Public Buildings of Interest.

The New Mint is now at Seventeenth and Spring Garden streets. The United States Mint is one of the city's great attractions to visitors. The first Government mint in this country was established in Philadelphia in 1792, near Seventh and Market streets, which had for its first director David Rittenhouse, the famous astronomer. Visitors are admitted daily, except Sundays, from 9.00 a. m. to 12.00 noon, and are escorted, from the door throughout the building, free, by conductors provided for the purpose. In making the tour of the mint the following route is taken: The deposit room, where the gold and bullion is received; the copper-melting room, in which ingots for minor coinage are cast; the gold and silver melting room; the rolling and cutting room; the coining room, where the coins are stamped; and, finally, the cabinet, in which is the finest collection of coins in the United States. This structure took two years to build and is constructed of Maine granite at the cost of about $2,400,000. The capacity of the new mint is three times as great as that of the old structure. The building is of fireproof construction throughout, and in every branch of the work the best materials were used, in order to obtain durability and strength. The exterior walls are of granite, while the floors and partitions are of steel and hollow tile. The roof is of steel laid in concrete and covered with vitrified tile laid in cement.

Post Office.—The post office stands at the northwest corner of Ninth and Chestnut streets. It is a splendid pile of four stories, built of dressed granite, and is surmounted by a dome reaching 170 feet above the pavement. It extends all the way on Ninth Street from Chestnut Street to Market Street, and 175 feet on each of these two last-named thoroughfares. Its many entrances are all on Ninth Street, and the different departments of the office are all located on the first floor. A long corridor extends from near Chestnut to near Market, and at each end are broad stairways and elevators reaching to the upper floors. The edifice cost the Government $8,000,000. In addition to the building at Ninth and Chestnut streets there are many sub-postal and receiving stations located in different parts of the city, as the exigencies of business demand. Other governmental offices here are the Circuit Court of Appeals, the Circuit Court, the District Court, and the United States Commissioners; the local offices of the Internal Revenue, Pension Bureau, Lighthouse Board, Coast Survey, Secret Service, etc.; and the Weather Bureau occupies quarters near the roof, where its signals are displayed.

Continuing down Chestnut Street past the Continental Hotel and many widely-known newspaper offices, the rambler soon reaches the most interesting spot in Philadelphia to the patriot, —

Independence Hall.— It stands on Chestnut Street, between Fifth and Sixth streets, and on the north side of Independence Square, which it was made to face, the city of that period being mainly to the southward; the Chestnut Street front is, therefore, properly, the rear of the building. It was built in 1729-'35, by the Province of Pennsylvania as the Colonial State House, and the present square was then the State House Yard. These earlier facts are overshadowed, however, by the greater one that in this building were arranged the preliminaries of the establishment of the United States. Here the Declaration of Independence was debated and proclaimed in 1776, and here the first Congresses met and preparations for the Revolutionary War were made. Hence, it is as *Independence Hall* that the building has been known and venerated since the foundation of the Republic. It was used for over a century by various public offices and societies, and underwent many minor alterations; but, in 1897-'98, these were mostly cleared out, and the whole of the main building renovated and restored as nearly as possible to its original condition. It is henceforth to be a national monument of the birth of the Republic, and is open freely to the public. The central building, or old State House, whose tower is surmounted by a wooden cupola built in 1828 and containing a clock, is flanked by low open structures leading on the east to the old Supreme Court House at the corner of Ffth Street, and on the west to Congress Hall at the corner of Sixth Street.

The Supreme Court House was built in 1791, for the Supreme Court of the United States, when it was supposed that this city was to be the national capital. Other lesser courts were lodged here in early times, and among the great jurists who have sat there are Jus-

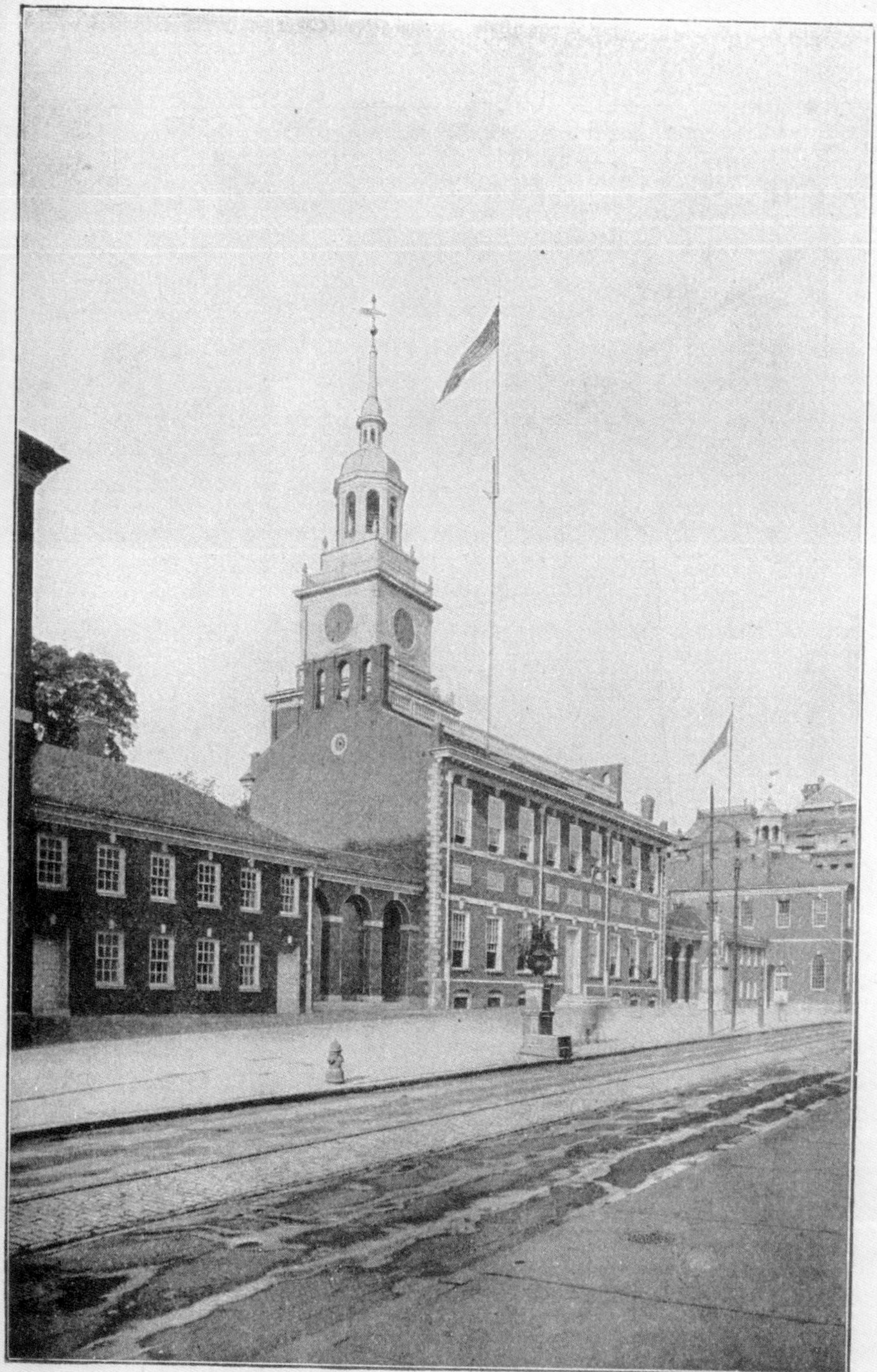

INDEPENDENCE HALL — Chestnut, between Fifth and Sixth Streets

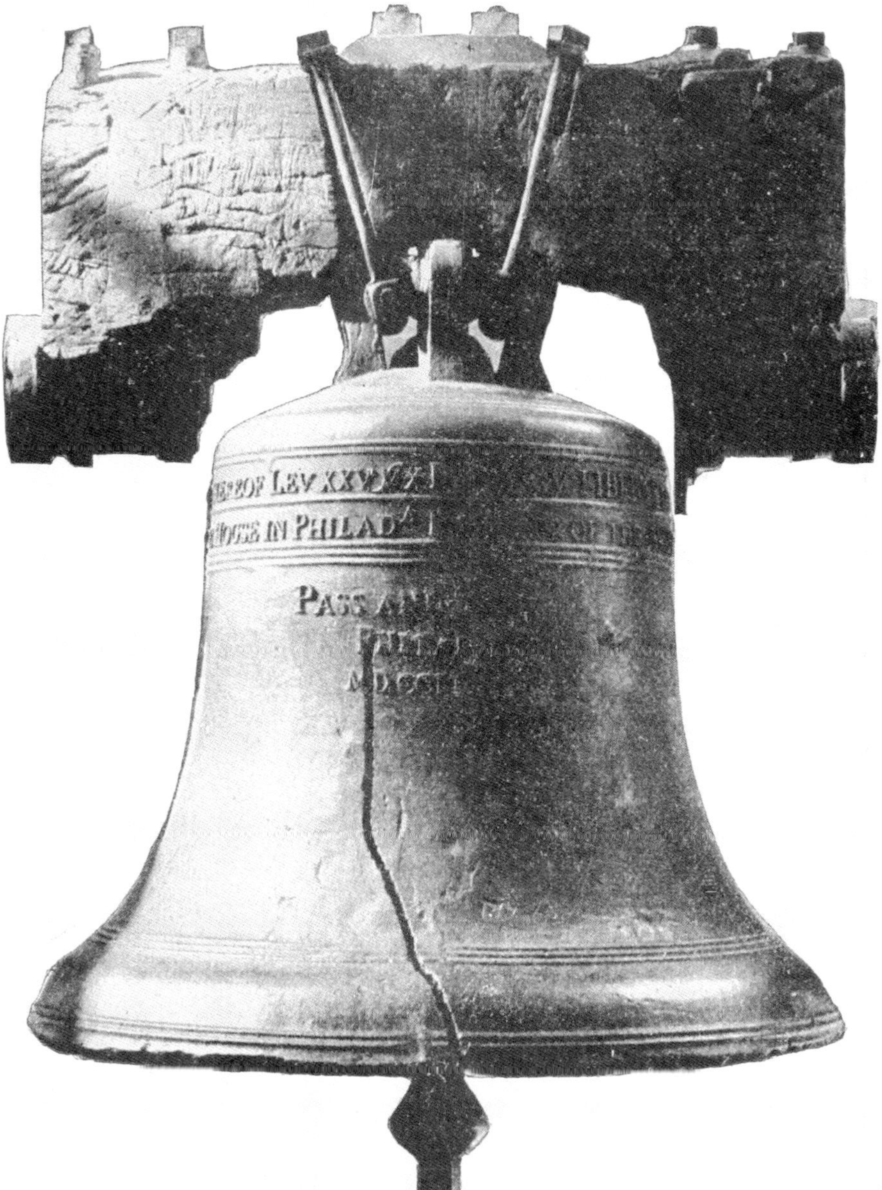

LIBERTY BELL – Independence Hall.

tices John Jay, Oliver Ellsworth, Francis Hopkinson, William **Lewis,** and Richard Peters. Upon the removal of the Supreme Court to Washington this building became the City Hall, and so remained until recently. It is now occupied chiefly by patriotic societies.

Congress Hall has even greater interest. Its site, before the Revolution, was occupied by a wooden shelter for visiting Indians. The present building was completed in 1790, and until 1800 was occupied by the Congress of the Nation. Here Washington was inaugurated President, in 1793, for a second term, and John Adams as Vice-President; and here Adams took the oath as President in 1797, and Jefferson as Vice-President. After 1800 it was devoted to criminal courts, and became popularly known as the "Slaughter House," on account of the many murder trials that took place there; but these courts now sit in the City Hall, and the old building is empty.

Independence Square, now one of the pleasantest spots in the city, extends to Walnut Street, and was the scene of the first public announcement of the Declaration of Independence, which was read to the public, July 8, 1776, from the platform of an observatory erected there in 1769 to observe a transit of Venus. It had been, and continued to be for many years, the assembly-place for citizens' meetings and public celebrations of all sorts, often addressed by Presidents of the United States. Its area is 4½ acres, and its arrangement dates from 1825, when the present trees were planted—many of them rarities.

The Interior of Independence Hall has been restored, and is gradually being filled with authentic historical relics under the superintendence of the Sons of the American Revolution. The first and most important object in the building is the **Liberty Bell,** whose tongue first announced the legal formation of the United States. It hangs from its original beam, within an ornamental frame in the main corridor, where it may be closely examined, but is carefully guarded against vandalism.

The bell was cast in London, and received in this country about the end of August, 1752. When it arrived it was found to be cracked, and it was re-cast in Philadelphia in April, 1753. The work was unsatisfactory, and it again went into the melting-pot, from which it emerged a satisfactory bell, and was placed in the steeple in June, 1753. It bore the same inscriptions which were cast in the original, and on the 8th of July, 1766, it did indeed "Proclaim liberty throughout the Land." When the British approached Philadelphia, in 1777, the bell was taken down and carried to Bethlehem for safe-keeping, and returned after the evacuation. After sounding its joyous notes in proclaiming liberty, the old bell was only used on very particular occasions, and while being tolled on July 8, 1835, in memory of Chief-Justice Marshall, it suddenly cracked, and since 1843 it has been silent.

The East Room is the one of most interest, since it is the one occupied by the Second Continental Congress, which there made and signed the Declaration of Independence, July 4, 1776. The recent restoration has not replaced the hangings and furniture which gave the room an elegant appearance at that time; but a number of the ancient desks and chairs are there, including the table upon which the Declaration was signed. A *fac simile* of the document hangs above the Speaker's rostrum, and portraits of most of the signers hang upon the walls.

The West Room, opposite, was for a century the sitting-place of high Provincial and State courts.

The National Museum, of the Sons of the Revolution, now occupies the restored upper floor of the building, reached by a winding staircase in the tower. A large number of portraits, all well labelled, adorn the walls; most of these are copies of ordinary merit, but some are spirited originals, notably that of George III, by Allan Ramsay. Other notable objects are the original charter of Pennsylvania (1701), signed by William Penn; a slab of the Penn Indian Treaty Elm of Shackamaxon; two chairs that once belonged to Penn; a portion of George Washington's pew in Christ Church, and other pieces of furniture; and the small table upon which George Mason drafted the famous Declaration of Rights of Virginia. To this collection constant additions will be made of authentic historical relics illustrating the Revolutionary period of American history.

Other Historic buildings are numerous in Philadelphia, some of which are described elsewhere under "Parks," "Churches," etc. A few may better be mentioned here,— first,

Carpenters' Hall.— Carpenters' Hall is looked upon by many with nearly the same amount of veneration they accord to Independence Hall. The venerable structure is at the head of a court running south from Chestnut Street, between Third and Fourth. It is a brick structure, with steps leading to it, and surmounted by a little cupola. Within the walls of this building assembled the first Continental Congress, on September 5, 1774. Among its members were Washington, Patrick Henry, Richard Henry Lee, and Peyton Randolph. From this Congress emanated the resolutions and measures which led to the existence of the present national government. Here that liberty was conceived that had its birth in Independence Hall. The building was erected in 1724, by the Carpenters' Company, a society of carpenters and architects. After the vacation of the building by the first Congress, the place was occupied at different times by various bodies representing the Province of Pennsylvania. During the Revolution it was used as a hospital for sick American soldiers, and it was also occupied at various times by the Philadelphia Library, the land office of the United States, and the Bank of Pennsylvania. It is open to visitors.

House of the Declaration of Independence.—On the west side of Seventh Street, next to the building on the corner of Market, is an ancient house occupied as an oyster saloon. In this building, it is claimed, Thomas Jefferson drafted the Declaration of Independence. There is a difference of opinion, however, in regard to this.

Free Quaker Meeting House.—The Free Quaker Meeting House stands at the southwest corner of Fifth and Arch streets, and is now occupied by a firm of wholesale leather-dealers. The original members of this body were known as "Fighting Quakers," because, during the Revolutionary War, they abandoned their principles of peace to fight for American liberty. A tablet on the north gable states that the building was erected by subscription in 1783.

Christ Church Cemetery (Franklin's burial-place) is immediately opposite. The entrance is on Arch Street, and an attendant will answer questions, and sell photographs. This interesting old burying-ground was opened by Christ Church (on Second Street, see below) over a century ago, after it outgrew its own small yard, and is enclosed in a wall of bricks brought from England. The old house on Fifth Street (opposite, at the corner of Cuthbert) was then standing, and the great mulberry tree is said to have been planted by Benjamin Franklin, who, with his wife and an infant son, is buried in the northwest corner, where the slab above his tomb may be read from the street; his death occurred in April, 1790. Other noted persons interred here are Dr. Benjamin Rush, one of the Signers; Generals Cadwallader and Jacob Morgan of the Continental army; Commodores Truxton, Bainbridge, and Dale, of the Navy, and many once prominent Philadelphians.

Betsy Ross or *First Flag House.*—On Arch Street, near Third, is a quaint little shop, marked by a rude tablet-sign, where, at the time of the Revolution, John Ross kept an upholsterer's shop. He died in the Continental army, and his wife Betsy continued the business. In May, 1776, Washington and a committee employed Betsy Ross to make a sample flag of thirteen stars and thirteen stripes, which was adopted as the national ensign. At the time she made the flag, Betsy Ross was twenty-four years old, and is described as having "bright, winning eyes, which sparkled with expression and intelligence, and goodness seemed to breathe in every lineament of her beautiful countenance." Nevertheless, she was compelled to bear for some time the jeers and taunts of her neighbors, and be called a "little rebel" for her loving work in making the first ensign of an unstable and locally unpopular government.

Chew House.—Another interesting relic, among many in Germantown, is the Chew House. In this edifice the British made their desperate stand, which finally turned the tide of the battle of Germantown, on October 4, 1777, in their favor. Until this point was reached, the Continental army had driven the British before it; but once lodged in the staunch old Colonial mansion, neither the army nor its cannon could dislodge them, and the Americans were held in check from early in the morning until late in the afternoon, when re-enforcements of the British came from the city and gained the day. The marks of the cannon balls on the old house are still plainly visible, and the mutilated marble statuary still stands on the lawn.

League Island Navy Yard.—In 1876 the United States removed its Philadelphia navy yard to League Island, which lies in the Delaware, just off the mouth of the Schuylkill, about seven miles from City Hall. To reach it take the Fifteenth Street trolley-line to Porter Street, and there change to the electric line running down South Broad Street to the Island. League Island is about two miles long, and contains nearly one thousand acres. A broad avenue extends from the entrance to the wharves, and upon each side of this highway are arranged the buildings of the yard,—officers' quarters, storehouse, machine shops, etc. Here are displayed cannon captured from British ships in the War of 1812, Parrot guns that saw service in the Civil War, and pyramids of old-style shot and shell. A feature of the yard is the immense fresh-water basin in which many vessels may lie at once without their bottoms becoming fouled by sea-growth, or other injury overtaking them. The monitors remaining from the Civil War, which had been anchored here for thirty years, were in good order when summoned for harbor defense in the recent war with Spain. The Government has neglected this yard until lately, but now proposes to make a great naval station of it. Already facili-

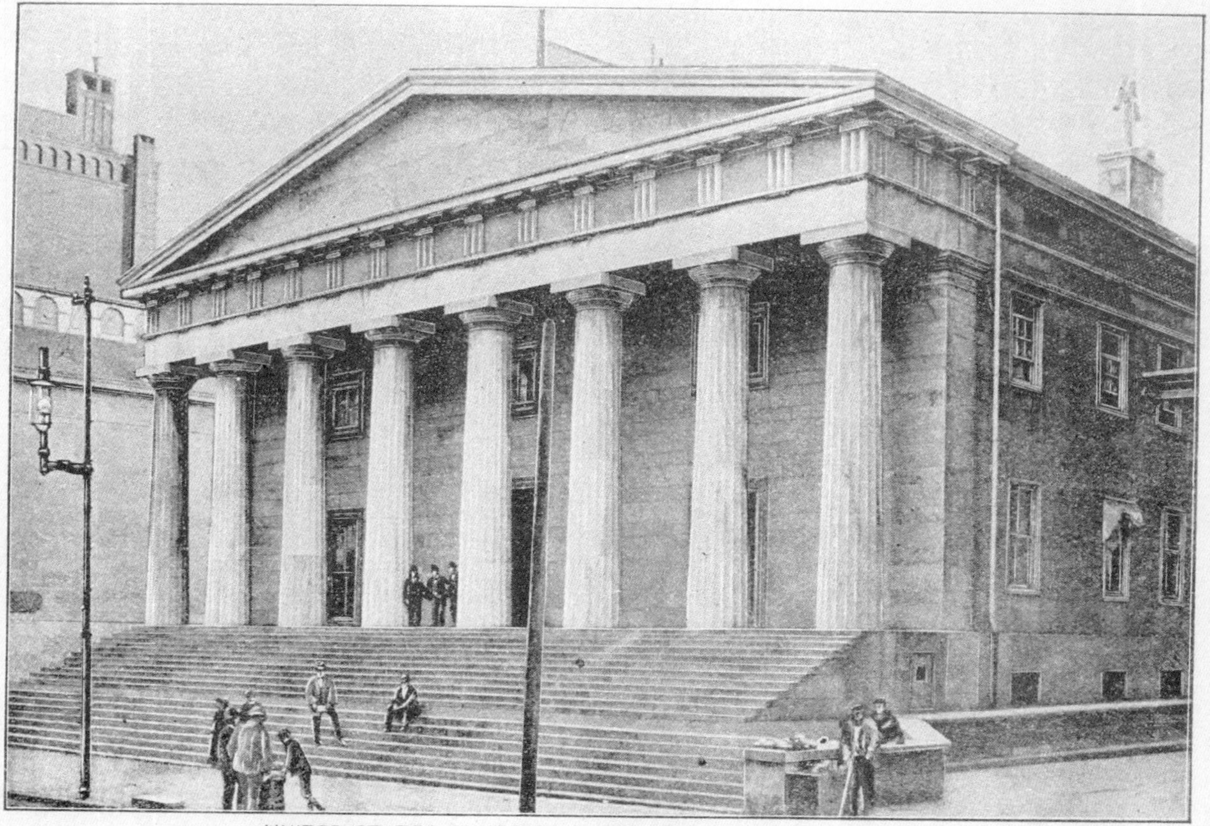

UNITED STATES CUSTOM HOUSE — Chestnut and Fourth Streets.

DENTACURA

Tooth Paste is **"The Ideal Dentifrice."** It cleans the teeth perfectly.

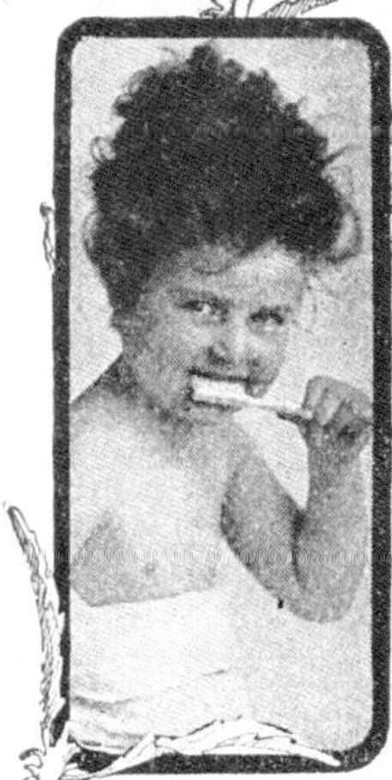

By destroying the harmful bacteria in the mouth it minimizes or entirely removes the chief cause of decay. This prophylactic action is of the utmost importance. Dentacura is a delightfully flavored creamy paste in collapsible tubes, unbreakable, convenient, and economical. Its use insures the aseptic condition of the mouth, leaves a delicious sense of coolness and cleanliness, and a perfumed breath.

PERMIT NO SUBSTITUTION.

THE PRICE IS 25 CENTS PER TUBE.

Let us send you our free booklet on Taking Care of the Teeth, which contains much valuable information concisely written. Address,

DENTACURA COMPANY,
120 Alling Street, Newark, N. J., U. S. A.

The Mutual Benefit Life Insurance Company

NEWARK, NEW JERSEY.

FREDERICK FRELINGHUYSEN, President.

THE LEADING ANNUAL DIVIDEND COMPANY

Has During the Past Sixty Years Paid to Policyholders $218,668,480.65.

ASSETS, Jan. 1, 1905, $93,237,790.27 : SURPLUS, $7,319,562.97

NO COMPANY HAS EVER ACCOMPLISHED BETTER RESULTS FOR ITS POLICYHOLDERS.

ties are at hand for building war-ships there (where several auxiliary cruisers were equipped in 1898), and these facilities will be much enlarged, and a vast drydock will be built. The yard is a highly interesting place to visit, and is open to the public all day.

Business Men's Organizations.

Custom House.—On the south side of Chestnut Street, between Fifth and Fourth, is a strikingly handsome white marble building, approached by a long flight of steps. This is the United States Custom House. The structure, which was completed in 1824, is modeled after the Parthenon at Athens, and is regarded by connoisseurs as a fine specimen of architecture.

The Bourse.—A few years ago a large class of the business men of Philadelphia felt the need for a great central building in which their common affairs could be best transacted. The Bourse was the practical outcome of this feeling, and forms a general commercial exchange modeled upon those in Europe, and especially at Hamburg. It has erected in the business center of the city, on Fifth Street, between Chestnut and Market (reaching through to Fourth Street), an immense and imposing building of red-stone and brick in the Renaissance style, at a cost of $2,250,000 (with the lot), where every business man is welcomed, and strangers will find much to interest and profit them. It was opened early in 1896, and since that time has concentrated under its roof all but two of the organized exchanges and wholesale associations of the city, namely: The Board of Trade, Trades' League, Commercial Exchange, Maritime Exchange, Grocers and Importers' Exchange, Drug Exchange, Lumbermen's Exchange, Hardware Merchants and Manufacturers' Association, Coal Exchange, Oil Trade Association, Paint Club, Quaker City Association, and the National Association of Manufacturers.

The great hall of the Bourse, in which the daily meetings are held, is on the ground floor, a room 240 feet long by 126 feet wide, with a height of 45 feet in the center to the skylight; and it is estimated that from 4,000 to 5,000 persons could gather here for business purposes daily. Certain portions of it on the north and south sides are given over to the uses of the Commercial, the Maritime, and the Grocers and Importers' exchanges, the center of the floor being kept for the use of those members of the Bourse who are not members of the exchanges mentioned. The Commercial Exchange looks after the interests of the grain, flour and provision trade of the city, and corresponds to the Produce Exchange in New York, or the Board of Trade in Chicago. Its section of the floor, on the north side, is fitted up with small tables on which grain and flour can be displayed for the inspection of buyers, and blackboards, upon which are posted, all through the day, the fluctuations in the prices of wheat, corn, oats, etc., received by direct wire from New York, Chicago, and other principal points. The Maritime Exchange looks after all marine and shipping interests, and maintains signal stations at the capes of the Delaware, where the movements of ships, etc., are reported. The Grocers and Importers' Exchange holds daily auctions in the south-west corner of the hall of staple groceries. In the center of the floor are three large quotation boards, on which are kept posted the prices of various commodities as fast as received by "ticker" service; and the London, New York, and other large markets are reported daily. The galleries contain rooms where statistical books, etc., may be consulted, newspapers from all over the country may be seen, and writing and chatting done comfortably. The third to the sixth floors contain over three hundred and fifty offices, many of which may be rented by the day or week, as sample-rooms, by commercial travelers; and special conveniences are offered to induce buyers as well as sellers to make this building their business headquarters. The building contains a branch post office, railroad and steamship ticket offices, telegraph and telephone offices, restaurants, etc. *Exhibition Rooms* are open in the basement (machinery and heavy goods), and on the seventh floor, devoted to displays of manufactured goods, like so many shop-windows.

Builders' Exchange.—In 1886 the Master Builders' Exchange was organized, at the suggestion of the Master Plasterers' Association, and soon after an ornate structure for the use of the new and important body was erected on Seventh Street above Chestnut. Within the buildings are located The Lumbermen's Exchange, and the meeting places of The Stonecutters' Association; The Bricklayers' Company; The Master Carpenters; The Builders' Company; The Master Plasterers' Association; Planing Mill Association; Master Painters' Association, and Metal Roofers' Association. In addition there is a Mechanical Trades School, under the direction of the Builders' Exchange, for the instruction of young men in any branch of the trade they may select, and a permanent exhibition. This last is well worth a visit, for here is arranged and classified exhibits of all kinds of materials and devices which are employed in the construction of a building. Admission is free, daily, from 8.00 a. m. to 5.00 p. m., except legal holidays and Sundays.

Banks.—Philadelphia has more that eighty National banks and

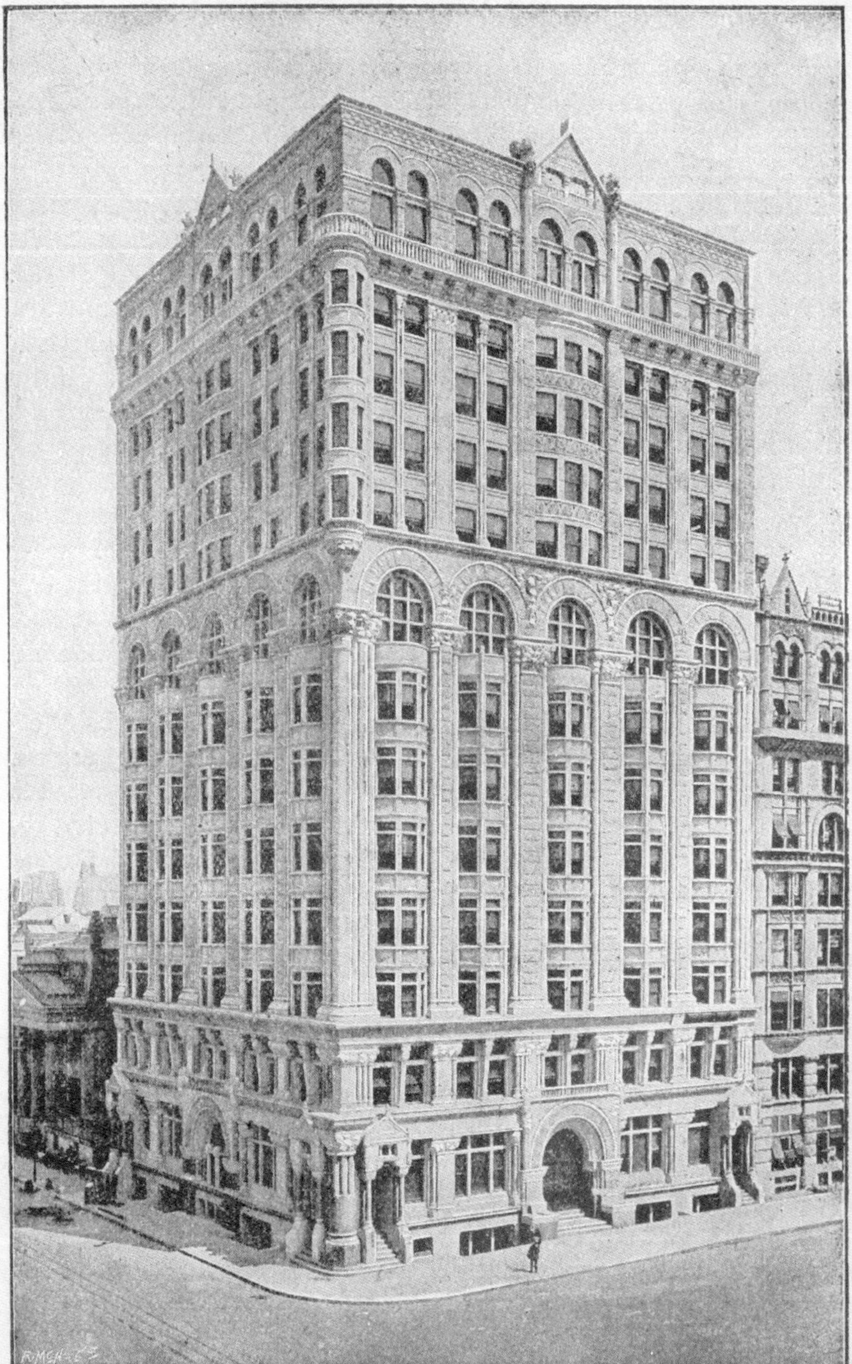

BETZ BUILDING—Broad Street and South Penn Square.

other banking institutions, having a combined capital of about $55,-000,000, which declare annual dividends amounting to over $2,250,-000. Of these institutions forty-four are National banks.

Almost without exception, these institutions occupy magnificent edifices, the equal of which in architectural finish and interior embellishment would be hard to find anywhere on the continent. Philadelphia has the distinction of possessing, in the Bank of North America, the oldest institution of the kind in America. It was founded in 1781 by Robert Morris, the organizer of the Pennsylvania Bank, the first public bank of the United States. Immediately on the close of the Revolution, the Bank of North America became the financial agent of the American Government; and its building on Chestnut Street, near Third, is almost upon the site of its original home. The Philadelphia National Bank, 421 Chestnut Street, having been established in 1803, is the next oldest institution of the kind in the city. Philadelphia has also the honor of possessing the oldest fire insurance company in America. This is the Philadelphia Contributorship, on South Fourth Street, below Walnut, which was incorporated March 25, 1752.

Commercial and Office Buildings.—Philadelphia can boast of its stately buildings, although, on account of its vast area, they are much more widely scattered than in either New York or Chicago. Thus, at first appearance, it would seem as though, for a large city, there were singularly few handsome structures for commercial purposes. Broad, Chestnut, Market, Third, and a number of other streets, however, can exhibit some splendid specimens of architecture, and year by year many others are being added. The large area given over exclusively to business renders unnecessary very many buildings of what are known as the "sky-scraping" type. But some of these are to be found also. The finest group, all things considered, is in the neighborhood of Broad and Chestnut streets, the north side of Chestnut Street, from Ninth to and beyond Tenth. These are the structures of the Post Office, the *Record*, the Mutual Life, the Penn Mutual, the City Trust Company, the Sharswood, and the Mutual Life Insurance Company (of New York). Although built at various periods and from the plans of different architects, care has been taken in each instance that the last structure erected should harmonize with those preceding it. Thus the general effect is of one great palatial edifice, with graceful curves and bold outlines.

Between Tenth and Third streets are clustered many of the finest bank, insurance, trust, and other financial institutions in the city, but this last year or so they are gradually going toward Broad and Chestnut streets. Each seems to have endeavored to outdo the other in architectural effects, expressing solidity and security. All of these institutions have their names plainly on the fronts where they may be seen at a glance. Further particulars of some of these financial institutions will be found in a chapter by itself.

An alphabetical list of the names and locations of the principal commercial buildings of the city follows:

Bank of North America, 307 Chestnut Street.

Betz Building, South Broad Street and Penn Square.

Bourse, South Fifth Street.

Brown Brothers' Building, southeast corner Fourth and Chestnut streets.

Bullitt Building, 131-141 South Fourth Street.

City Trust Safe Deposit and Surety Company, 927-929 Chestnut St.

Crozer Building, 1420 Chestnut Street.

Drexel Building, Fifth and Chestnut streets.

Fidelity Mutual Life Association, Broad Street, above Arch.

Fire Association, 409 Walnut Street.

First National Bank, 315-319 Chestnut Street.

Girard Trust Company, Broad and Chestnut streets.

Girard National Bank, 120 South Third Street.

Guarantee Trust Company, 316-320 Chestnut Street.

Independence National Bank, 436 Chestnut Street.

Insurance Company of the State of Pennsylvania, South Fourth, opposite Harmony Street.

Land Title Building, Broad and Chestnut streets.

Lehigh Building, 106-108 South Fourth Street.

Manhattan Life Insurance Company, South Fourth and Walnut sts.

Mutual Life Insurance Company of New York, Tenth and Chestnut streets.

North American Building, Broad and Sansom streets.

Penn Mutual Insurance Company, 921-925 Chestnut Street.

Pennsylvania Company for Insurance on Lives, 515 Chestnut St.

People's Bank, 435 Chestnut Street.

Philadelphia Saving Fund Society, Seventh and Walnut streets.

Provident Life and Trust Company, Fourth and Chestnut streets.

Real Estate Trust Company, Broad and Chestnut streets.

Real Estate Title Company, 523 Chestnut Street.

Record Building, 917-919 Chestnut Street.

Sharswood Building, Tenth and Chestnut streets.

Stephen Girard Building, Twelfth Street, above Chestnut Street, corner Girard Street.

Union Trust Company, 715-719 Chestnut Street.

United Gas Improvement Company, Broad and Arch streets.

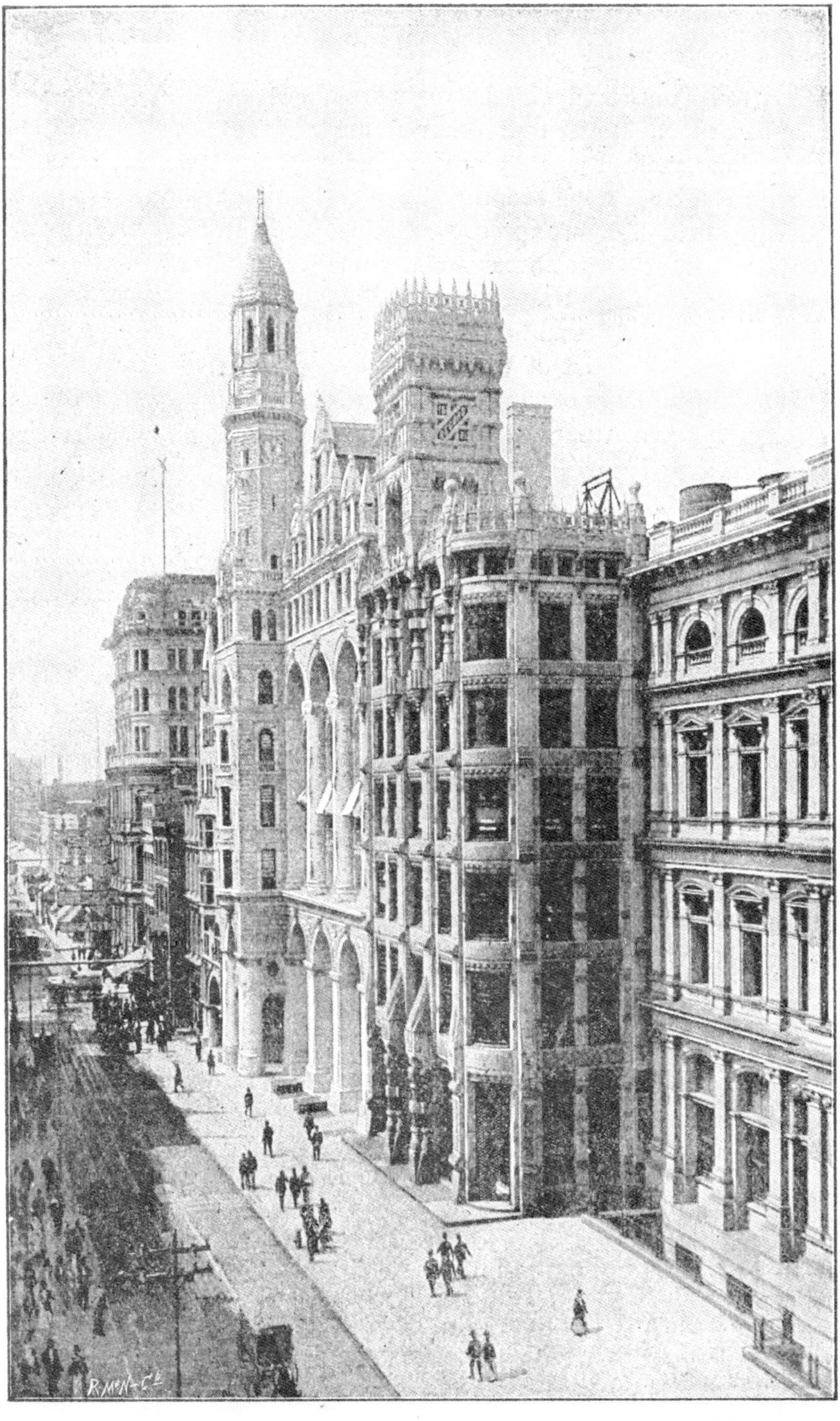

CHESTNUT STREET, LOOKING WEST FROM NINTH STREET.

Weightman Building, 1524 Chestnut Street.
West End Title & Trust Co. Building, Broad and South Penn Square.
Western Savings Fund Society, Tenth and Walnut streets.
William Mann Company, 27 North Fifth Street.
Witherspoon Building, Walnut and Sansom streets, below Broad.

A Shopping Trip.

Women visiting this city, who wish to go shopping, will find abundant places in which to gratify their desire. In the center of Philadelphia the stores on Chestnut and Eighth streets, and portions of Market, devoted to goods particularly attractive to womankind, are large, handsome, and well stocked. Some of them are unsurpassed in America in size and in the assortment and variety of goods displayed. This is true particularly of Wanamaker's, Strawbridge & Clothier, Gimbel's, Lit Brothers, Sharpless Brothers, and the Marks Brothers. All these have monster establishments, and sell both low and high priced goods. Columbia Avenue is a noted up-town shopping street, and South Street, in the lower section of the city, has a reputation peculiar to itself, and which may be likened, in a measure, to the Bowery in New York. In Northeast, North, and Northwest Philadelphia the main thoroughfares of the original villages or boroughs are given over to shops and stores, some quite pretentious, but generally of a minor character. As the lady shopper, presumably, will be stopping at one of the hotels on or in the neighborhood of Chestnut Street, the shopping tour will be confined to Chestnut, Eighth, and Market streets, beginning with Broad.

Chestnut Street.—Chestnut Street is recognized as the leading thoroughfare for the great stores carrying the heaviest stocks of the richest fabrics and other rare articles for retail sale. The first place of interest to every woman, no matter what her special quest may be, is *John Wanamaker's.* It is a huge establishment, reaching half a square on Chestnut Street from Juniper to Thirteenth, and extending north one square to Market Street. It was originally the freight depot of the Pennsylvania Railroad Company. It has been deepened by a basement, heightened by building, and added to by the absorption of other edifices until it has assumed its present huge exposition-like character and national reputation. Millions of persons visit this store annually, and, at scarcely any time of the day, despite its many acres of area, can one pass along its miles of aisles without constantly elbowing other shoppers or sight-seers. For the convenience of the patrons, many waiting, reading, and toilet rooms are provided, and a large restaurant is established in the store.

Eighth Street.—Eighth Street is a thoroughfare much visited by ladies who delight in making bargains. The large and handsome stores between Chestnut Street and Race are filled with a bewildering array of cheap goods and bargains. Besides Lit Brothers, Gimbel's Brothers, and Strawbridge & Clothier, who all have entrances on Eighth Street, there are several other very large firms having immense establishments and doing an enormous business. Among these are Marks Bros., Eighth and Arch; Shoneman Bros., Eighth, above Arch, and Partridge & Richardson, nearly opposite. Fully a day can be spent by a lady on Eighth Street, profitably and enjoyably, for although Eighth Street has the reputation, and deservedly so, of being a "cheap" street, it is by no means the case that the goods offered for sale are proportionately inferior to those displayed on the more aristocratic thoroughfare, Chestnut Street. On Eighth Street also, for the convenience of shoppers, are several choice restaurants, where excellent meals are served at reasonable rates.

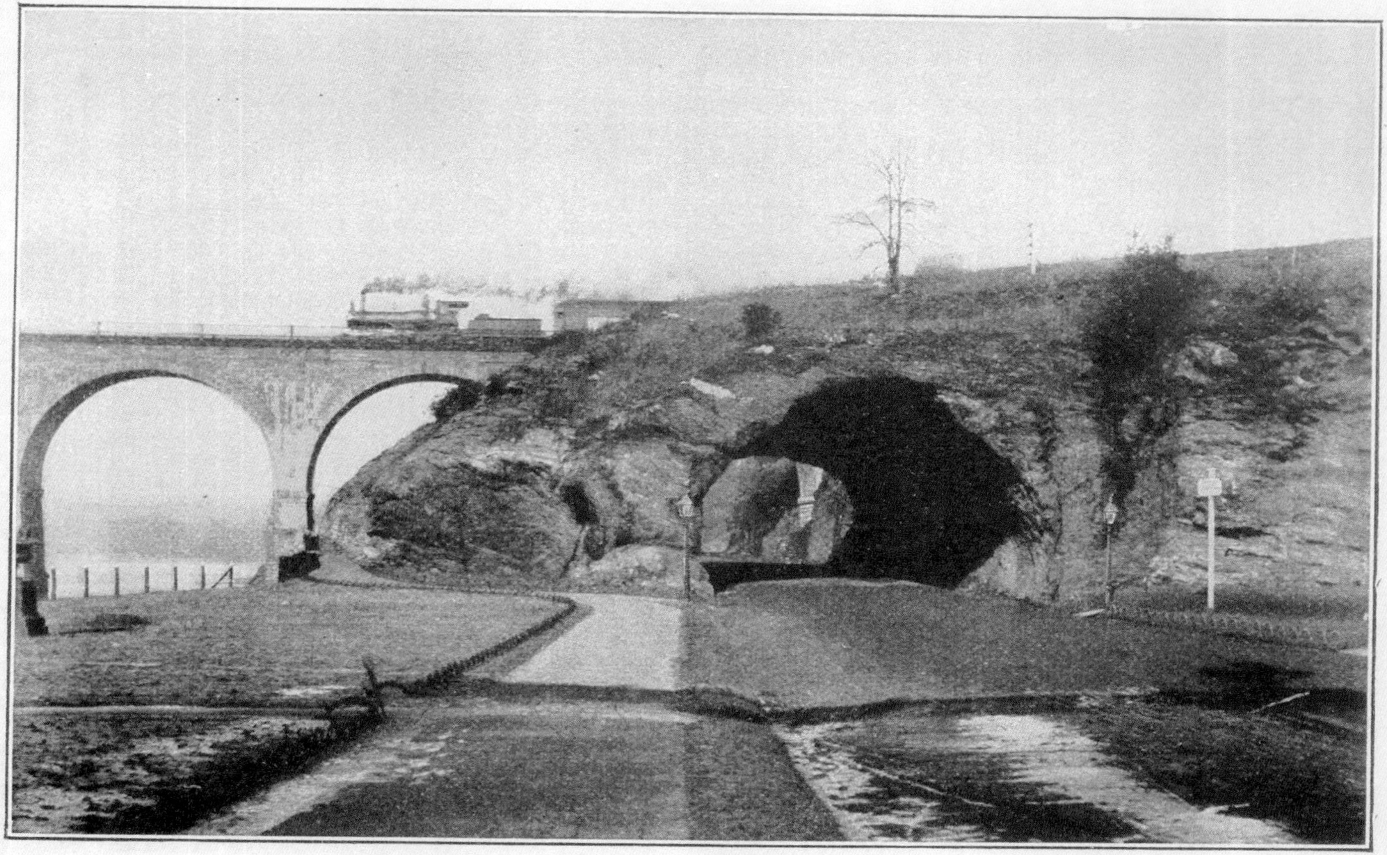

THE RIVER DRIVE TUNNEL.

The Zoölogical Garden

(FAIRMOUNT PARK.)

One of the Great Gardens of the World.

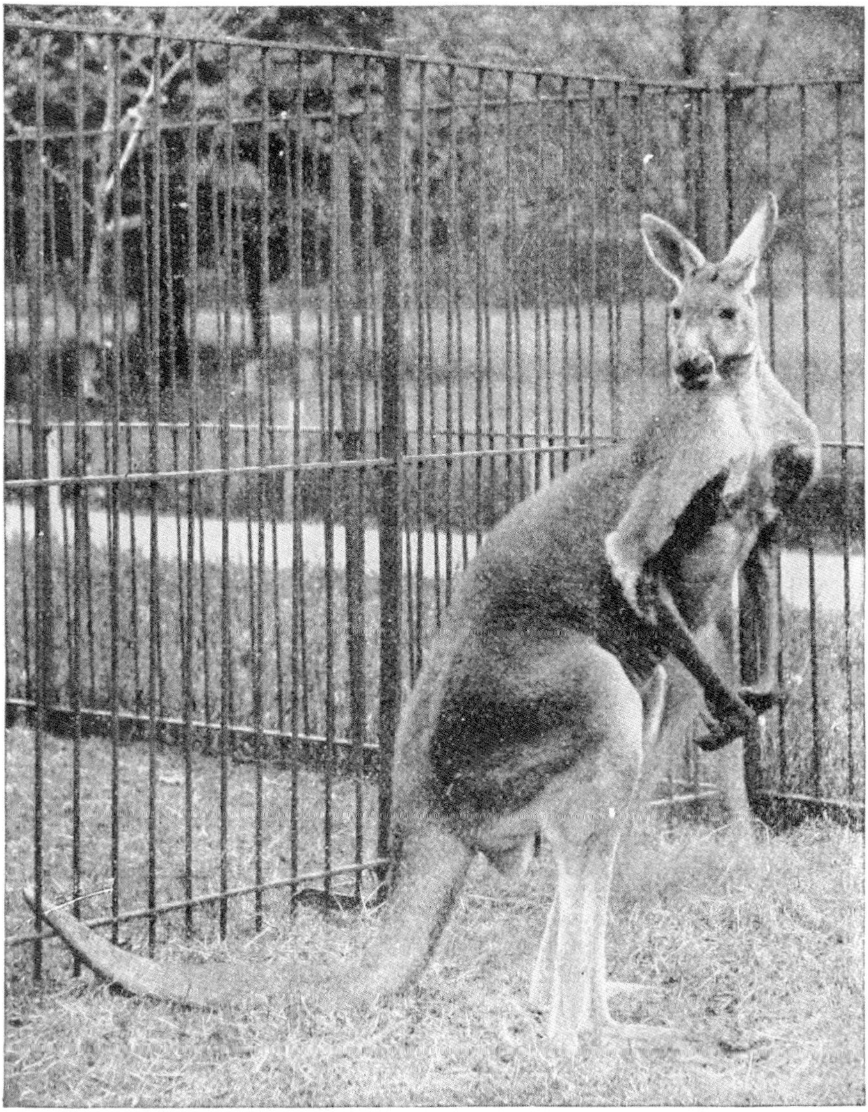

OPEN EVERY DAY FROM 9.00 A. M. UNTIL SUNSET.

ADMISSION: 25 Cents for Adults; 10 Cents for Children. On Saturday, 10 Cents for Adults; 5 Cents for Children.

SPECIAL RATES TO LARGE EXCURSIONS.

Reached by all street car lines connecting with Girard Avenue line.

(See page 36.)

V.

THE CITY'S PARKS AND DRIVES.

Philadelphia possesses a vast area covered by public parks. Nearly 4,000 acres are devoted in this manner to the people's health and pleasure. Of this, Fairmount takes over 3,000 acres, League Island Park about 340 acres, and Hunting Park a little more than 43 acres. Of these three, the first and last are open, and have been laid out under the best skill of the landscape gardener. The second, League Island Park, located in the lower part of the city, on the Delaware, was only recently placed in the city plan, and the ground has not yet been improved, although a beginning has been made. The plan for it is unique, for this great space is to be utilized as a pleasure resort, a children's playground, and a place for civic display on a grand scale. The remaining acreage is taken up by a large number of smaller plots ranging from half an acre to ten acres each, some of which are improved and beautified, while others as yet remain much as they were when first taken by the city, and are only used as playgrounds for the little ones.

When Penn founded Philadelphia he placed five "public squares" upon its plan, one on each corner and one in the center; these were known respectively afterwards as Washington, Rittenhouse, Logan, Franklin, and Penn or Centre Square. Although the acquisition of Fairmount Park began as early as 1812, the real movement—which is now one of great magnitude—for a large number of breathing places was begun about the year 1880, and was undertaken by Prof. Thomas Meehan, an eminent botanist, and a member of common council from Germantown. Through him the City Parks Association was formed; and through him, and this organization, and the newspapers, public sentiment was aroused to such an extent that within the last five or six years more than $500,000 has been spent annually by the city on parks, and many plots have been given to the municipality by public-spirited citizens. A new organization, called the Culture Extension League, has as its chief object the provision by the city of a large number of children's playgrounds in the different wards. A beginning has been made in John Dickinson Square, where an extensive central area has been prepared for all sorts of children's games and amusements, two shelter-houses have been built, and a flooded area for skating in winter.

Fairmount Park.

This grand pleasure ground contains over 3,000 acres. Its southern end is at Callowhill Street bridge; from here it extends north on both sides of the Schuylkill River in varying widths to the Wissahickon Creek. Here it branches off and follows the latter stream, with its embracing hills, to the north side of Chestnut Hill. At Rittenhouse Street, about one mile above the mouth of the Wissahickon, a branch goes off to the right, follows the line of the Monoshone Creek, or Paper Mill Run, and enters a short distance into Germantown.

Fairmount Park may be reached by almost countless routes, any one of which would prove satisfactory to the visitor. The Arch, Vine, and Callowhill street cars all go directly to Old Fairmount Water Works, near Callowhill Street bridge. The Eighth Street cars, Fairmount Avenue branch, and Eleventh Street cars to Fairmount Avenue (passes given west on application when fare is paid), go to the Green Street entrance, near the Schuylkill River Steamboat landing, by which various points along the river to the mouth of the Wissahickon may be reached in the summer months. The Spruce and Pine street cars also run to the Fairmount Water Works. The Eighth Street line goes to the West Park and the old Centennial grounds, via Girard Avenue; and several branches of the Philadelphia Traction Company reach the latter spot through transfers. The Electric Traction Company lines, by transfers and direct cars, go to the upper end of the East Park; and the People's line, by transfer with the Chelten Avenue Germantown branch, reach the Monoshone Creek, part of Fairmount Park, not far from the Wissahickon. This last is a particularly desirable trip, and will be mentioned more fully in its proper place. The Pennsylvania Railroad, Chestnut Hill branch, and certain trains on the New York branch stop at Zoölogical Garden Station; Chelten Avenue Station, one mile from Wissahickon; Allen's Lane, one mile from Devil's Pool, on Wissahickon; and each station thereafter to Chestnut Hill is but little, if any, farther from various points on the same stream, and the approaches of all are full of beauty.

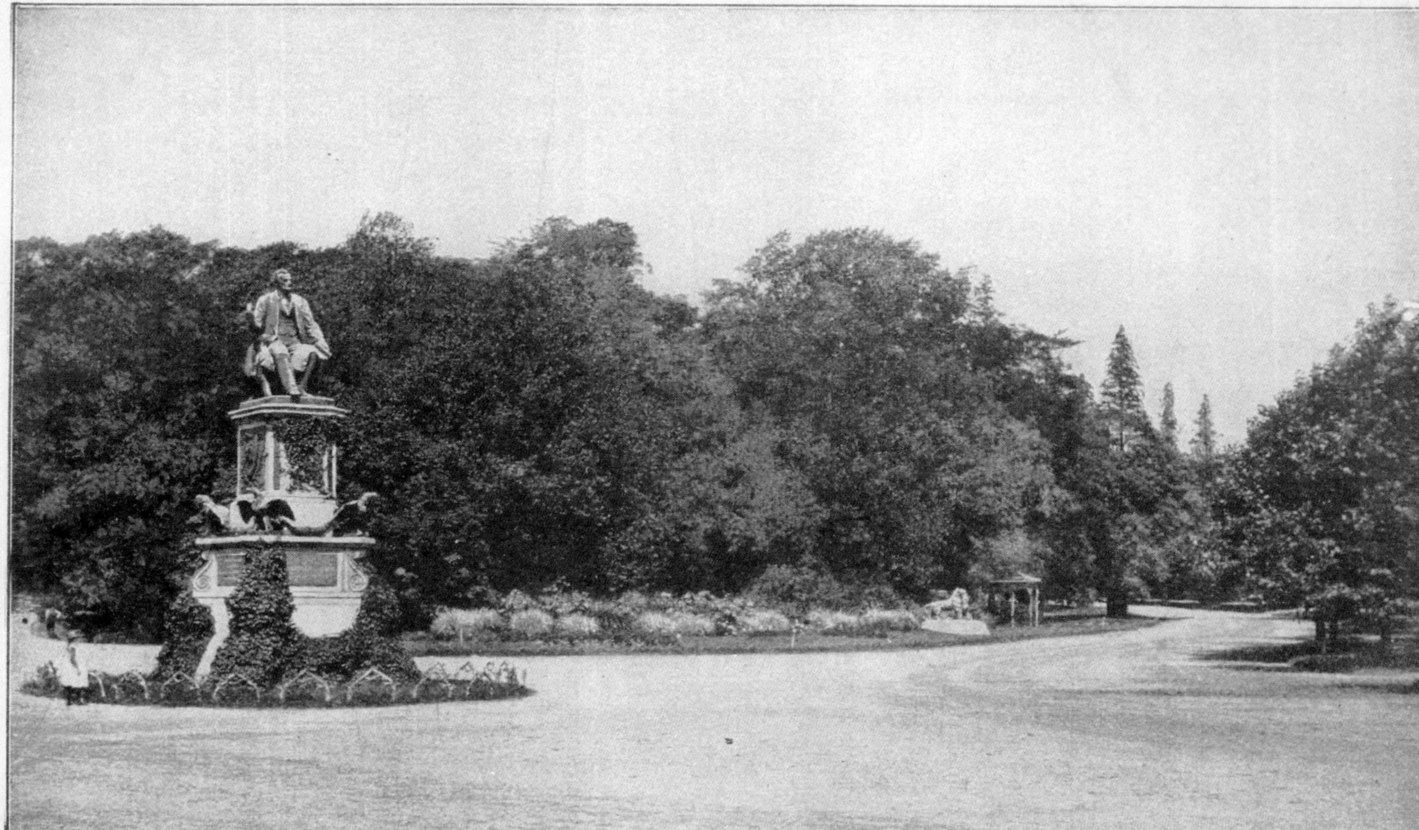

Lincoln Monument. Mineral Spring.

THE RIVER DRIVE FAIRMOUNT PARK.

THE OLD PARK (LEMON HILL).

The first acquisition of land by the city within the bounds of Fairmount Park was made in 1812, for the purpose of obtaining a supply of water free from impurities. This site was known in the earliest days as "Faire Mount." Here is situated the chief water-works of the city, one of the many attractions for visitors. This and the land on the east side of the Schuylkill to Girard Avenue is called the Old Park, where a vast amount of skill in landscape gardening is displayed, and a large grass-plot is set apart for croquet, lawn-tennis, and children's games. Here, at Green Street entrance, stands the

Washington Monument.—This imposing memorial to the Father of his Country was erected by the Pennsylvania Society of the Cincinnati during 1896, and unveiled by President McKinley, amid rejoicing ceremonies in which the whole city participated, in May, 1897. It is the result of a movement and of accumulating subscriptions that began in 1811; and the fund had increased to about $280,000 when the time came to use it. Professor Rudolph Siemering of Berlin designed the monument, which was constructed abroad and brought to this country. The work of erecting the monument began in the spring of 1896. Thirteen steps, symbolical of the thirteen original States of the Union, lead up to a platform from which rises a pedestal of granite, rich with carving and bronze ornamentation. On the pedestal stands the equestrian figure of Washington, twenty feet high. The entire height of the monument is forty-four feet. Its cost was about $250,000.

The top of "Fairmount," which rises just beyond, is covered by the old reservoir, and on the edge of the river at its further base are the old water-works, with their quaint Grecian architecture. Following the main pathways and driving northward, past a plaza containing a statue to Lincoln, we come to another eminence,—

Lemon Hill.—Upon it stands a former country-house of Robert Morris, the great financier of the Revolutionary government, now a restaurant. This locality is one of the most popular afternoon resorts in the Park. Concerts are given daily by a band employed by the city, in an open-air amphitheater with over three thousand seats, amid surroundings of extraordinary beauty and historic association. Along the river bank at the foot of Lemon Hill are a dozen or more pretty stone boat-houses, belonging to clubs in the Schuylkill

Navy; walking on north, we pass the *Grant Cottage* (the log hut used as winter quarters by Grant at City Point in 1864-'65, and brought here later), and the statue to the late Hon. Morton McMichael, and reach, about a mile from the Washington Monument, Girard Avenue and the *Girard Avenue Bridge* (a magnificent structure, 120 feet wide), where there stands a monument to Humboldt, erected by the German citizens. This marks the limits of the original park; but many years ago the city, partly to protect the water supply, and partly in appreciation of the need of pleasure grounds, began to acquire the parklands north of Girard Avenue, on both sides of the river, which are next to be explored. That on the same, or eastern, side of the Schuylkill may first be considered, by following the broad driveway along the river bank.

THE EAST PARK (MOUNT PLEASANT, ETC.).

The East Park begins at Girard Avenue, and extends northwardly in a comparatively narrow strip to the Wissahickon, and probably has more romantic and picturesque spots than any other part of Fairmount Park except along the Wissahickon. The Spring Garden Water-works and the Pennsylvania Railroad's great bridge are public works at its lower end, but beyond that it is all hills and ravines, dotted with colonial mansions "old in story," traversed by a system of roads and paths, — an ideal place for bicycling or rambling. The People's and the Ridge Avenue lines of street cars give direct routes to this region. The principal park road is the continuation of the East Drive along the bank of the river. Following that, half a mile above Girard Avenue Bridge, brings one to *Fountain Green*, built a century ago by Samuel Meeker; and a third of a mile more to *Mount Pleasant*, opposite the Columbia Bridge (Philadelphia & Reading Railway), once the home of Benedict Arnold. It was built, however, by Capt. John McPherson, a privateer of great celebrity during the French and Spanish wars preceding the Revolution, and John Adams, in 1774, pronounced it "the most elegant seat in Pennsylvania." At the outbreak of the Revolution, Arnold, then military governor of the State, purchased the property for his wife, *nee* Peggy Shippen; but when Arnold's treason became known, the State confiscated the life interest which he had retained. Between 1781 and

1782 the place was tenanted by General the Baron de Steuben. The house is now utilized as a restaurant.

A short distance above Mount Pleasant is *Rockland* (with Rockland Steamboat landing), a residence built about 1810, near a promontory from which there is a beautiful view of the river and of the heights beyond it. Other old estates are passed as we move on, especially *Ormiston* and *Edgeley*, below the great East Park Reservoir, beyond which we turn inland, and, making a long detour past the old Woodford mansion (now used as a Park Police office, and noted for the "Franklin trees" in its garden), we reach the Dauphin Street or Ridge Avenue entrance to the park, and the populous precincts of Strawberry Hill. This is the terminus of several lines of street-cars marked "Strawberry Mansion," and of the Park Trolley. *Strawberry Mansion* is an old-fashioned country-house surrounded by big trees, and commanding a large view of the river and the parks beyond it. Here are croquet and play-grounds, and open-air band concerts are given daily to large audiences, who may listen to the music while taking ice-cream or other light refreshment on the broad piazzas. The East Drive continues to skirt the river past Laurel Hill Cemetery (which begins just above), and leads to Wissahickon Park.

The Park Trolley Line is a new and important element in visiting Fairmount Park, and enables the hurried visitor to get a fair idea at very small expense of time and money. It starts at this point (Dauphin Street entrance), and its cars take a course of over six miles (or 9½ miles, if you add the line to West Philadelphia), yet nowhere covers a driveway or path at grade, and nowhere duplicates the route. The fare is 5 cents.

Skirting Strawberry Hill, the line crosses the Schuylkill, then turns up the river, which, with the Philadelphia & Reading Railway on this side and Laurel Hill Cemetery on the other, is kept in view for some time. *The Lilacs*, *The Willows*, and *Chamounix* are the names of stopping-places, at the last of which are boats on a small lake. The northern end of the West Park is reached at Woodside (a popular summer amusement resort), where a change may be made (additional fare) to a longer route terminating in West Philadelphia. After leaving here, the return road bears to the left and takes a charming homeward course through the woods past Belmont and Beechwood to the starting-point. This ride gives a rapid but very charming idea of the wilder regions of the West Park.

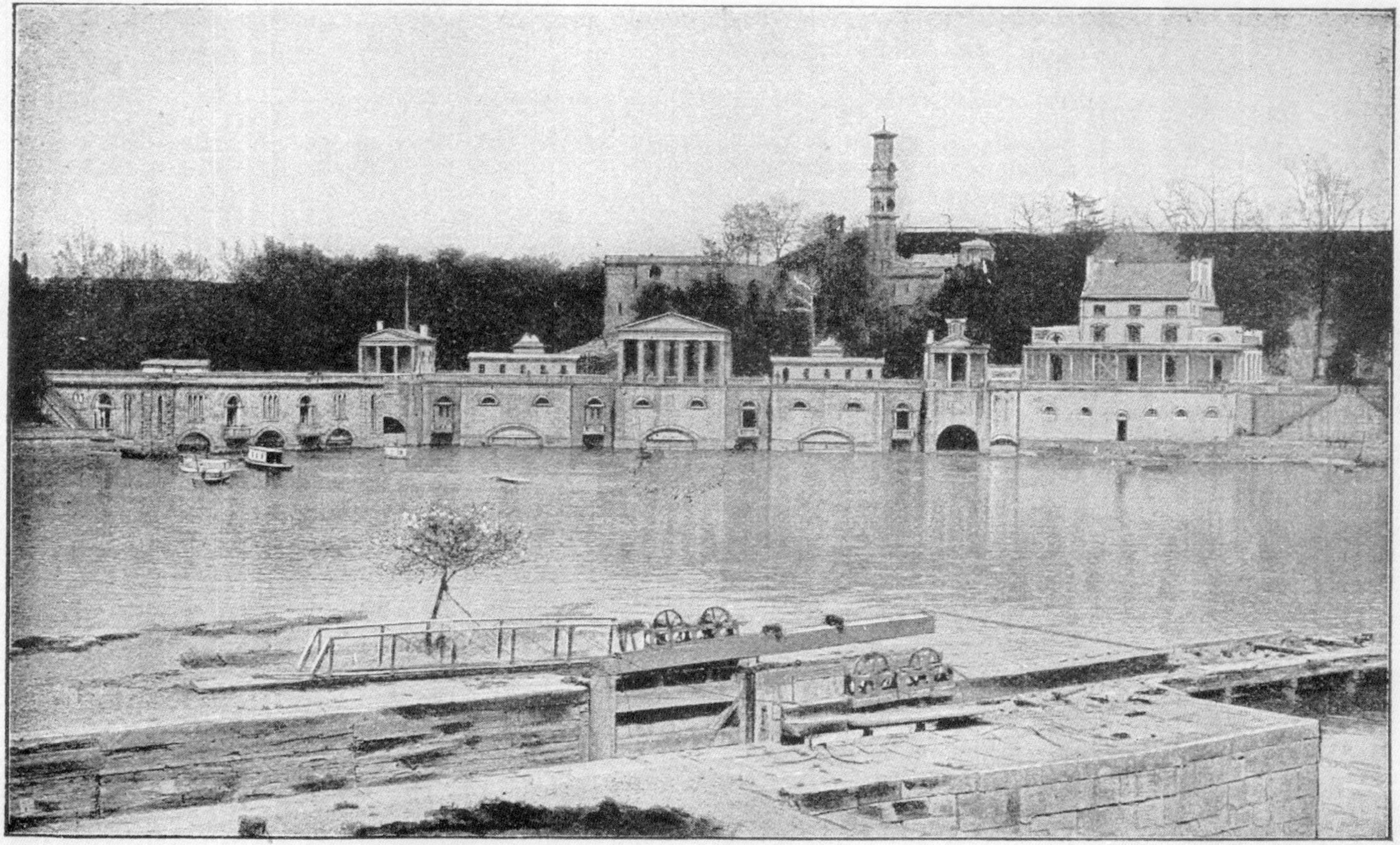

FAIRMOUNT WATER WORKS — From West Side of Schuylkill River.

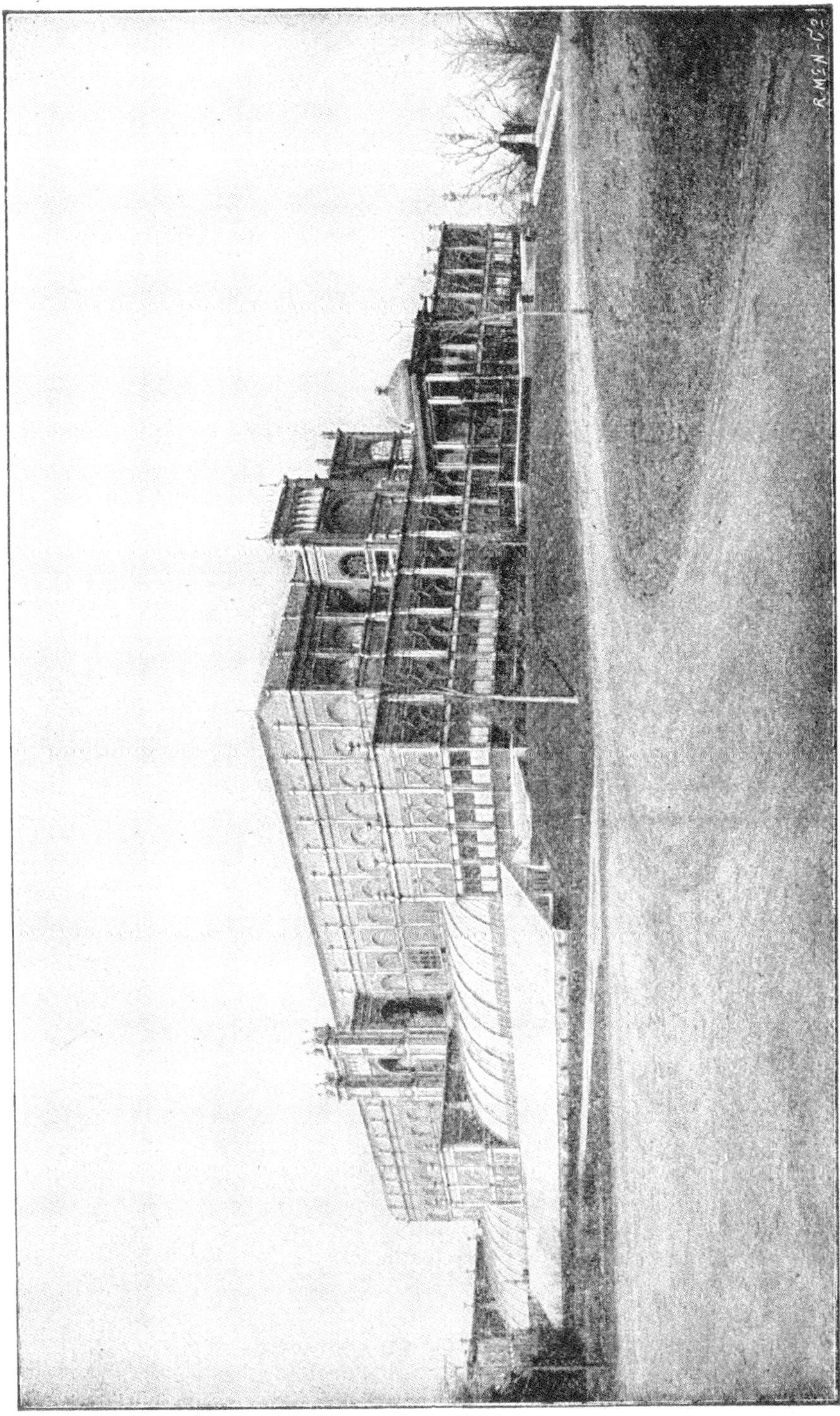

HORTICULTURAL HALL — Fairmount Park.

THE WEST PARK (CENTENNIAL GROUNDS, ETC.).

That part of Fairmount Park west of the Schuylkill is much larger than the area east of the river. The southeast angle is occupied by the Zoölogical garden, but the main portion begins on the north side of Girard Avenue. On this section the Centennial Exposition was held in 1876, and of the principal buildings, the Art Gallery and Horticultural Hall are still standing and in public use. Many Pennsylvania Railroad trains on Chestnut Hill branch, from Broad Street, stop at the Zoölogical Garden, and others at Park Station. Some Reading trains stop at Girard Avenue Station. The Chestnut and Walnut streets, and certain cars of the Market Street line; the Arch Street line; and the Girard Avenue line, through its feeders, go to the West Park. If carriages are used from the center of the city, the finest route is up Broad to Spring Garden Street, thence to Fairmount, through the old park to Girard Avenue, and west across Girard Avenue bridge.

The Lansdowne Drive is the fine road which exhibits the best features of this great pleasure-ground. It begins at the western end of the Girard Avenue bridge, and takes its name from the estate of "Lansdowne," of John Penn, called the American, whose nephew, John, built near here a house known as Egglesfield, in which he lived during the Revolution. Here, at its beginning, stands a relic of the time of Penn, in the little *Letitia* or *Penn House*, the first brick structure erected in Philadelphia. It was built in 1682, and for many years was used as the State House for the Province of Pennsylvania. It was taken to its present location many years ago from its original site in Letitia Street. Somewhat beyond it stands the old *Sweet Brier* mansion, built about 1810 by Samuel Breck, an eminent citizen and politician of that period. It commands one of the many wide and interesting views of the river, and immediately beyond it a rustic bridge carries the drive across *Lansdowne Ravine* into that part of the Park occupied by the Centennial Exposition. Some of the buildings remain, and offer inducements to the visitor to enter them.

In Horticultural Hall are still kept the magnificent tree ferns and other tropical plants which delighted visitors during the Centennial. The Conservatory measures 230 by 80 feet, and is 55 feet high. At the west end of the old hall is stored a splendid collection of blooming green-house plants, gathered many years ago by George

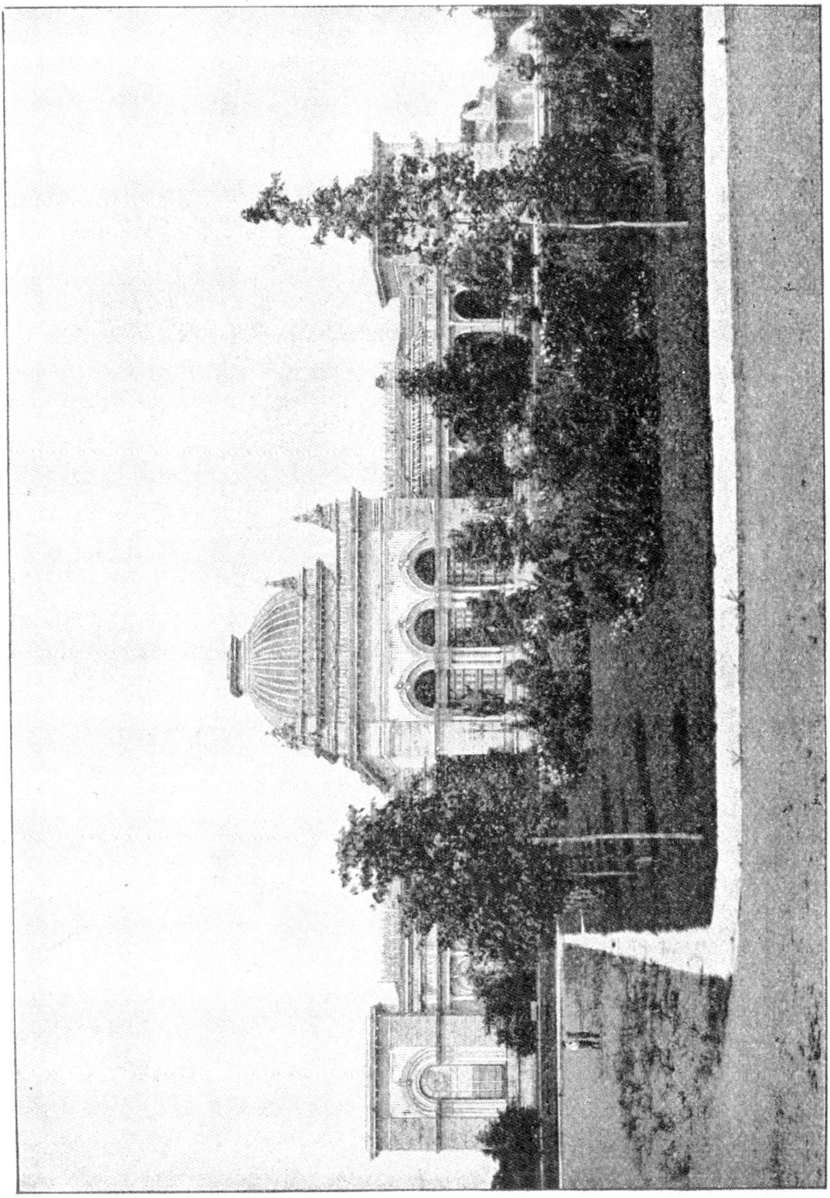

MEMORIAL HALL, FAIRMOUNT PARK.

W. Carpenter, and presented to the city by his widow. A restaurant is maintained here.

Memorial Hall, built in 1876 by the city, at a cost of $1,500,000 as a permanent memento of the Centennial, is now partly occupied by the School and Museums of Industrial Art elsewhere described.

George's Hill is an eminence 210 feet in height, north of these grounds, from which a very wide landscape is to be surveyed, and it is a favorite resort for picnic parties and carriage-drivers. Its summit bears the Belmont Reservoir (40,000,000 gallons), and at its foot is the allegorical fountain erected here in 1876 by the Catholic Total Abstinence Society.

Continuing along the beautiful drive, a mile further brings one to *Belmont Mansion*, the Revolutionary country-seat of Judge Richard Peters, an eminent patriot, who was acting as Secretary of War when his friend Morris, of Lemon Hill, was practically Secretary of the Treasury. Both Washington, when President, and Lafayette, were entertained here, among many other distinguished persons of a century ago; and the latter planted a white walnut, which still flourishes. The mansion now serves as a restaurant, and has a station on the Park trolley-line. On the bank of the river below Belmont, and opposite Peter's Island, may still be seen a little house which is called *Tom Moore's Cottage*, though it is not certain that the story that he once lived in it is true. The shady walks of *Belmont Glen* connect the two houses.

North of Belmont the park spreads out in a spacious area of hills and dales and beautiful woodlands, and the drive passes over high ground, giving views of the Belmont Driving Park, Park Nursery, and the river, with the marble-studded slopes of Laurel Hill beyond. The old mansion of Chamounix is an interesting item at the northern end of the park, where one may turn backward along the West Drive, and thus follow the river bank down to the starting-point at Girard Avenue Bridge.

WISSAHICKON PARK.

Many who have traveled much pronounce the scenery along the Wissahickon Park among the most charming in the world. The Wissahickon Creek winds in short curves for miles between high and thickly-wooded hills, which are frequently split into romantic gorges, with little streams dashing down them in rapid rifts and small cascades. There is a quiet loveliness attached to every foot of this portion of the park that leaves a deep impression which grows with each succeeding visit. The lower portion of the Wissahickon may be reached by the Ridge Avenue Cars and the Norristown Branch of the Reading Road to Wissahickon Station, and to the upper portion by the Pennsylvania Railroad, Chestnut Hill Branch, by taking a walk of some distance. The best method of seeing the whole of this portion of Fairmount Park is to hire a carriage and make a complete day of it. In this case, after reaching Girard Avenue and the park, take the East River Drive to the Wissahickon, and enter at the point where the stream and valley are spanned by the handsome stone bridge of the Norristown Branch of the Philadelphia & Reading Railway.

Fishing.—As the visitor enters the Wissahickon Valley, he finds the stream near its outlet dammed, and the water above placid and deep, and having on its bosom numberless boats which may be hired at the hotels. But a mile or so above, the quiet appearance of the stream ceases, the waters rush rapidly over a shallow bed, dash madly over and around large boulders, flash in rifts, and darken in deep pools. To the eye of an angler, this pellucid creek smacks of a trout stream, which indeed, some twenty miles above the park limits, it is, to a limited extent, but, favorable as it appears, few trout are seen or caught as far down as Chestnut Hill. For some years the State and United States Fish Commissions have been stocking its waters with black bass, and good sport for anglers may be had again in the Wissahickon. Besides these fish, the stream is literally alive with white chubs, which rise eagerly to the artificial fly. As many as fifty fish, ranging from six to ten inches, have been taken from the stream in a single afternoon. By an order of the Fairmount Park Commissioners, fishing is only allowed in the Wissahickon on Wednesdays and Saturdays.

Drives and Pathways.—The Wissahickon drive enters the park on the left bank of the stream, but a little above Rittenhouse Street it crosses by a wooden bridge to the right bank, and follows its sinuosities to the far side of Chestnut Hill, where it enters the Barren Hill Pike, a short distance to the north of St. Joseph's Roman Catholic Seminary. From the river road a footway, termed a bridle path, enters the valley and cuts along the hillside on the right bank of the creek, and extends to the bridge above Rittenhouse Street. At this point the bridle path is transferred to the left bank of the stream, from whence it runs high up the hillside through deep shade to the northern limits of the park. For convenience of description, we will follow this bridle path. For the first mile above the outlet of the creek the path winds about towering rocks and along the verge of

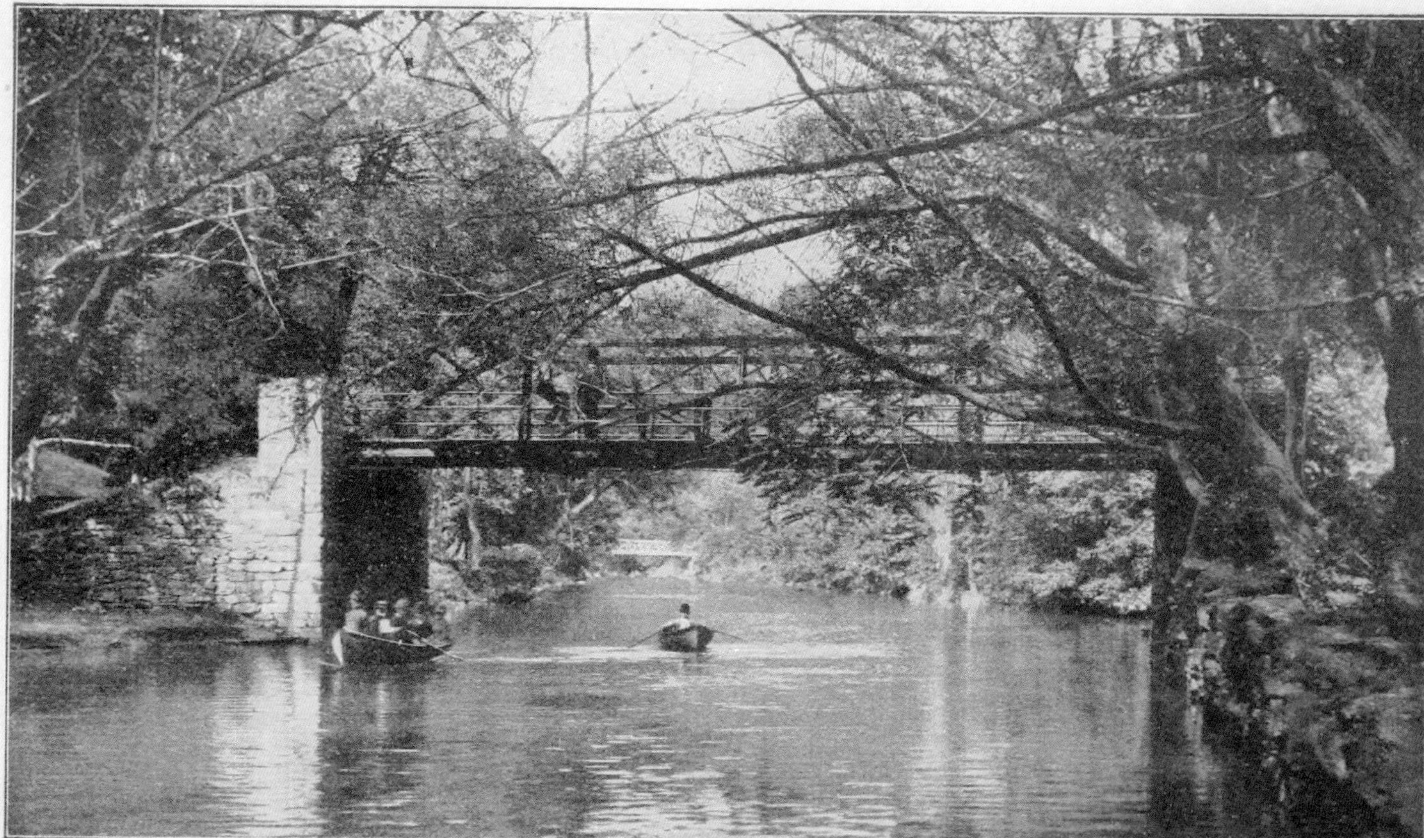

ON THE WISSAHICKON.

steep but low precipices; then the valley broadens out, and a series of fine picnic grounds are reached. From here is a steep ascent for two or more hundred feet to a pretty rustic summer-house.

The Monastery, Etc.—Near here is the "Monastery," a building once occupied by the "Hermits of the Ridge," the remains of a peculiar sect which settled in this neighborhood early in the eighteenth century under the name of the "Women of the Wilderness."

At the head of this body of men was John Kelpius, a young scholar and mystic, who prayed and waited for the coming of the "woman clothed with the sun, with the moon under her feet, and twelve stars on her forehead. She who had fled into the wilderness." The sect came from Germany to America because, from many events and signs, in which the thirty-years' war, the newness of this country, its peculiar situation, etc., it was believed America was the place for the coming of the promised one. The sect did not exist long after the death of Kelpius, which occurred a few years after his arrival in this country.

On the opposite side of the creek is a fine spring named after Kelpius, and not far away is a romantic Hermit's Glen. The huge rock just below the drive bridge is known as Washington's Rock.

Mom Rinker's Rock.—Taking the bridle path on the east side of the stream for perhaps a short mile, "Mom" Rinker's Rock is come upon. Diligent investigation has failed to satisfactorily explain this peculiar title, though the name Rinker is a familiar one among the early Germantown families. On the top of this rock is placed a statue of William Penn, a gift of the Hon. John Welsh, once minister to England, and who owned the place where the statue stands, before it was utilized for park purposes.

The Caves.—Beyond pretty scenery and romantic spots there is nothing particularly noteworthy until Livezey's Lane is reached. Here, by crossing the bridge to the drive and walking north about two hundred yards, a little stream is come upon, which empties into the Wissahickon, and on the north side of that little stream, twenty-five or thirty feet from the road, is a mysterious artificial cave. It once was entered from the brook, but with years portions have fallen in until now not more than forty or fifty feet of cavern remain. It has two chambers. A hundred yards farther on is a second cave, also the work of man, and a third, now entirely obliterated, existed a few years ago a short distance beyond. There is a tradition that these caves were made by the "Women of the Wilderness," and also that

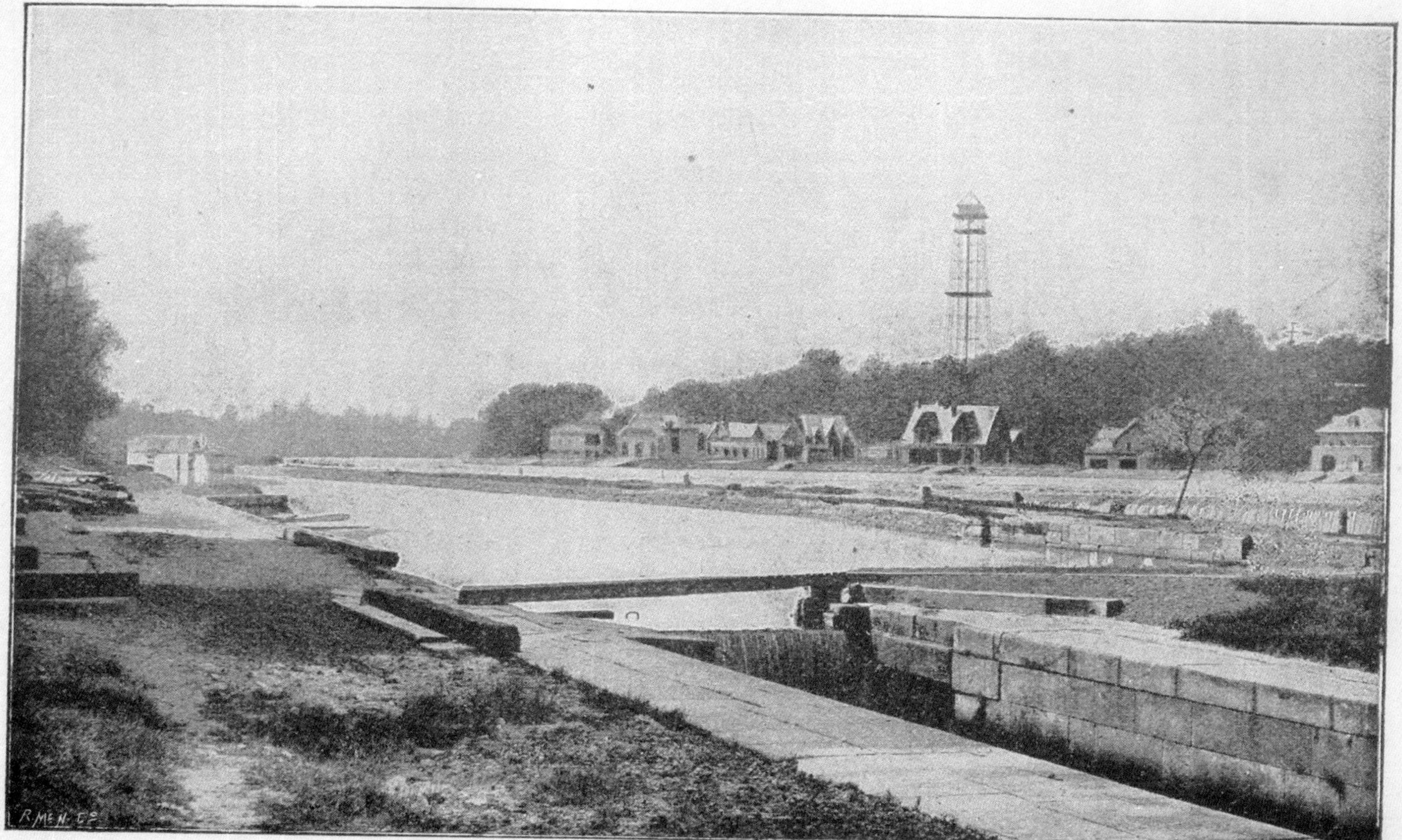

Lemon Hill Observatory.

THE SCHUYLKILL RIVER AND BOAT HOUSES—Fairmount Park.

they were the work of Indians. This, however, can not be, since they were made by blasting and drilling tools. What is more probable, is another story that they were made by prospectors for lead and silver during the early part of the present century.

The Sneaking Indian.—A short distance below the caves, right on the driveway, is a natural curiosity which has lately received a great deal of public attention. At that point a rock, fifteen or twenty feet high, stands on the west side of the road; when one approaches it from the north, and arrives within about a hundred yards, this rock takes the form of a stooping Indian, bow and arrow in hand, stealing upon his prey. The resemblance is so perfect and striking as to require no imagination to assist one to perceive it; yet, on nearer approach, it wholly disappears, and only formless fissures and knobs meet the surprised gaze.

Livezey House.—Crossing again to the bridle path and following it a short mile, the old Livezey House is reached. This old edifice, which was in the hands of the Livezey family for a century and a half before the city included it in the park, was, during the Revolutionary War, a sort of neutral ground where British and American officers met and forgot for a few hours, in the company of the charming ladies, that they were at war with each other. The remains of a pre-Revolutionary mill still stand beside the house.

Devil's Pool.—A short distance above Livezey House the Cresheim Creek empties into the Wissahickon. At the point where the bridle path crosses it, by a pretty rustic bridge, is a large, dark, square body of water known as the Hermit's Pool. At one corner, beneath an overhanging rock, thrown there, according to an Indian legend, by an evil spirit, is a pretty little cascade. On the other side of this overhanging rock, and at the junction of another huge mass, is a small, deep pool, continually frothing and seething. This is the "Devil's Pool," believed by children to be bottomless.

The rock on the west side of the Devil's Pool, crowned by a rustic pavilion, is *Lover's Leap.* It derives its name from an Indian legend, and the vicinity is a favorite picnic ground. Above Cresheim Creek is *Valley Green*, where boats may be hired and a comfortable meal obtained at the quaint old wayside Valley Green Hotel. Half a mile above Valley Green, on the drive, is the first public fountain erected in Philadelphia. It has a lion's-head spout, framed by a granite arch, and the water falls into a deep basin cut from a single block of stone. Above are cut the words, "Pro Bono Publico," and below the basin, "Esto Perpetuo." It was presented to the city in 1854, by Mr. Joseph Cook. Not far above "Pro Bono Publico," on the east side of the creek, high up on the steep hill, stands a huge rock projecting from among the tall trees and having cut in its face a large cavern. Surmounting this rock is the wooden effigy of an Indian. According to a legend, a hunted Indian sought refuge in this cavern, and thus escaped his foes. Not far above, the park limit is reached.

Wissahickon Park is kept, as nearly as possible, in its original wild state, and it is estimated that more than 200,000 trees clothe its steep and picturesque sides.

Bartram's Gardens.

Bartram's Gardens is in the Twenty-seventh Ward. It was placed in the city plan July 2, 1888. Its area is about thirty acres, and it is situated between Fifty-third, Fifty-fourth, and Eastwick streets and the Schuylkill River. To reach this park, take the Baltimore & Ohio Railroad, or the Woodland Avenue branch of the Union Traction Company, Walnut Street Line. This park is one of the most important in a historical point of view of any of the city's public grounds, and is besides an exceedingly interesting place to visit. It is a portion of the farm of the celebrated botanist, John Bartram, and of his almost equally distinguished son, William. On these grounds the two established probably the first botanic garden in this country, and nearly every specimen of tree planted was brought by one or the other of them from its native place. A large number of these trees still exist; among the most noteworthy is a huge cypress, which now has a girth of more than twenty-five feet, and is the largest specimen in cultivation. This was brought on horseback from Georgia by the elder Bartram.

Another tree which is still there, though in a dying condition, is one which is surrounded in some respects by the greatest mystery. It is called the Franklin Tree. On one of William Bartram's explorations in the South, he came upon three acres of a wonderfully beautiful plant, with long, shining green leaves, and large, single, white, camellia-like blossoms. He brought home with him four seeds and planted them in his garden. One of these seeds grew, and in time reached maturity and blossomed. Then Bartram discovered that the plant, although its flower parts were apparently perfect, would not seed. As he recognized the great value of the Franklin Tree for cultivation, he made a second visit to the locality where he first found it, to gather more seeds or secure some plants. But when he arrived every plant had disappeared, and, although the whole country has since been thoroughly searched, not another plant was ever found in a wild state. Botanists since have decided that the Franklin Tree's mission on earth was about fulfilled when Bartram discovered it, and soon after became extinct, except for the plant then growing in Philadelphia. Nurserymen now only keep the stock up by layering it, and the product in this way is extremely small. From the Bartram Tree are a few fine specimens in Fairmount Park, near the old Woodford Mansion.

Another feature of interest in the Bartram Gardens is the old Bartram House, which was built by John Bartram without any outside assistance. It is a quaint structure, with a still more quaint inscription, cut by himself in a stone, built in the wall over the front window of the room which he used as a study, and which reads as follows:

"'Tis God Alone, Almighty Lord,
The Holy One, by me adored."

An old stone cider-press still stands on the place, and from one portion of the grounds a magnificent view down the river is obtained.

Other Parks and Public Grounds.

Of the lesser parks of the city only a few require any special notice. William Penn left five squares upon his original plot of the city. The central one was the ground now covered by the City Hall, and latterly known as Penn Square; the others are Franklin, Washington, Rittenhouse, and Logan. *Franklin Square* is an area of 6.7 acres, bounded by Race and Vine, Sixth and Seventh streets. It was used for many years as a burying-ground, and headstones still lie flat above graves whose bones have long ago mouldered into dust. It is filled with large, handsome trees, has a fine fountain, and is surrounded by old-fashioned streets. It has been suitably named, for Franklin lived and is buried in this quarter. *Washington Square* adjoins Independence Square at its southwestern corner, and in the early days was the principal Potter's Field, where hundreds of victims of the yellow-fever epidemic of 1793-'94 were buried. Later it was improved, and became noted all over the country for its trees, no two of which were alike, and many were very uncommon, but as these died they were replaced by ordinary species, so that now this peculiarity has been lost. The streets about it were formerly fashionable, and many old mansions remain, but are mostly devoted to offices. A neat soldier's monument adorns it.

Rittenhouse Square is still the center of a highly fashionable district, and is well cared for. Its ornament is a bronze group by Barye,—the "Lion and the Serpent." *Logan Square* was in early days a Potter's Field, and place for the execution of criminals; and here was held, during the Civil War, the great Sanitary Fair. It is now a handsome park among fine residences, and has a soldier's monument. Another square identified with old times is the *William Penn Treaty Park*, on the Delaware River, in Kensington. It is a small tract, and owes its existence to the fact that there grew the traditional Treaty Elm (destroyed in 1819) beneath which William Penn is said to have made that agreement with the Delaware Indians in 1682, which, as Voltaire remarked, "was never signed and never broken." The site of the tree is marked by a small, plain monument.

Other park-areas have been opened as the city enlarged, but few call for special mention. John Dickinson Square, in the First Ward, has been fitted up lately as a children's play-ground, with shelter-houses for boys and girls, and arrangements for out-door games. Other parks are to be similarly provided. *Girard Park*, in the southern part of the city, was the homestead and farm of Stephen Girard. Germantown Park is a small plot, interesting only because it contains a handsome soldier's monument. Opposite it is the Elliston P. Morris house, the executive mansion during the yellow-fever scourge of 1793-'94, and occupied during that time by President Washington and cabinet. McPherson Square, in Frankford, was originally the homestead of Gen. William McPherson, a patriot of the Revolution. Prior to that struggle, he was an officer in the British Navy, but when the war for independence opened he resigned and gave his sword to the land of his birth. The old homestead is still standing. Another rustic area, with fine possibilities, in Frankford, is Juniata Park; and the same may be said of Stenton Park, near Chestnut Hill. This was the home of William Penn's Colonial Secretary, James Logan. The mansion is still in perfect order, and is occupied by descendants of the family. The little Ontario Park, at Thirteenth and Stiles streets, is worthy of note only as having a handsome electric fountain, presented by William L. Elkins, whose lights work automatically. *Vernon Park* is a place especially interesting to botanists. It contains eight acres, and on the occasion of its ceremonious opening, July 4, 1893, a great meeting was held in honor of Prof. Thomas Meehan, the father of the Small Parks Movement, who resides in that ward; and a large silver memorial was presented him by the citizens of Philadelphia, for his successful efforts in behalf of the increase of public greens. Vernon Park was the homestead of one branch of the Wister family, and the old mansion, one of the handsomest of the Colonial residences, stands amid a great grove of trees in the center of the park. Many of the trees in this place were collected by Kin, an eccentric botanical collector of the early part of the present century.

Cemeteries.

Philadelphia contains a number of notable "cities of the dead," to which visitors are attracted either for the beauty of their situations, adornments and monumental marbles, or for their historical associations. Among the latter class that of the Old Swedes Church and of Christ Church are elsewhere described. Many of the Friends' burying-grounds are highly interesting to those acquainted with local families and history; and the suburban churches often stand in the midst of beautiful little graveyards where the ashes of the founders of the city and the commonwealth have long reposed. The foremost cemetery of the city, however, answering to Greenwood in its relation to New York, is that of

Laurel Hill.—This great and highly ornamented burying-ground covers the high eastern bank of the Schuylkill, between the East (Fairmount) Park and Wissahickon Park. It is bounded on the east by Ridge Avenue, whose cars go to its North Gate, and on the west by the East Drive, which runs along the river margin, and past the South Gate. The Schuylkill steamboats land there, and the Philadelphia & Reading Railway has a station for the cemetery on its Norristown Branch.

Laurel Hill was founded in 1835, and therefore is, next to Mount Auburn (near Boston), the oldest suburban cemetery in the country. It now contains nearly one hundred acres, all of which has been laid out with artistic skill, and beautified by the managers as well as by owners of burying-lots. If the intentions of the present managers are carried out, the Park Drive along the western base of the cemetery slope will "resemble the Appian Way, leading out of Rome, where the road is lined with monuments."

This cemetery is divided into three parts,—North, South, and Central. North Laurel Hill is the original part, and took its name from the fact that it was previously "The Laurels," the homestead of the Sims family. South Laurel Hill was "Harleigh," the country-seat of the Rawle family; while George Pepper formerly occupied Central Laurel Hill as an estate named "Fairy Hill." The south entrance is through rather an old-fashioned but dignified gateway, whose massive posts are crowded by symbolic urns; but the principal entrance is that to North Laurel Hill, where an archway through a fine temple-like structure admits one to the sacred grounds. Just within this stately entrance is a group of statuary, cut in brownstone by Thom, which is the chief ornament of the grounds in a public way. It is a group exhibiting Old Mortality at his favorite occupation of restoring defaced tombstones, pausing a moment to converse with Sir Walter Scott. Readers of Scott's *Old Mortality* will recall the scene:

"An old man was seated upon the monument of the slaughtered Presbyterians," writes Sir Walter, "busily employed in deepening with his chisels the letters of the inscription, which, announcing in scriptural language the promised blessings of futurity to be the lot of the slain, anathematized the murderers with corresponding violence. A blue bonnet of unusual dimensions covered the gray hairs of the pious workman. His dress was a large, old-fashioned coat of the coarse cloth called *hoddin-gray*, usually worn by the elder peasants, with waistcoat and breeches of the same, and the whole suit, though still in decent repair, had obviously seen a train of long service. Strong clouted shoes studded with hob-nails, and *gramoches* or *leggins*, made of thick black cloth, completed his equipment. Beside him fed among the graves a pony, the companion of his journey, whose extreme whiteness, as well as its projecting bones and hollow eyes, indicated its antiquity. It was harnessed in the most simple manner, with a pair of branks or bridle, a hair tether or halter, and a *sunk*, or a cushion of straw, instead of bridle and saddle. A canvas pouch hung round the neck of the animal, for the purpose, probably, of containing the rider's tools, and anything else he might have occasion to carry with him. Although I had never seen the old man before, yet, from the singularity of his employment, and the style of his equipage, I had no difficulty in recognizing a religious itinerant whom I have often heard talked of, and who was known in various parts of Scotland by the title of Old Mortality."

VI.

THE RIVERS AND HARBORS.

Two large rivers touch Philadelphia — the Delaware and its great tributary, the Schuylkill. The first divides Pennsylvania from New Jersey, and separates Camden from Philadelphia by about a mile. The Schuylkill divides the city into two unequal parts before it empties into the Delaware. From the latter stream, which is only navigable by moderate-sized vessels for a short distance, Philadelphia draws the greater part of its water supply, impounding it first by two large dams, one at Fairmount and the other at Shawmont, and secondly by large subsiding reservoirs in various parts of the city. The Delaware is a navigable stream for a distance of about one hundred and thirty-one miles, or some thirty miles above Philadelphia.

The general Improvement of the harbor and waterways of Philadelphia, which has been carried forward, under the combined efforts of the Federal and City governments, since 1891, is now completed. A channel from 300 to 600 feet wide is now opened through all the shoals from the city to the sea, having a depth at low tide of not less than 26 feet. Improvements of value, not only to the city, but to commerce generally, have also been made at the Delaware Breakwater, at the entrance to Delaware Bay, in the formation of a "harbor of refuge" suitable for vessels of the deepest draft. The improvement of the harbor proper has been at the expense of the city, and has resulted in the removal of the islands that used to obstruct the river between the city and Camden, and the transference of a large part of their material to enlarge and elevate the area of League Island, and to fill in and make useful flatlands along the shore. There is now a channel 1,000 feet wide and at least 26 feet deep at low tide along the water front, between the Delaware River bridge, at Bridesburg, and Kaighn's Point, a distance of 6½ miles, and the other parts of the channel have a least depth of 12 feet at low tide, so that a large, deeply-laden vessel can now go to sea without waiting for a high tide to lift it over shoals. The lower part of the Schuylkill, whence much of the grain, all the petroleum, and much other freight, are exported, has also been deepened.

The reconstruction of the Philadelphia Water front, a con-

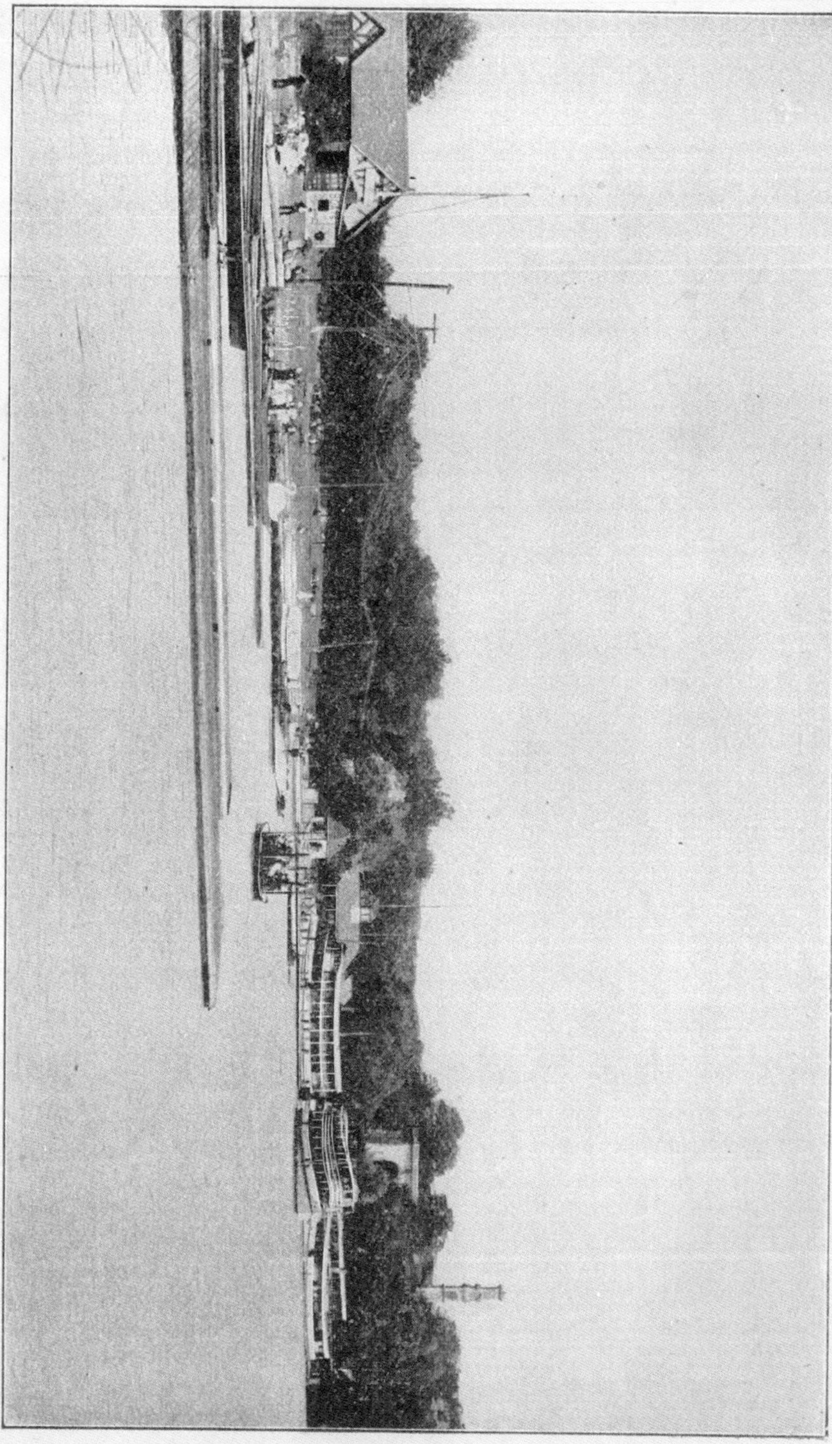

STEAMBOAT LANDING, FAIRMOUNT PARK.

GOING TO BOSTON? TRY THE

NEW AMERICAN

and its RATHSKELLER, the most unique room of its kind in the country.

HANOVER STREET, near Scollay Square Station of Subway, **BOSTON, MASS.**

EUROPEAN PLAN.

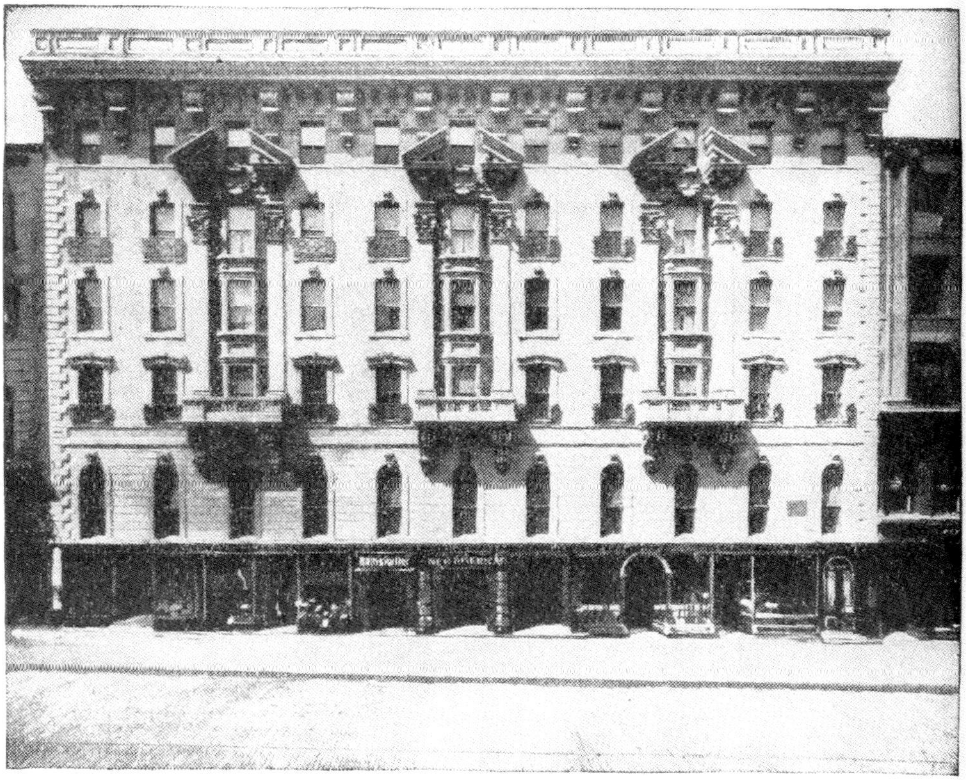

SITUATED IN THE BUSINESS PORTION OF THE CITY.

The House is convenient to the historical places of interest, shopping districts, amusements, Steamboat Lines, Railroad Stations, etc. Best rooms in the city for the price: $1.00 per day and upward—baths, $2.00 per day and upward. Running hot and cold water in every room, also **Public Telephones.**

Every room with steam heat and lighted by electricity. Our extensive refurnishings and additions, including tiled bathrooms and new open plumbing, give our patrons all the modern conveniences at moderate rates.

From South Station, take Federal Street surface car, stop at Washington Street, corner Elm Street; or take elevated train to Scollay Square. From North Station, leave surface cars at Washington Street, corner Elm Street; leave elevated train at Scollay Square. *Commercial men will find the House conveniently located for visiting the surrounding towns without loss of time.*

C. A. JONES, Proprietor. **A. C. JONES, Manager.**

temporaneous work with the channel improvement, has been in progress since 1894, and many new piers have been constructed, providing facilities for the largest steamships. The widening of Delaware Avenue, the street running along the river front, by extending the bulkward into the river, was commenced in October, 1897. The work is to be continued, and will result in a street 150 feet wide.

A Trip up the River.

A steamboat trip up the Delaware River is a very enjoyable experience, and one to be honestly recommended. Excellent boats depart mornings and afternoons from both the Chestnut Street and Arch Street wharves, and the fare is less than a dollar.

The northerly part of Philadelphia first passed (after the vast export and coal-delivery yards of the Philadelphia & Reading Railway at Port Richmond have been left behind) is *Kensington*, whose shore is a "forest of masts" and a wilderness of mills, factories, and grain-elevators. In their midst is the little park where stood Penn's "Treaty Elm." A recent intelligent commentator upon Philadelphia has characterized this part of the city as follows:

"Kensington, the paradise of small houses, where every laboring-man is a landed proprietor and every woman the mistress of her own house. There are miles and miles of these little brick houses, encircling the old town on all sides, with their white facings and marble steps. Here is the first cause of the prosperity, the vast magnitude, and, above all, the health and happiness of this great manufacturing city, in which the skilled laborer with small pay must necessarily play so important a part. Here also is to be found the inspiration for that name which so aptly tells the secret of the Philadelphian's love for his Philadelphia — the 'City of Homes'."

The steamboats pass near the Pennsylvania shore (leaving Petty's, or "Treaty," Island on the right), and give good views of *Cramp's Ship-Yards*,— a place of almost universal interest, of late, on account of the well-known "ocean greyhounds" and warships that have been constructed there. Philadelphia has always been a leader in naval architecture, and this firm was founded as early as 1830, and during the three-quarters of a century since then over three hundred vessels have been built in its yards, including some of those best known to the world.

A vast bridge spanning the river has attracted all eyes since passing Petty's Island, and now, 5½ miles above the Market-Street wharf, the steamer glides under it. It is the property of the Pennsylvania Railroad, which began it in January, 1895, and opened it for traffic in March, 1896, under the name "Delaware Bridge."

This bridge is of steel, and rests on stone piers with a weight of about fifteen million pounds, requiring the foundations to be sunk seventy feet below the surface of the river. There are three fixed spans, each 533 feet in length, and a draw 325 feet in length, and 50 feet above high tide, making a total length over the river of 1,950 feet, to which must be added the approaches. By this bridge it is now possible to run through trains, both passenger and freight, not only between Broad Street Station and Atlantic City, but to and from any part of the west.

Bridesburg and the United States Arsenal, at the mouth of Frankford Creek, appear just above the bridge, and above them is *Tacony*, where, a short distance from the shore, is located the Tacony Iron & Metal Works, in which was manufactured the colossal statue of William Penn that surmounts the tower of City Hall. Just above the metal works, spreading broadly upon the shore and stretching far inland, is the Keystone Saw Works, owned by the Disstons.

To this point the steamboat plies near the Pennsylvania shore, but, on leaving Tacony, it crosses to the New Jersey side, and makes a stop at Riverton, one of the most attractive places on the Delaware. The Riverton Yacht Club has erected on the shores an ornamental club-house, and around it the shores, beautifully sodded, slope from the water's edge upward and back through groves of majestic trees. Crossing the river again, the steamboat moves northward to *Torresdale*, the northern limit of Philadelphia. Attractive villas peep from among the trees, and some distance back, nearly hidden by the foliage, is the "Forrest Home," the bequest of Edwin Forrest, as a retreat for aged actors. Delightful pastoral scenery on both sides of the river now greets the visitor, increasing steadily in beauty, mile by mile, as the river narrows perceptibly. Frequent stops are made by the boat, but the most important after leaving Torresdale is *Beverly*, once one of the terminal points of a famous crossing-place known as Dunk's Ferry. Above Beverly the river widens again, forming two channels around a spot of land known as Burlington Island. Here, on the Pennsylvania side, is *Bristol*, and on the New Jersey shore, Burlington, connected by a steam ferry. During the last century Bristol enjoyed a great reputation as a watering-place, and an inn of Colonial days, remodeled, is still in use there. A place of great interest and curiosity there is the State fish hatchery, supplying young shad for the river.

Burlington, which lies nearly opposite Bristol, antedates Philadelphia five years, and the site was first suggested by George Fox, the founder of the "Quakers," in 1672. In 1677, 228 members of thi society landed here from the "goode shippe London," and occupied the lands just below the Assiscunk Creek, the property being regularly purchased from the Indians. Burlington, since then, has grown to be quite a large town, is comfortably wealthy, is noted for its schools, and is filled with places of historic interest, among which may be noted the old dwelling of Fenimore Cooper, the novelist.

Above Burlington the Delaware, never straight, begins to be extraordinarily crooked, and a short distance in a straight line below Trenton, the capital of New Jersey, it takes a sharp curve from the northwest to the northeast, making the journey by water one of fully fourteen miles. The tongue of land formed by this great curve is one of the most famous on the river, being known as *The Manor of Pennsburg*. Here was located Penn's country home, on a tract originally comprising 8,000 acres. The founder of Pennsylvania occupied this mansion only one year, between 1700 and 1701, and then finally returned to England. Another sharp turn in the river takes the visitor past *Florence Heights*, on the Jersey shore, where there is a large iron foundry and pipe factory. Here the stream narrows, with numerous pretty islands interspersed over its surface, and the shores become heightened and roughened into miniature mountains. Beyond is *White Hill*, another spot interesting historically, and further noteworthy as being the most eastern point of Pennsylvania. Here, too, the Delaware bends so sharply to the southward that for some distance the boat's head is pointed directly toward Philadelphia.

Bordentown is the next noted landing place. Here dwelt for many years Admiral Charles Stewart, "Old Ironsides," of the United States Navy, and on his estate dwelt the late Mrs. Delia Parnell, daughter of the old admiral, mother of the noted Irish leader, Charles Stewart Parnell. To Bordentown came, in 1816, Joseph Bonaparte, ex-king of Naples and Spain, to live as Count de Survelliers after his dethronement. He occupied a mansion at Point Breeze, since called Bonaparte Park; the house is still standing, though in a dilapidated condition. Another famous resident of Bordentown was Prince Murat, nephew of Napoleon and Joseph, a son of Prince Joachim Murat, king of the Sicilies. He occupied a farm near his uncle Joseph. At Bordentown is a curious little monument of granite to commemorate the sixtieth anniversary of the first running of the "John Bull" locomotive at this point. A bronze tablet on the monument represents old "John Bull," a notable inscription accompanying it.

Above Bordentown the river shallows suddenly, and the channel through which the boats pass is tortuous in the extreme all the way to *Trenton*, the terminus of the navigable waters.

A Short Trip Down the River.

A trip down the river may be made on the steamer *Republic*, which in summer runs regularly to Cape May from Arch Street wharf.

At the outset, great business houses line the banks of the river; huge sugar refineries, among which that of the Spreckles is conspicuous, and other lofty buildings almost hide the city in their rear; but near the American Line Steamers' wharves a glimpse may be had of the *Old Swedes Church*, the most ancient edifice of worship in the city of Philadelphia. It was built about 1700, and through all the years which have elapsed it has been maintained in its primitive and refreshing country-church-like appearance. Below are the old navy-yard wharves, where, before the present site on League Island was taken, the Government cared for its war vessels in Philadelphia. Nearly opposite, on the New Jersey shore, is Kaighn's Point, the starting-place of the Philadelphia & Reading's line to Atlantic City. Many of the large factories that have lately increased Camden's prosperity are in this neighborhood.

Below Kaighn's Point, on the Pennsylvania shore, begins that part of Philadelphia known as the Neck — the narrow stretch of land terminating with the confluence of the Delaware and the Schuylkill. The approach to this spot is heralded by odors not from "Araby the blest," the cause of which are numerous fertilizing-making and bone-boiling establishments. Below them are the Pennsylvania Salt Company's works, with their extensive wharves at which the vessels from Ivigtut, Greenland, unload the kryolite gathered in that far-off arctic land. Marshes are now the rule, and across them, looking northward, is plainly to be seen the huge tower of City Hall, and the dim outline of the statue of William Penn surmounting it. As the river approaches the southern limits of Philadelphia, it makes a curve to the westward known as Horse Shoe Bend, and on the right are the Greenwich piers, where the Pennsylvania Railroad Company ships its coal, and the various gas coal companies put the soft coal from the western part of the State on board vessels.

On the left, on the sloping New Jersey shore, is the town of *Gloucester*, which for some years bore a malodorous reputation on account of the race-track and the gambling which existed there. But the place has a better fame than this, because of the quality of its "planked" shad, a delicacy which epicureans love, and which brings thousands to Gloucester every season to enjoy. At Gloucester is the largest shad fishery on the river, and, when this toothsome fish is on its annual journey to the spawning grounds, multitudes go purposely to Gloucester to witness the hauling in of the huge seine, the largest of the kind in the United States.

During the month of May and the first two weeks in June, the United States Fish Commissioner's steamer, "Fish Hawk," usually anchors at Gloucester, for the purpose of hatching shad eggs to be deposited in the river. Admission to this vessel is free, and her apparatus and methods are interesting.

Below Gloucester the river sweeps grandly around the Horse Shoe Bend, and the voyager can see the "Neck" in all its glory. Across the lowland, with its green, marshy grass, rise the buildings of League Island Navy Yard, the Government naval construction and repair station. Big Timber Creek empties its waters into those of the Delaware, just below Gloucester, and on its lower side, running to the banks of the latter, is *Washington Park*, a new pleasure resort of five or six hundred acres, where the longest pier on the river (1,600 feet) juts out to the deep channel. Just below is *Red Bank*, once well patronized as a summer resort, but now best remembered as a Revolutionary battle-ground, where, on October 21, 1777, a British force of 1,200 Hessians, under Count Donop, was repulsed with great loss by the American garrison of Fort Mercer. The old earthworks can still be traced, and a marble monument marks the battle-ground. The southern side of this village is the *Sanitarium*, of an association which brings here in summer thousands of poor children from the city and gives them an outing.

8

The mouth of the Schuylkill is here passed; and so hidden is it, by the peculiar shore lines, that one does not wonder it was passed and repassed by the early explorers before it was discovered, and there is a realizing sense of the fitness of the name Schuylkill, the Dutch term meaning "hidden river," which was given it. Below it, on the Pennsylvania shore, is old *Fort Mifflin*, built upon the site of a Revolutionary battery captured by the British, and likely soon to be replaced by a less picturesque but more effective fortification. Hog Island, the pasture land of herds of Shetland ponies, and *Tinicum Island*, in regard to which many romantic tales have been told, follow quickly, and then is seen the *Quarantine Station* and Lazaretto of the harbor, marked by the yellow flag. There is a charming view down the Delaware River below the Lazaretto, although the shores are low and the river wide. It shows one of the finest industrial sights the eye can look upon, backed by sloping banks of greensward and woodland. Chester Island is in mid-stream, and the city of *Chester* is broadly stretched on the right bank of the river. At the lower end of the latter are located the once famous Roach ship yards, and below them immense mills at intervals along the banks. The Christiana River empties into the Delaware near here, and back over the meadows is seen the thriving town of *Wilmington*, along the base and partly up the slope of the Brandywine Hills, which run far away inland toward the northwest. A low green shore extends below Wilmington on the Delaware side, and on the Jersey boundaries is a narrow streak of yellow beach with trees in the rear. Then comes *New Castle*, that town which a certain ironically-inclined person designated as the only "finished town in the United States."

The rapidly widening Delaware now warns the visitor that the head of Delaware Bay is near, and just before that broad expanse of water is reached, Pea Patch Island, on which *Fort Delaware* is, comes in view in mid-stream. The fort is a high stone structure with barracks inclosed, their roofs showing above the outer walls. Fort Delaware was used during the Civil War as a place of imprisonment for political offenders and Confederate officers; and nearly the whole island is made land.

Delaware Bay is now entered, and there is little to see beyond a waste of waters, and little for the tourist to do until Cape May is reached, except to enjoy himself as best he may.

A Trip up the Schuylkill.

All that portion of the Schuylkill which can be continuously traversed by steamboat lies within the confines of Fairmount Park. Several steamers ply on the river during the summer months, all starting near the Green Street entrance to Fairmount Park, and stop at every interesting point as far north as the ancient Falls Village, at the mouth of the Wissahickon Creek.

Row-boats may be hired near the Fairmount water-works, above the steamboat landing, by the hour or by the day, but all persons employing such craft for a pleasure outing are cautioned not to proceed down the river, lest they be caught in the current and carried over Fairmount Dam.

"In Philadelphia rowing comes next to cricket in popularity, because there is no city which offers the same advantages to the man who believes in this sort of exercise. The sport is not confined to the racing set, but to men who find time to leave their offices on a summer afternoon and take a spin of several miles up the river, and return late in the evening, after a fish dinner. Unlike the wooden affairs one finds along the Harlem, the club-houses that line the Schuylkill are made of stone with broad piazzas, from which the members can look out either upon the river or the grassy slopes and broad drives of Fairmount Park. Every clear afternoon, large barges, filled with young men in flannels and girls in their smartest summer clothes, put out from the down-river boat-houses and wind their way up the clear waters of the Schuylkill."

VII.

LIBRARIES AND MUSEUMS.

The City's Free Libraries.—About 1891 free libraries were ordered to be established throughout the city at public expense and under the direct charge of the Board of Education. A miscellaneous collection of books was placed in the Wagner Free Institute of Science, at Seventeenth Street and Montgomery Avenue, which was opened to the public on October 18, 1892. This branch was such an instantaneous success that others were established throughout the city, and in 1895, when six branches had been started under the Board of Education, Councils ordered that the management be transferred to the Directors of the Free Library of Philadelphia, which had been founded through a bequest of George S. Pepper of $250,000, and which had been carrying on its work in the City Hall. Since the time of this coalition, the Free Library has advanced very rapidly in the number of books acquired and in its circulation, which is now the largest of any library in the world, distributing, in 1897, 1,587,157 volumes. Any one may use these books, or take them home by obtaining a ticket signed by two reputable citizens of his neighborhood. The Main Library is in temporary quarters at 1217-1221 Chestnut Street, in addition to which the following branches have been opened:

Wagner Institute Branch, Seventeenth Street and Montgomery Avenue.
Broad and Federal Branch, Broad and Federal streets.
Frankford Avenue Branch, 1858 Frankford Avenue.
Roxborough Branch, Ridge and Lyceum avenues, Roxborough.
West Philadelphia Branch, Fortieth and Ludlow streets.
Germantown Branch, Vernon Park, Germantown.
College Settlement Branch, Seventh and Lombard streets.
Evening Home Branch, 25 South Van Pelt Street.
McPherson Park Branch, Indiana Avenue and F Street.

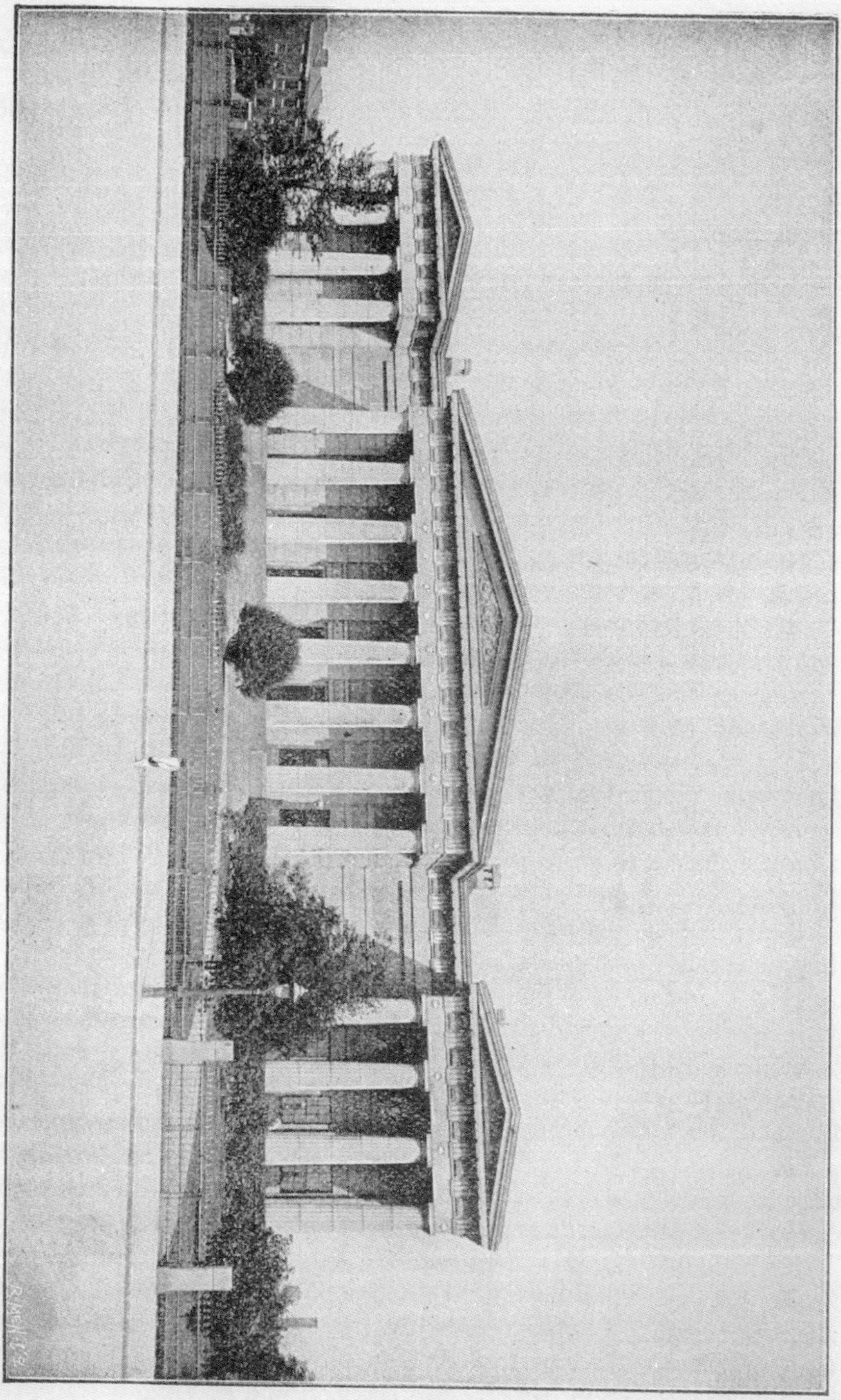

PHILADELPHIA LIBRARY, RIDGWAY BRANCH — Broad, Christian, Thirteenth, and Carpenter Streets.

Chestnut Hill Branch, Germantown Avenue, below Chestnut Hill Avenue.

Nicetown Branch, 4013-15 Germantown Avenue.

These branches lend a prodigious number of volumes each year; the average at the Wagner Institute Branch being one thousand a day. The Library has, in addition, a number of collections of books in cases, which are sent from point to point, constituting a Traveling Library System. These libraries are sent to places where the population would not justify the building of a branch, and also to Fire Stations and Telegraph Stations. Special collections are made in this way also for some Unversity Extension centers and the Girls' Normal School. The number of volumes in the Library at the present time is about 160,000.

Philadelphia Library.—Locust and Juniper streets. This library, together with the Loganian Library in the same building, is the oldest subscription library in the United States. The Philadelphia Library was founded by Benjamin Franklin, Thomas Hopkinson, and a few others, July 1, 1731. It first attracted wide attention by importing from London, in 1732, a large quantity of books, and before the Revolution had absorbed no less than three local libraries. It was first located on Pewter Platter Alley, between Front and Second, and in 1773 was removed to Carpenters' Hall. In 1790 it occupied a handsome building of its own on the northeast corner of Fifth and Library streets, between Chestnut and Walnut. A few years ago a beautiful structure was erected at Locust and Juniper streets, where it now is, with some 70,000 volumes, many of which are of the rarest character. The Loganian Library, which is united with the Philadelphia Library, is a collection of books bequeathed by James Logan, the first secretary to William Penn, and at one time Chief Justice of the Province of Pennsylvania. Under his will the library, which contains many rare and curious books in ancient languages, was to be maintained forever for the free use of the citizens of Philadelphia. The Philadelphia Library is open to any respectable person who wishes to utilize it, and books may be taken out under certain simple regulations for 10 cents a week, while those of the Loganian department are free. Open on week days from 9 a. m. to 6 p. m.

Ridgeway Branch.—This well-known branch is on South Broad Street, between Carpenter and Christian. The history of its founding is of more than ordinary interest. Dr. James Rush, a son of Dr. Benjamin Rush, died in Philadelphia May 26, 1869, and by his will left over $1,000,000 in trust for the erection of a building suitable for the use of a library of large proportions, for the support of which an additional sum was left. The library was to be called the Ridgeway Branch of the Philadelphia Library, the name of Ridgeway being derived from the maiden name of his wife, a daughter of Jacob Ridgeway, a rich merchant of the city. The trustees erected a magnificent structure of Doric Greek style at Broad and Carpenter, of dressed granite, with a frontage of 220 feet and a depth of 105 feet. It contains the tomb of its founder, at the rear of the main hall. This library now contains about 120,000 volumes, is very strong in Americana, especially of the Revolutionary period, in works relating to Pennsylvania, and in geology, where it is excelled only by the library of the U. S. Geological Survey. This library is open weekdays, and all of Sunday afternoon.

Mercantile Library.—18 South Tenth Street. This is probably one of the best known libraries in the United States. It was incorporated in 1822, and contains at the present time 180,000 volumes and 10,000 pamphlets. The association was formed in 1820, and opened to the public in 1821, and has now a membership of over 12,000. The reading-rooms are free to the public, but members only are entitled to take books from the building.

Other Libraries in the city are of less general interest, though many are exceedingly useful to the public of their neighborhood, or by reason of strength in specialties. Mention is made of many of them elsewhere, in connection with the scientific and learned societies, educational or beneficent institutions, to which they mostly belong.

Museums and Galleries.

Academy of Natural Sciences.—The Academy of Natural Sciences, at Nineteenth and Race streets, is the oldest institution of the kind in America. It was founded in 1812, and to-day has a large museum of natural history. It has the largest collection of shells in the world, surpassing even the famous one of the British Museum, and numbering more than 100,000 specimens. The collection of birds consists of about 27,000 mounted specimens, and some 4,000 unmounted skins, and is excelled by few other collections. The collection of fossils is one of the most important in the country. In addition to the regular geological collection, the Academy cares for and exhibits the collection of the Pennsylvania State Geological Survey. The herbarium contains upward of 35,000 species of plants, and, with the exception of the one at Harvard, is the most extensive in America. There are 1,700 human skulls illustrating race peculiarities, and the archæological collection is among the foremost in the United States; very important, also, are its collections of minerals, insects, and the alcoholic specimens of all forms of animal life indispensable to the modern student.

The building on Logan Square is partly of green serpentine and partly of brick and terra cotta. The museum and library are open daily, without charge, and on Sunday from 1 to 5 P. M. The section of the museum recently erected south of the old building has afforded an opportunity for the proper arrangement of a fine mineral collection and a series of remains illustrating the habits of the Mound Builders of Florida and the southern coast. These are placed with other interesting anthropological material. The fine collection of mounted mammals is displayed on the floor above.

Lectures on the several departments of natural history are delivered free of charge during the fall and winter months, and do much to extend the influence of the society, which is placed in constant communication with all parts of the scientific world by means of its publications, an annual volume of Proceedings and a Journal, published from time to time. Over 500 copies of the former are distributed to corresponding societies, the volumes received in exchange therefore constituting a most important portion of the library, which consists of nearly 50,000 volumes, forming especially in the department of journals and periodicals, perhaps the largest collection of exclusively scientific books in America. It is especially rich in old works which cannot now be bought, and in superb illustrated folios, including those of Audubon, Gould, and Elliott.

American Philosophical Society.—Independence Square, Fifth Street, below Chestnut. This venerable society was founded in May, 1763, and in 1785 it erected the present building on Independence Square, adjoining the old City Hall. Its first president was Benjamin Franklin; the second, David Rittenhouse, the astronomer; the third, Thomas Jefferson. The building is of Pennsylvania marble, and contains a library, lecture-room, and museum. Visitors are admitted daily on application. Historical sketches in regard to this important society were published in the *Philadelphia Ledger* during May, 1893, and by the Trades League in the autumn of 1893.

Commercial, Educational, and Economic Museums.—In the former offices of the Pennsylvania Railroad, South Third Street. This institution is the property of the city, but is controlled by a board of trustees. It originated in 1893, and is the conception of Prof. William T. Wilson. Its object is to gather, exhibit, and publish materials and information likely to be of use to manufacturers and business men. The closing of the Columbian Exposition enabled representatives of the city to obtain, by the promise of a permanent exhibition, the collections of raw products and materials sent to Chicago by many countries, especially those of Central and South America; extensive exhibits were also secured from Africa, Australia, Japan, and India; and, through the work of special commissions and agents in foreign countries, these collections are constantly increased. These are now arranged according to countries, so that the manufacturer, merchant, or consumer, interested in any particular commodity, may here find systematically arranged and displayed samples of the various products which interest him, accompanied by all obtainable data whereby he may judge of their commercial value. "For instance, the manufacturer of woods finds displayed for his benefit thousands of samples, embracing nearly all the woods of the world in sufficient size and quantity, and with data necessary for him to determine their value in his particular industry. Likewise, the textile manufacturer here finds samples of the wools, silks, cottons, vegetable fibers, etc., from every foreign country, comprising the most varied and complete collection of its kind in existence. The collections of hides, skins, leather, tanning materials, dye stuffs, food products, oils, medicinal drugs, and herbs, minerals, etc., are intended to enable the dealers in these products to keep fully posted upon the constantly changing conditions of the markets of the world. These collections are renewed and augmented as the progress of industry may require." The collections are of such a character, and include so many real curiosities, that they are highly interesting to the casual sight-seer. The Institution also carries on a system of scientific analyses and tests, is gathering a large commercial library, and has an elaborate system of collecting and disseminating information useful to merchants and manufacturers. It is open daily, without charge.

Franklin Institute.—15 South Seventh Street. This society was organized in 1824, for the encouragement of the mechanical arts. It occupies a plain edifice on the east side of Seventh Street, between Market and Chestnut, erected in 1825. From the beginning, it has been a prominent educational force by means of lectures, classes for instruction in science and the mechanical arts, drawing, etc., and many other institutions and men of reputation owe their origin and success to its initiative and guidance. Ever since 1826, it has published the *Journal*, a periodical of importance in science, and among the oldest of its class in the country. This work is sustained. A very valuable special library has been accumulated, and a reading-room is open to members and students. In these rooms, on the second floor, may be seen, freely, many relics of Benjamin Franklin, some curious models of early electrical and other apparatus, old maps, pictures, etc., of considerable interest.

Historical Society.—The Pennsylvania Historical Society, founded in 1824, occupies the old residence of Gen. Robert Patterson, at Thirteenth and Locust streets, to which extensive additions have been made to accommodate the collections. The valuable library of this active society is spoken of under LIBRARIES. Its museum contains a great quantity of relics and souvenirs of the history of the city, state and country, and ought not to be missed by any visitor interested in such matters.

The College of Physicians, also at Thirteenth and Locust streets, has an extensive library and museum of pathological and surgical books and specimens that can be seen by any one who wishes to examine them.

Memorial Hall.—The important museum of art and industry housed in Memorial Hall, on the Centennial grounds, Fairmount Park (see PARKS) is the result and property of the "Pennsylvania Museum and School of Industrial Art," an educational institution which grew out of the impetus given in this direction by the Exhibition of 1876, and to whose purposes the city's permanent art-hall has been devoted.

The Memorial Hall museum collections ought to be examined by every visitor as well as citizen. They include a great variety of objects illustrating the arts as applied to industry in textile fabrics, including exquisite embroideries from all parts of the world; in pottery of various nations and periods; in wood-carving, and so forth, and notably in artistic metal work, especially of the Japanese. The collection is exceedingly useful to students of decoration, etc., as well as pleasing to the more idle eye. Here, also, are exhibited at present the numerous and valuable *Wilstach Paintings*, regarded as one of the foremost picture galleries in the country, for which it is proposed to erect a separate memorial building. Rothermel's colossal painting, the "Battle of Gettysburg," is another object of popular interest here.

The Schools of Textile Art conducted by this society are now housed in the old Deaf-Mute Asylum at Broad and Pine streets, where instruction is given in the nature of fibers, yarns, and threads of all sorts, their adaptability to various fabrics, the history, methods and styles of weaves, and the effect of treatment and dyeing. This means a complete technical education in the making of textile fabrics, and fits the pupils to take high places in the conduct of mills and factories, as a large number of the graduates have already done. Another important branch of study is the art of design as applied to textile fabrics of every character; and exceedingly satisfactory results have been obtained by manufacturers of carpets, silks, and other cloths from the designs and drawings of the young men and women of this school.

Museums in the University of Pennsylvania, Independence Hall, etc., are described under the headings to those institutions.

Picture Galleries open to the public in Philadelphia are few. The Wilstach collection and other pictures in Memorial Hall, the portraits in Independence Hall, and notable pictures scattered in the rooms of libraries and societies have already been mentioned. The annual exhibitions of the work of the local art societies and of individual artists, which are held in the Academy of Fine Arts, and occasionally elsewhere, are features of each autumn and spring here, as in other cities. Occasional loan-exhibitions are open to the public (see newspapers), and these are likely to be of the very highest interest, as Philadelphia possesses, in its private houses, many pictures and art-objects of the highest excellence and rare value. Of private picture-galleries, those of Wm. B. Bement and of Mrs. Henry C. Gibson are especially noteworthy. The only permanent and public art-gallery of importance is that of

The Academy of Fine Arts.—This owns and occupies the conspicuous Venetian building at Broad and Cherry streets, built in 1876. The society was founded in 1805, and has collected a large library and a priceless assemblage of art-treasures, including the Phillips collection of over sixty thousand etchings and engravings. It supports schools in drawing, painting, and sculpture, which are among the foremost in America, and have trained many of our best artists and sculptors. Admission to the gallery, 25 cents.

Among the most notable of the three hundred or more *paintings* upon its walls are: (*American artists*) C. W. Peale's portraits, of himself and of Robert Morris; Gilbert Stuart's replica of his Lansdowne portrait of Washington, and his portrait of Mrs. Blodgett; Benjamin West's "Rejection of Christ"; John Vanderlyn's "Ariadne in Naxos"; Washington Allston's "Dead Man Resuscitated by the Bones of Elisha"; Thomas Sully's "Cook as Richard III"; T. B. Read's "Sheridan's Ride" (well remembered by Centennial visitors); F. A. Bridgman's "Roumanian Lady"; Thomas Hill's "Yosemite"; John Neagle's "Pat Lyon at the Forge," and many others; (*foreign artists*) W. Bougereau's "Orestes and the Furies"; Peter Janssen's "Peter's Denial"; C. R. Leslie's "Murder of Rutland by Clifford"; Van der Helst's "Violinist"; Witt Kamp's "Deliverance of Leyden"; Vernet's "Cardinal and Friends"; Wylie's "Story-teller"; Carolus Duran's portrait of Modjeska, and many more illustrating the various European schools. Of *sculptures*, notable marbles are: W. W. Story's "Jerusalem"; Hiram Powers' "Proserpine," and a cast of John Lough's "Battle of Centaurs and Lapithæ." A growing feature is the Temple Gallery of Modern Paintings, now numbering nearly fifty canvasses

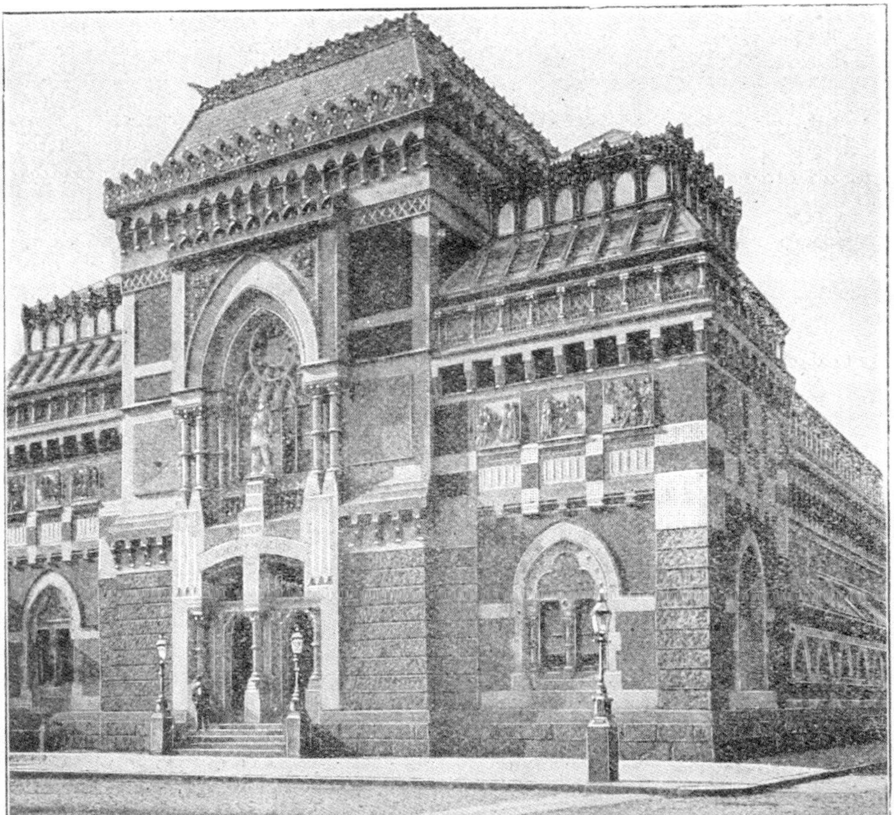

ACADEMY OF FINE ARTS—Southwest Corner Broad and Cherry Streets.

VIII.

CHURCHES.—RELIGIOUS AND BENEVOLENT WORK.

There are more than seven hundred churches in Philadelphia, comprising over forty independent and semi-independent denominations. They are so scattered over the great city that the worshiper need not go far from his home or stopping-place in order to find a place in which to pursue his devotions in the form to which he has been accustomed. Most of the leading Protestant and many of the Roman Catholic churches advertise their services for the succeeding Sabbath in the religious-notice column of the *Public Ledger* on the preceding Saturday. In all the churches strangers are cordially welcomed and given seats by the ushers. As a rule, the services in the Protestant churches begin at 10:30 in the morning and 7:30 in the evening. Alphabetically arranged, the principal denominations are as follows:

Baptist.—The Baptist denomination has a powerful hold on the affections of the church-going people of Philadelphia, and about one hundred of its edifices are scattered within its limits. Its headquarters and publication house are at 1420 Chestnut Street. The denomination has been established in the city since 1698, and the *First Baptist* congregation now worships at the northwest corner of Broad and Spruce streets, in a greenstone Gothic edifice, half hidden beneath ivy. The *Fifth* church, now at Eighteenth and Spring Garden streets, was founded in 1811.

Tabernacle.—Chestnut and Fortieth streets. Occupies a temporary structure since its removal from Seventeenth and Chestnut.

Memorial.—Broad and Master streets. A handsome church of greenstone, with light stone trimmings.

Grace.—Broad and Berks streets. This is probably the handsomest church of the denomination in the city. It is of light stone mixed Gothic, and with elegant interior fittings and furnishings. It is ordinarily known as the Temple Baptist.

Other noted churches of the Baptist denomination, having popular clergymen in charge, are:

East, Hanover and Girard Avenue.
Fourth, Fifth and Buttonwood.
Gethsemane, Columbia Avenue and Eighteenth.
Mantua, Fortieth and Fairmount Avenue.
Roxborough, Ridge Avenue, near Lyceum.
Second, Seventh Street, below Girard Avenue.

Congregational.— There are but eight Congregational churches in the city, and but one has any fame outside the locality in which it is situated. This church is known as the *Central*, Eighteenth and Green streets. It is a Gothic building, attractively placed.

Friends.— The Society of Friends is very strong in Philadelphia, and has a number of large meeting-houses in different parts of the city. These are severely plain, and this characteristic, together with their surroundings of venerable trees and large yards, gives the visitor the impression he is in the country amid the fields and meadows.

Jewish.— Fourteen Jewish congregations have tabernacles in Philadelphia, and all are large and flourishing. *Mikve Israel* is the oldest congregation of the Jewish faith, and occupies a commodious building on Seventh Street, near Arch. It was organized in 1747. The synagogue of *Rodeph Shalom*, at Broad and Mount Vernon streets, is built in the Moorish style, and forms a conspicuous object.

Lutheran.— The Lutheran denomination is among the oldest in Philadelphia, dating its beginning as early as 1638. It was not, however, in full formation until the arrival of Muhlenberg in 1742. Of the Lutheran congregations, the one occupying the handsomest structure is that of the *Holy Communion*, southwest corner Broad and Arch streets, one of the finest churches in the city, built of greenstone. The interior is richly fitted up, and the whole church cost over $200,000.

Methodist Episcopal.— There are in all over one hundred Methodist churches in Philadelphia, the greater number of which are plain structures.

Arch Street.— Southeast corner Broad and Arch streets. This church is built of white marble, and is of the Gothic style.

Grace.— Broad and Master streets. This church resembles the preceding in general design, and is decorated in a costly manner.

Spring Garden.— Twentieth and Spring Garden streets. The Spring Garden Church is a plain, early English Gothic style, without any of the usual ornamentations, and is built of brownstone, with a tower at one corner.

Kensington, Marlborough and Richmond.
Park Avenue, Park Avenue and Norris.
Seventh Street, Seventh and Norris.

Moravian.— There are but four Moravian churches in the city, as follows:

First, Fairmount Avenue, below Seventeenth.
Second, southeast corner Franklin and Thompson.
Third, Kensington Avenue, below Venango.
Fifth, Germantown Avenue, above Dauphin.

The Moravian Church is noted for the sweetness of the music rendered, especially at Easter and Christmas.

Presbyterians.— More than one hundred churches of various shades of this denomination are located in the city. The local headquarters of the church and its bureau of publication are in the Witherspoon Building, which is owned by its Board of Publication. Among the most prominent churches are:

First.— Seventh and Locust streets. This church was the first organized in Pennsylvania (1698), and built its present Ionic structure in 1822.

Second.— Twenty-first and Walnut streets. This celebrated church had its origin in 1743, and was a split-off from the First, through the preaching of George Whitefield. Few churches in the city are richer in ornamentation. Its pulpit is a splendid work of art, and its organ one of the finest in Philadelphia.

Bethany.— Twenty-second and Bainbridge streets. Bethany is one of the largest churches of any of the Protestant denominations in the city. It can seat 2,000 persons with ease, and it is frequently filled with worshipers. Its Sunday-school is still larger, and more than 2,000 scholars are enrolled on its books. It is at this church that John Wanamaker worships, and this is the Sunday school of which he is superintendent.

West Arch.— Eighteenth and Arch streets. The church edifice here is of the Corinthian style of architecture, with a portico, and it is surmounted by a central dome 170 feet high.

Other churches of the Presbyterian denomination are the
Bethlehem, Broad and Diamond.
Calvary, Locust, near Fifteenth.
Central, Broad Street and Fairmount Avenue.
Holland Memorial, southeast corner Broad and Federal.
MacDowell Memorial, Twenty-first and Columbia Avenue.
Memorial, Nineteenth Street and Montgomery Avenue.
North Broad, Broad and Green.
Northminster, Thirty-fifth and Baring.
Olivet, Twenty-second and Mount Vernon.
Oxford, Broad and Oxford.
Princeton, Saunders Street and Powelton Avenue.
Tabernacle, Thirty-seventh and Chestnut.
Walnut Street, Walnut, west of Thirty-ninth.
Tenth, Seventeenth and Spruce.

Protestant Episcopal.—Of the churches in Philadelphia, the Protestant Episcopal denomination owns nearly one-seventh of the whole. The oldest is the Old Swedes Church at Front and Christian streets, and among the most fashionable are St. Marks, Locust and Sixteenth Streets; St. James, Twenty-second and Walnut streets; Holy Trinity, Nineteenth and Walnut streets. Next to the Old Swedes, the two churches having the greatest historical interest are Christ Church, Second Street, above Market; and St. Peters, at Third and Pine streets. Among the High churches is St. Clements, at Twentieth and Cherry streets; and another, of the Protestant Episcopal denomination, which draws large congregations on Sunday, is St. Stephens, Tenth Street, above Chestnut. The Diocesan "Church House" is at Walnut and Twelfth. Prominent among the churches of this denomination are:

Atonement, Seventeenth and Summer.
Calvary, Manheim Street, Germantown.
Christ, Tulpehocken Street, Germantown.
Epiphany, Eighteenth and Chestnut.
Holy Apostles, Twenty-first and Christian.
Incarnation, Broad and Jefferson.
Mediator, Nineteenth and Lombard.
Savior, Thirty-eighth, above Chestnut.
St. Andrew, Eighth, above Spruce.
St. Luke, Thirteenth and Spruce.
St. Mark, Locust, above Sixteenth.

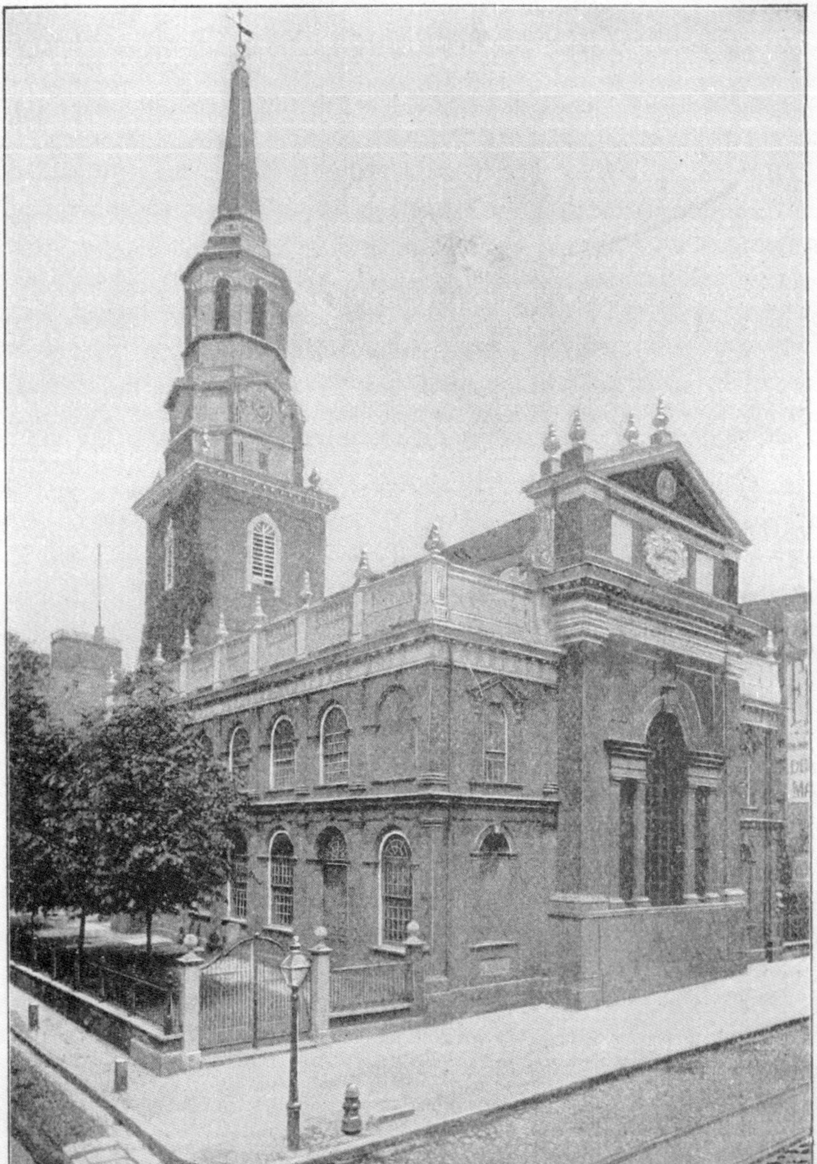

CHRIST CHURCH—Second, near Market Street.

St. Mary, Locust, at Thirty-ninth.
St. Matthias, Nineteenth and Wallace.
St. Paul, Chestnut Hill.
Transfiguration, Thirty-fourth and Woodland Avenue.

All of these churches are fine specimens of architecture, and all have elaborate and elegantly decorated and furnished interiors.

Old Swedes.—Old Swedes Church, as it is generally called, or Church of the Gloria Dei, as it is legally known, is the oldest in the city, and until 1843 belonged to the communion of the Swedish Lutheran Church, and for 130 years was under the charge of ministers sent from Sweden. The edifice now standing was begun May 28, 1698, and dedicated July 2, 1700. Among the dead in the venerable churchyard surrounding the sacred edifice are the remains of Alexander Wilson, the celebrated naturalist, and the dust of the first man buried there, Peter Sandel, in 1708.

Christ Church.—Second Street, above Market. This historical church occupies the site of a frame building erected in 1695. A portion of the present edifice was built in 1727, and the remainder was erected at various intervals. In this church President Washington worshiped. President Adams also was a worshiper here, and Benjamin Franklin had a pew in this church for many years. John Penn, one of the former proprietors of Pennsylvania, was buried in the place in 1795, and a tablet to his memory yet remains, although the body was removed to England a long time ago. Other great patriots of the Revolution are interred in the adjacent ground or under the floors of the church. Some of the communion service in use was presented to the church by Queen Anne, in 1708. It was "restored" a few years ago, but is still an object of great historical interest and value, and may be visited from 9.00 a. m., to 3.00 p. m., any week-day.

St. Peter's, Third and Pine streets, is another remarkable church of this denomination. It was commenced in 1758, and completed three years later. The building, both as to its exterior and interior arrangements, is kept as nearly as possible in the original state. In the churchyard repose the remains of Commodore Decatur.

St. Paul's, Third Street, below Walnut, is within a few months of being as old as the preceding. The edifice now standing is the original one, although the interior is greatly altered. Edwin Forrest is buried in one of the vaults of the church.

St. James', northwest corner Twenty-second and Walnut streets, is one of the wealthiest Protestant Episcopal churches in the city. Its building is of the Gothic style, of stone of different colors, and the interior is fitted up with rich decorations.

Holy Trinity.—Nineteenth and Walnut streets. This is another very wealthy congregation, and the building is a massive brownstone Gothic structure.

St. Stephen's.— Fourth Street, above Chestnut. This church is of a peculiar style of architecture, with two high octagonal towers fronting it. The interior is Gothic, and on the northern side is a small chapel in which is the Burd Monument, consisting of three figures in pure white marble, erected by Edward Shippen Burd in memory of his family.

Reformed Episcopal.— Three churches among the Reformed Episcopal have reputations beyond their fellows; these are: *Christ Memorial*, northeast corner Chestnut and Forty-third streets; *Our Redeemer*, Sixteenth and Oxford streets, and *St. Paul*, Chestnut Street, above Twenty-first.

Roman Catholic.— There are seventy-eight Roman Catholic churches in Philadelphia, and all the churches are commodious and have laıge congregations. Several have considerable historical interest.

Cathedral of St. Peter and St. Paul.— Eighteenth Street, between Race and Vine streets. The Cathedral of the Roman Catholic Church in Philadelphia is a conspicuous object for many squares, and from the higher points may be seen several miles away. Surmounting the Cathedral is a huge dome, 51 feet in diameter and 156 feet above the pavement. The interior of the Cathedral is cruciform and designed in the most elaborate Roman-Corinthian style. The pavement is of marble, and the light is all received from above. Over the grand altar is a painting of the Crucifixion, by Constantine Brumidi (the early decorator of the Capitol at Washington). The corner-stone of the building was laid September 6, 1846, and services were first held in it on Easter Sunday, 1863, but it was not dedicated until November 20, 1864.

St. Joseph's.— Willings Alley, below Fourth Street. On this site was built the first Roman Catholic church in Pennsylvania, by a member of the Society of Jesus, who came from Maryland, in 1731, for that purpose. The present structure was consecrated in 1839.

St. Mary's.—Fourth Street, near Spruce. This church was the second of the kind erected in Philadelphia. The present building, not quite so large as now, was consecrated in 1763, and for many years, beginning with 1810, it was the Cathedral Church.

St. Augustine's.—Fourth Street, below Vine. St. Augustine Church has had an eventful history. Built in 1801, under the direction of hermits of the Order of St. Augustine, it had over the altar Rush's great work, sculptured in wood, of the Crucifixion. In 1826 a cupola was built to the church, and possession was gained of the clock of the old State House, which belonged to Pennsylvania in Colonial times. When the anti-catholic riots broke out in Philadelphia in 1844, the anger of the mob was directed especially against this church, and on May 8th it was set on fire by a rabble and destroyed. The present edifice was built two years later.

Swedenborgians.—The Swedenborgians, although they originated in this city through the preaching of the Rev. Manning B. Roche, have but two churches, both of which are handsome and commodious. These are the *First*, Chestnut and Twenty-second, and the *Frankford*, Paul and Unity.

Unitarian.—This denomination, while it has not the strength in Philadelphia it has in Boston, has yet a large following, and supports three large and wealthy congregations. The most noted of these is the *First Church*, Chestnut and Aspen, near Twenty-first. For more than fifty years this congregation was presided over by the scholarly Rev. Dr. Furness.

Universalist.—There are but two churches of this denomination in Philadelphia, but both have flourishing congregations. One of these two, the *Church of the Restoration*, is a handsome building at Master and Sixteenth streets. The other is the *Church of the Messiah*, at Broad Street and Montgomery Avenue.

Humane and Benevolent Institutions.

Philadelphia has been foremost among American cities in the development and management of organized means of education, assistance, and charity for the less favored classes of the community. It would be out of place in a book of this kind to attempt a full account of them, since few offer anything of interest to the general traveler or may be visited with special permission. Those especially interested in a study of the city's philanthropies, or curious as to any particular institutions, will find a complete list of them, and their addresses, in the city directories; and an annual "City Mission Directory" of benevolent, charitable, and humane institutions, containing descriptive details, is published by the Protestant Episcopal Mission, 411 Spruce Street. A few remarks may call attention to certain institutions of special note.

The Pennsylvania Bible Society, at Seventh and Walnut streets, was founded in 1808, is the oldest society of its kind in the country, and has distributed over 5,500,000 copies of the Scriptures. Other very old institutions are the *Prison Society*, dating from 1787; the *French Benevolent Society*, founded in 1793; the *Magdalen Society*, founded in 1799, and the parent of several younger agencies for the rescue of fallen women, and several founded during the first quarter of the century. Associations for the protection and care of poor, neglected, and feeble women and children are especially numerous, and support a large number of seaside or rural "homes," where ailing women and the children of the poor are given summer vacations. The *Law and Order Society*, 920 Walnut Street, exists to "enforce laws and uphold decency and good order in the community." Two downtown societies seek to ameliorate the misfortune of broken-down merchants and business men in an unostentatious way. Seamen ashore are also looked after, a sailors' home, now at 422 Front Street, giving these wanderers a safe and comfortable refuge from "boarding-house sharks." A singular charity is the *Sunday Breakfast Association*, which provides a great number of free breakfasts for the poor on Sunday morning, amid Christian surroundings. The *Women's Directory*, 238 South Tenth Street, offers "sisterly sympathy and practical assistance" to women in distress; and another society prosecutes gratuitously the claims of working-girls against employers, and legally protects them in other respects. An important society exists for the prevention of the spread of tuberculosis; and other "prevention" societies are those directed against cruelty to animals (1627 Chestnut Street) — a State institution, with a local Women's Branch; and against cruelty to children (217 South Broad Street). An attempt has been made to combine and regulate the work of all these agencies under a central bureau, — the *Society for Organizing Charity*, with headquarters at 1705 Chestnut Street, and many branches; but it has never reached the influence or effectiveness of the great Charity Organization Society in New York. *Homes* for the homeless of every class of persons are numerous in and about Philadelphia, and some are old and conspicuous. The only one that calls for mention here is the *Mary J. Drexel Home*, opposite Girard College. This is the handsomest institution of the kind in Philadelphia, and its interior is fully as beautiful as its exterior. It is the gift of John D. Lankenau as a memorial to his wife, Mary J. Drexel, his son, and his daughter. It comprises the Motherhouse, or institute for the maintenance, religious instruction, and education of deaconesses who are members of the Lutheran Church; the Old People's Home, for the reception and support of respectable aged couples, and aged single men and women of German birth or descent, and members of the Lutheran Church; the Children's Hospital, and the Girls' Boarding School, where a thorough education is given to little girls, from the kindergarten up, and where a tuition fee is charged.

Hospitals and Dispensaries.

Some of the oldest, largest and most advanced hospitals in the United States are in Philadelphia, where, alone, in the early history of the country, could proper surgical and medical treatment be obtained, and which for a long time took the lead in medical education, as, perhaps, they yet do. Of the fifty or more hospitals and dispensaries, the oldest (except the Municipal or "Philadelphia" Hospital) is the *Pennsylvania Hospital*, whose grounds occupy a block at Spruce and Ninth streets, and whose charter was procured by Franklin's aid in 1752. Since then nearly two hundred thousand patients have been admitted, and the most eminent physicians and surgeons in the history of the country have "walked" its wards, where the first clinical lectures in the United States were delivered. It has a large and very valuable library, in which are contained many objects of curious interest. A branch from it, separated in 1841, has grown into the great Hospital for the Insane (Kirkbrides) in West Philadelphia. Next to this, the most educational of the hospitals is probably that at the University of Pennsylvania, elsewhere mentioned. The *German Hospital* is a great institution under German auspices, near Girard College; the *Polyclinic* attracts many students; and the *Hahnemann*, on Fifteenth Street, above Race, is homeopathic in treatment, as also is the *Women's Homeopathic Hospital*, at Twentieth Street and Susquehanna Avenue. The *Maternity* and several others devote themselves to the lying-in and diseases of women, and to the needs of children. Each of the leading Christian denominations supports a hospital of importance. The Roman Catholics have several, the Friends an old and important hospital for the insane; the Protestant Episcopal church cares for two or more; the Methodists have one, and the Presbyterian Hospital, at Filbert and Thirty-ninth streets, is widely known. Special infirmaries and free dispensaries are numerous and widely scattered, as may be seen by consulting directory lists. *The City Almshouse*, popularly known as "Blockley," which occupies a large establishment south of the University, and has an average daily population of about four thousand derelicts, is often visited by strangers, and has attached to it the city's charity hospital, founded in 1732; admission tickets may be obtained from the Department of Charities, room 395A, City Hall. *The Morgue* is at 1307 Wood Street, and the *Quarantine Station*, on Tinicum Island, several miles down the Delaware.

Prisons are not counted among a town's "objects of interest," as a rule, but in Philadelphia one or two, at least, ought not to be omitted from the list, because the city's prisons and penitentiary methods have been copied all over the world, even so remote a government as that of Sicily using Moyamensing as a model. The *Eastern Penitentiary* is a State institution, occupying a lot of nearly eleven acres on Fairmount Avenue, near the Park entrance, and is used for the confinement of those convicted of serious crimes in Philadelphia and Eastern Pennsylvania. The prison proper consists of a central building, from which the corridors radiate as from the spokes of a wheel. By an arrangement of mirrors, the entire length of every corridor can be seen by the watcher in the center. Theoretically, only one person occupies a cell during his incarceration, and his identity is rigidly kept from his fellow-prisoners and casual visitors. When brought into the presence of each other or of visitors, a prisoner wears a mask, and is known by number only. The solitary-confinement principle of this penitentiary was severely criticised by Charles Dickens in his "American Notes," through being imposed upon by sundry prisoners with whom he held converse; one in particular, who afterward became known as "Dickens' Dutchman," hoodwinking him entirely, and arousing an undeserved commiseration

The prisoners are taught useful handicrafts, and have the use of a library containing nearly ten thousand volumes. Persons are permitted to visit this institution by ticket obtainable from the inspectors.

The County Prison, properly styled "Moyamensing," is in the southern part of the city, on Passyunk Avenue, near Tenth Street. It is a huge square stone building, resembling an old Tudor castle. The *House of Refuge* and *House of Correction* are great reformatories, in the suburbs, for the reformation of juvenile offenders and the punishment of persons guilty of minor offenses.

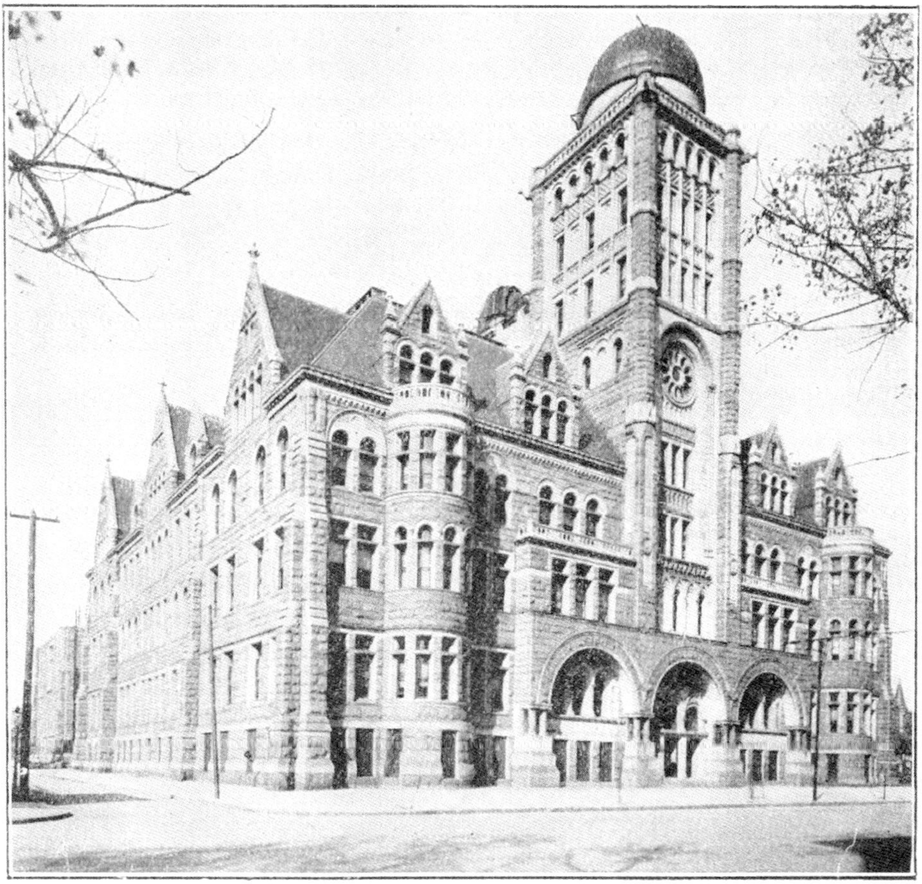

BOYS' CENTRAL HIGH SCHOOL.

IX.

EDUCATIONAL INSTITUTIONS.

Public Schools.

The public schools of Philadelphia are under the control of a Board of Education appointed by the judges of the courts, and by Ward School Boards elected by the people. The schools are graded into Sub-primary, Primary, Secondary, Grammar, High, and Normal schools. The Primary, Secondary, and Grammar grades are each subdivided into four grades, the highest called the Twelfth Grade. The office of the Board and Superintendent are at 713 Filbert Street.

The Philadelphia High School (for boys) occupies a new, spacious, and handsome stone building at Broad and Green streets, where many useful novelties in equipment and method may be seen by visiting teachers. It has sixty class-rooms, a gymnasium, etc.

Girls' Normal School and High School.—These two institutions are for the purpose of educating girls to be teachers and fitting them for business careers. One structure is at Seventeenth and Spring Garden streets, and the other at Thirteenth and Spring Garden streets.

The private and parochial schools of the city for general education number nearly, if not quite, as many as the public schools, while the institutions for special branches are exceptionally large.

Collegiate Institutions.

University of Pennsylvania.—This university was founded in 1740, as a charitable school, by the efforts of a body of men of whom Benjamin Franklin was the leading spirit, and the plans were characterized by a remarkable liberality in breaking away from traditions of classical education toward modern languages and non-sectarian, practical instruction. The first provost, or president, was the liberal-minded and energetic Dr. William Provost. It prospered, soon purchased and occupied the great building that popular enthusiasm had erected for the congregation of the reformer Whitefield, and its broad course of study became the model for American colleges. At the conclusion of the Revolution, a new charter was given by the State, and the present title was assumed in 1791.

It has graduated about 17,500 students — a number exceeded only by Harvard, chiefly from the Middle States south of New York. The Medical School was founded in 1765, the Law School in 1805, and each is the oldest of its kind in the United States. The Towne School, founded in 1855, has been reorganized and developed into the several technical and scientific departments now recognized, and which, meeting the local demand, have here overshadowed the classical departments. In 1875 the university was moved from its ancient site near the center of the city to the present extensive grounds west of the Schuylkill, where some thirty buildings have been erected and are constantly increased. In 1878 the Dental School was organized; in 1881, the Wharton School of Finance and Economy; in 1882, the Veterinary School and Hospitals; in 1883, the School of Biology, and the Graduate Department of Philosophy; in 1888, the School for Nurses; in 1891, the Graduate School for Women and the School of Architecture; in 1892, the Wistar Institute of Anatomy and Biology. These various branches, as they arose, have made necessary, one after another, the new buildings which now form a varied, but imposing and harmonious, collection, occupying several squares along each side of Locust Street.

A visitor to the university will enter at the main gate of the Campus, on Walnut Street, where Baltimore Avenue turns off, and find confronting him the Gothic front and tower of College Hall, where are the administrative offices, and which is flanked by chapel, dining-hall, dormitory, and class-room buildings also of green-gray stone. They contain little of interest to the casual sight-seer, and he may turn at once to the large *Library Hall*, at the left, an ornate structure of red stone and brick, open to view all day.

The Halls of the Library are adorned with pictures, some statuary, and many casts, carvings, and archæological relics from Babylonia, etc., but as these are liable to constant change it would be useless to speak of them particularly, except to call attention to Inman's portrait of Wordsworth and the picture of his house. Some cases, accessible to every one, contain works of reference and every-day use, including rare and costly German and French encyclopedias and collections of biography. Within glass cases are displayed a number of curious and valuable portraits, prints, and books, including the first edition of Horace, printed in Venice, about 1470; autograph copies of books of Martin Luther, Browning and other

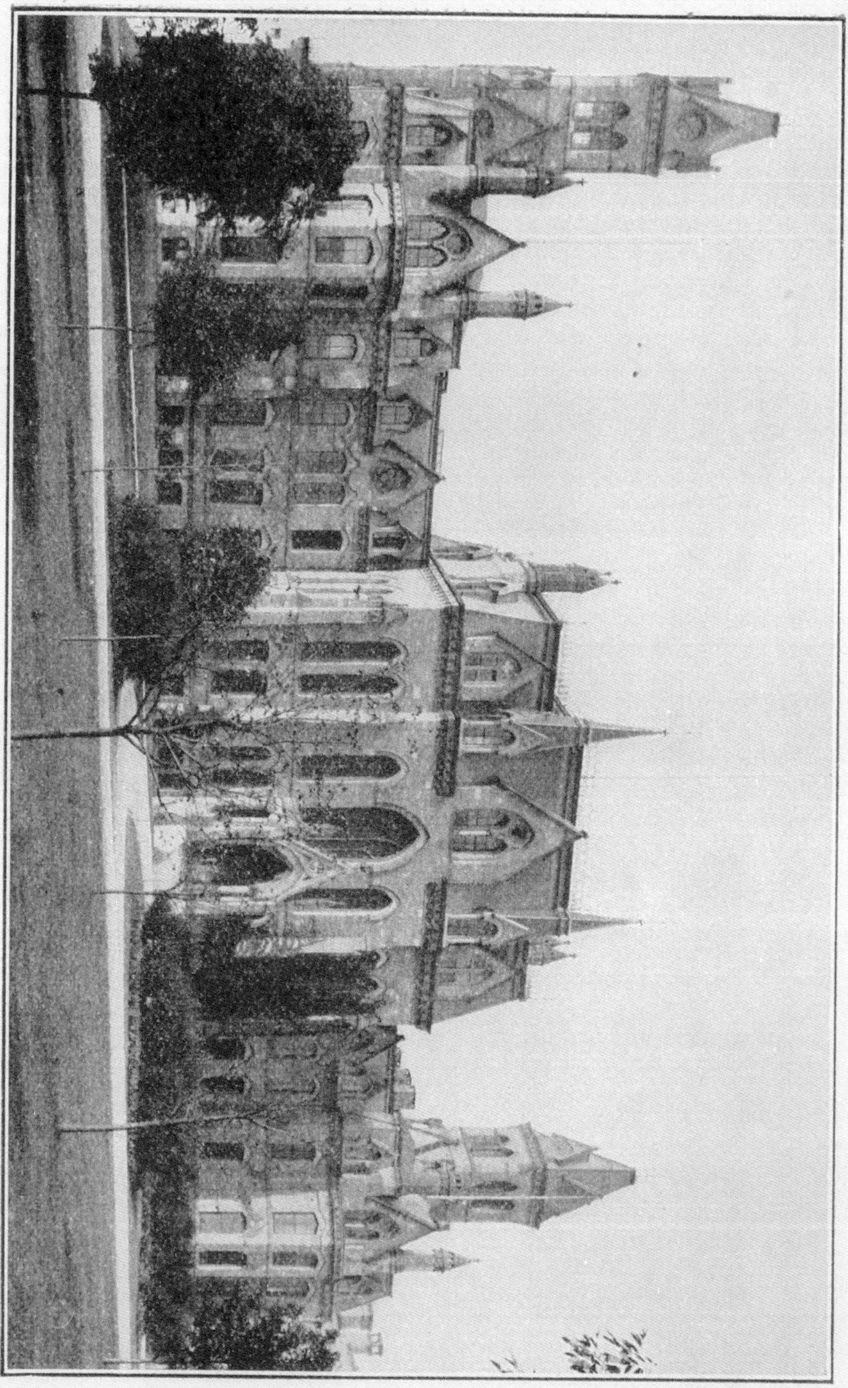

UNIVERSITY OF PENNSYLVANIA.—Thirty-fourth Street, near Pine Street.

eminent authors; a fine collection of book-plates, and another of sepia portraits by John Caspar Lavater; and a large number of very curious early German books, some illustrated, others in black letter, and others enriched by autographs or marginal notes of famous men of the past. The alcoves of the reading-room are named after conspicuous donors to the library, and are used to hold the classified periodicals, of which an extraordinary number (now about 800) are regularly received from all parts of the world, especially those of a scientific character a feature in which this library is particularly strong. Other curiosities exhibited are a hall clock and some astronomical apparatus made by David Rittenhouse over a century ago, and certain apparatus believed to have been used by Franklin in his early electrical experiments. The books of the library, which were only 3,000 in 1872, and now number about 150,000 bound volumes and over 50,000 unbound volumes and pamphlets, are kept in the fire-proof stock-room at the rear. They have been brought together for the needs of the University, and are not especially notable, except in certain particulars. Among them are books presented by Louis XVI, "including a set of the famous and now somewhat rare *Encyclopédie* to which Voltaire contributed, and which a century ago turned the world upside down." Of great importance are the almost complete sets of public documents, "blue-books," and published laws of the United States, Great Britain, France, and Germany, presented by the several governments. Two late additions of great importance have been the extensive Bechstein collection of works in German philology and literature, and the rich Macaulay library of Italian, Spanish, and Portuguese literature, particularly relating to Dante and Tasso.

The Archæological Museum, at present occupying the upper part of Library Hall, but soon to be moved to its new building south of Spruce Street, is one of the most interesting things of its kind in the United States, and should be visited by every reader; but any large account of it is reserved until it is arranged in its new halls. The collections are not only very extensive in American archæology and the illustration of folk-lore, but are among the richest in the country in remains of the extinct Babylonian and Egyptian civilizations,—the result of the long and careful explorations of the sites of Nineveh, Nippur, and several Egyptian localities conducted by the University and affiliated agencies.

The Museum of Anatomy and Palæontology, in the Biological department, which includes the collections of the late Dr. Joseph Leidy, will interest men of science, who will also be pleased at an opportunity to inspect the various laboratories.

The Medical Schools and Hospitals lying south of Spruce Street

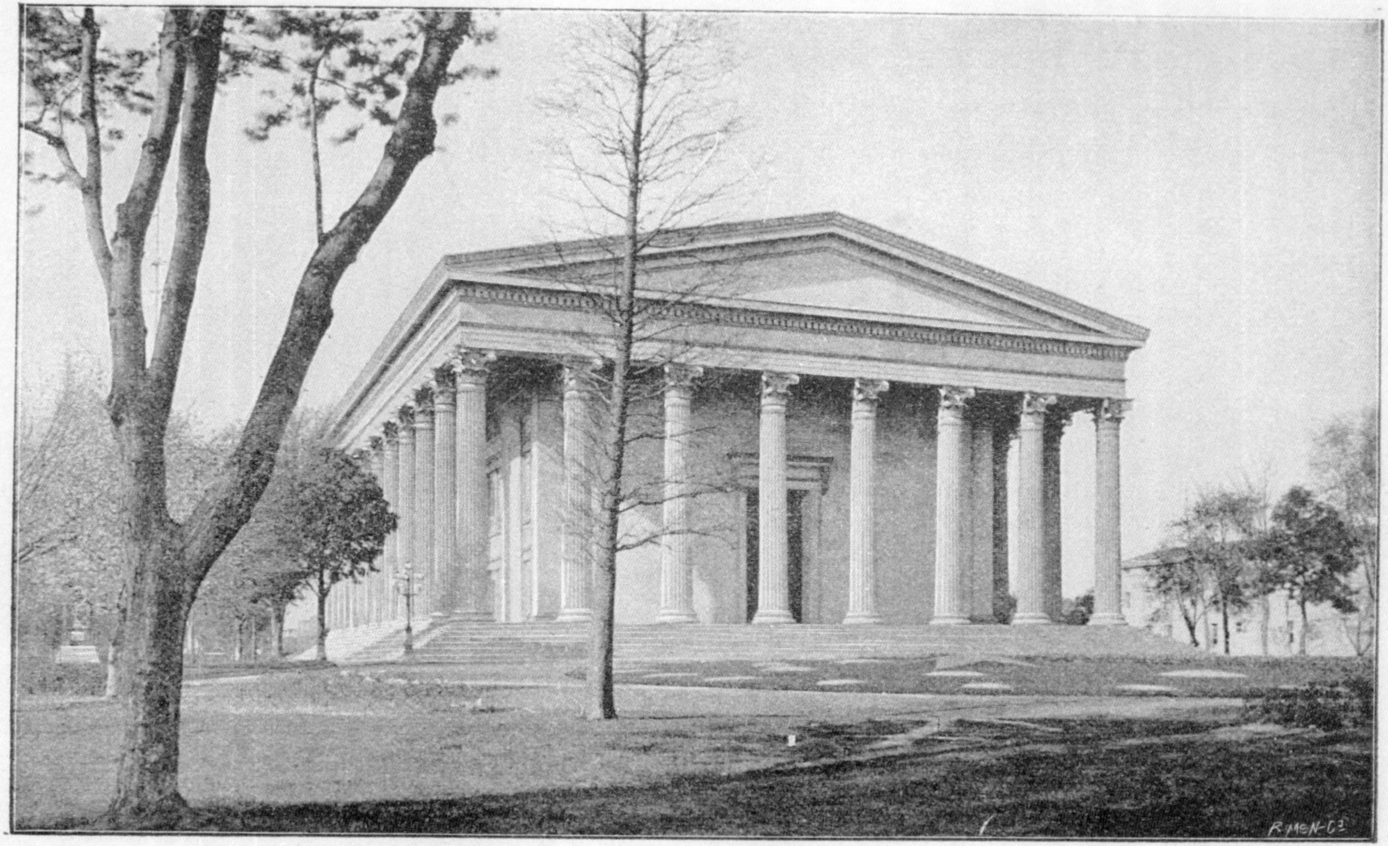

GIRARD COLLEGE, MAIN BUILDING — Twenty-second Street and Girard Avenue.

are very extensive, and may be visited, as also may the hospitals for horses and dogs near by. These form one of the strongest departments of the University, and have given it, perhaps, its greatest distinction. While they relieve a vast amount of suffering, their purpose is primarily educational, and their arrangements and methods are therefore well worth examination by specialists.

The Athletic Field, for student games, lies in their rear; but the great gymnasium has not yet been completed. The near neighborhood of the Schuylkill has always given "Penn" a leading place in college rowing, and the practicing of the crews on the river is something to see.

Girard College.—This noble institution, on Girard Avenue, from Ridge Avenue to West College Avenue, was founded by the will of Stephen Girard, a wealthy and eccentric Philadelphia merchant. He was a native of France, born May 21, 1750, near Bordeaux, and died in Philadelphia December 26, 1831. He began life as a cabin-boy, and became in time the master and part owner of a small vessel, through which he acquired money enough to establish himself in business in Philadelphia in 1769. By the close of the Revolution Girard was a wealthy man, and at his death was one of the richest men in the country. In 1812, when the United States Government needed money, he loaned it $5,000,000. By his will he left $500,000 to Philadelphia for the improvement of the streets and buildings; $300,000 to the State for the improvement of canals; and the rest of his property for the support and education "of poor white male orphans, between the ages of six and ten years, when admitted to the institution, giving the preference first to those born within the bounds of the city of Philadelphia; secondly, to those born in Pennsylvania; thirdly, to those born in New York; and lastly, to those born in New Orleans." By a further clause in the will the city was made trustee of the estate, and a provision inserted that the boys of the institution should be bound apprentices to the municipal corporation and bound out from the college between the ages of fourteen and eighteen. The corner-stone of Girard College was laid July 4, 1833, and the building opened January 1, 1848. Since then the growth of the institution has been so great that numerous other buildings have since been erected by the trustees, until now the place resembles a small suburban town of handsome buildings and residences. The original college edifice is an imposing structure of a rich Corinthian style of architecture. It is 111 feet wide, and 169 feet long, and surrounded by a range of fluted columns. The total height of the building is 97 feet, and it is arched throughout with brick and stone, and roofed with marble tiles. The weight of the roof alone is estimated at nearly 1,000 tons. In the south vestibule is a large sarcophagus in which repose the ashes of Stephen Girard, and above it is a statue of the founder, by Gevelot, said to have been a wonderful likeness, both in expression and pose. Visitors are admitted daily except Sunday by ticket, which may be procured at the office of the Girard Trust, on Twelfth Street, above Chestnut.

Drexel Institute.—Chestnut Street, corner Thirty-second. The late Anthony J. Drexel, one of the most famous of America's bankers, decided to found an institution in which the young of both sexes could acquire knowledge likely to be of practical use to them in ordinary life. In this he was encouraged and assisted by the advice of his life-long friend, George W. Childs, the philanthropist. The structure was completed and formally opened December 17, 1891, and the ceremonies were attended and conducted by many distinguished men and women. The building is constructed of light buff brick, with terra cotta ornamentations, and measures, on the ground floor, 200 by 200 feet. A richly-ornamented portal on Chestnut Street leads into a spacious entrance hall, the ceiling of which is supported by pillars of red Georgian marble. Beyond this is the central court, or quadrangle, 65 feet square and the entire height of the building, the ceiling being a skylight of stained glass, whence stairways lead to the upper floors and to the basement. Broad galleries surround the central court, giving access to the various class-rooms, etc., and affording a view of the whole interior. At the rear of the central court, and having an entrance of its own on Thirty-second Street, is the auditorium, with a seating capacity of 1,500 persons, and an organ of great size. Students are admitted to the Institute who can pass an examination in elementary English subjects, and pay a small tuition fee. The Drexel Institute may be reached by the Chestnut and Walnut street lines of surface cars, and visitors are admitted daily, except Sunday, from 9.00 a. m. to 6.00 p. m., and in winter months, from 7.00 to 10.00 p. m., to the grand central court, the library, and the museum. The last mentioned is particularly worthy a visit, as here, among other valuable things, is the George W. Childs collection of manuscript books of famous authors, including manuscript works of Dickens and Thackeray. The library, which contains a large and valuable collection of books, is open to the general public under certain restrictions.

Other Institutions of Learning.—Historically interesting are the *William Penn Charter School*, chartered by William Penn in 1701, and maintained by the Friends, latterly at Twelfth and Clover streets; and the *Germantown Academy*, which dates from 1759, and still occupies the building in School Lane, erected for it in 1761, in whose belfry hangs a bell received from George III, of England. *The Spring Garden Institute* is a well-known semi-free school at Broad and Spring Garden streets, which maintains a library and free reading-room, gives courses of free lectures, and holds night schools in drawing and mechanical handiwork at a nominal fee, and day schools. To give additional efficiency in mechanical trades, the students are required to labor daily, at their various trade studies, the same number of hours as do regular journeymen mechanics when in actual employment. *Bryn Mawr*, *Strathmore*, *Haverford*, and *Villa Nova* colleges, though out of town, really belong to Philadelphia; and a long list might be made of medical, theological, commercial, and other colleges and seminaries which, though important, are not of interest to the casual tourist.

The Young Men's Christian Association is strong in Philadelphia, carrying on extensively the elevating and educational work characteristic of that institution generally. Its central building is at Chestnut and Fifteenth streets, and it has many branch houses, of which that in Germantown is most prominent.

X.

SOCIAL AND LEARNED SOCIETIES, CLUBS, ETC.

Secret Societies.—There are said to be nearly two thousand secret social or beneficial organizations in this city, some of which originated here. Among the prominent secret societies founded in Philadelphia is the Junior Order of American Mechanics, the original council of which, Washington No. 1, is not only still in existence, but is one of the wealthiest in the order. Most of the secret orders have large central quarters in Philadelphia, and two of them have temples famous all over the country. The oldest of these is

The Masonic Temple, at Broad and Filbert streets. It is pure Norman in architecture, rising 95 feet from the pavement, with two towers on the Broad Street front, one of which is 250 feet high. The temple is built of granite, and the front is exceedingly elaborate, having a Norman porch with three pairs of receding pillars, arches, moldings, and other decorations. The Temple contains numerous rooms for various purposes and for the subordinate lodges, all of which are fitted in a sumptuous manner.

Learned Societies are many, and their meetings are usually open to the public. Prominent among them are the *Academy of Sciences*, Race and Nineteenth streets, natural history; the *Philosophical Society*, Independence Square, and the *Franklin Institute*, Seventh Street, technical science; the *College of Physicians*, Thirteenth and Locust streets, medicine, etc.; the *Historical Society*, Thirteenth and Locust streets, American history; the *Horticultural Society*, Horticultural Hall, horticulture; and several societies connected with the University, interested in archæology, political economy and the like.

Social Clubs.—Many splendid social clubs have existence in

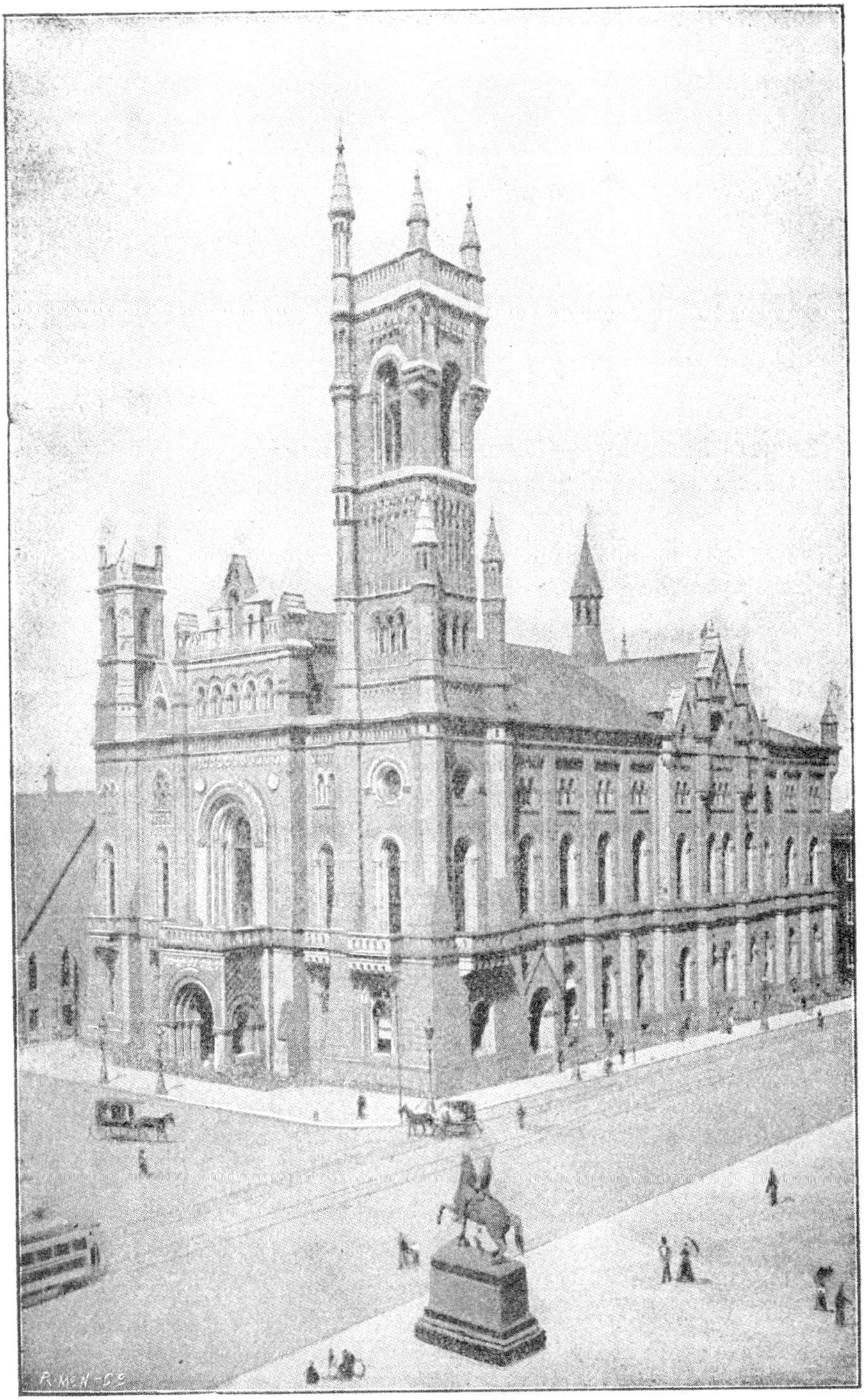

THE MASONIC TEMPLE—N. E. Corner Broad and Filbert Streets.

Philadelphia, some of which have a national fame not only because of the features of the organizations themselves, but for the elegance of the buildings they occupy. One of the oldest and best known of these institutions is the *Philadelphia Club*, at the northwest corner of Thirteenth and Walnut streets. This club occupies an unpretentious brick building, and is probably one of the most exclusive organizations in the country. The *Rittenhouse Club*, at home in two adjoining buildings on the north side of Rittenhouse Square (No. 1811), is also very exclusive. The *Columbia Club*, which has an elegant club house at Broad and Oxford streets, represents the more recently wealthy element which constitutes the "new Philadelphia" that has built up the northern part of the city. The *Union League* is a well-known organization that originated at the time of the Civil War, and has been ever since the representative of the Republican party in Pennsylvania, though its purposes are now social rather than political. In its conspicuous club house on South Broad Street, at the corner of Sansom, which contains many fine paintings and marbles, most of the recent presidents and distinguished foreign visitors have been entertained. Two or more women's social clubs exist. One is the *New Century*, having a charming club house at 124 South Twelfth Street; and the other the *Acorn*, in a fine old house at 1504 Walnut Street. The *Mercantile* and the *Manufacturers'* are social clubs of business men; the former has a large and handsome house at Broad and Master streets, and the latter a five-story building on Walnut Street, west of Broad. The *Penn Club* is composed of literary men, who frequently entertain eminent men and women of letters at receptions and dinners, in their pleasant rooms at Eighth and Locust streets; and the *Pen and Pencil* and *Sketch* are clubs of artists, rather more Bohemian in their nature than the *Art Club*, whose elegant building at 220 South Broad Street is one of the ornaments of the city. To this list might be added a large number of social assemblages having particular characteristics, such as the ancient State in Schuylkill, the irreverent Clover, and other dining clubs, the thoughtful Contemporary, the critical Browning, and various "country clubs," which have suburban houses and go in for out-door sports and ruralized recreation.

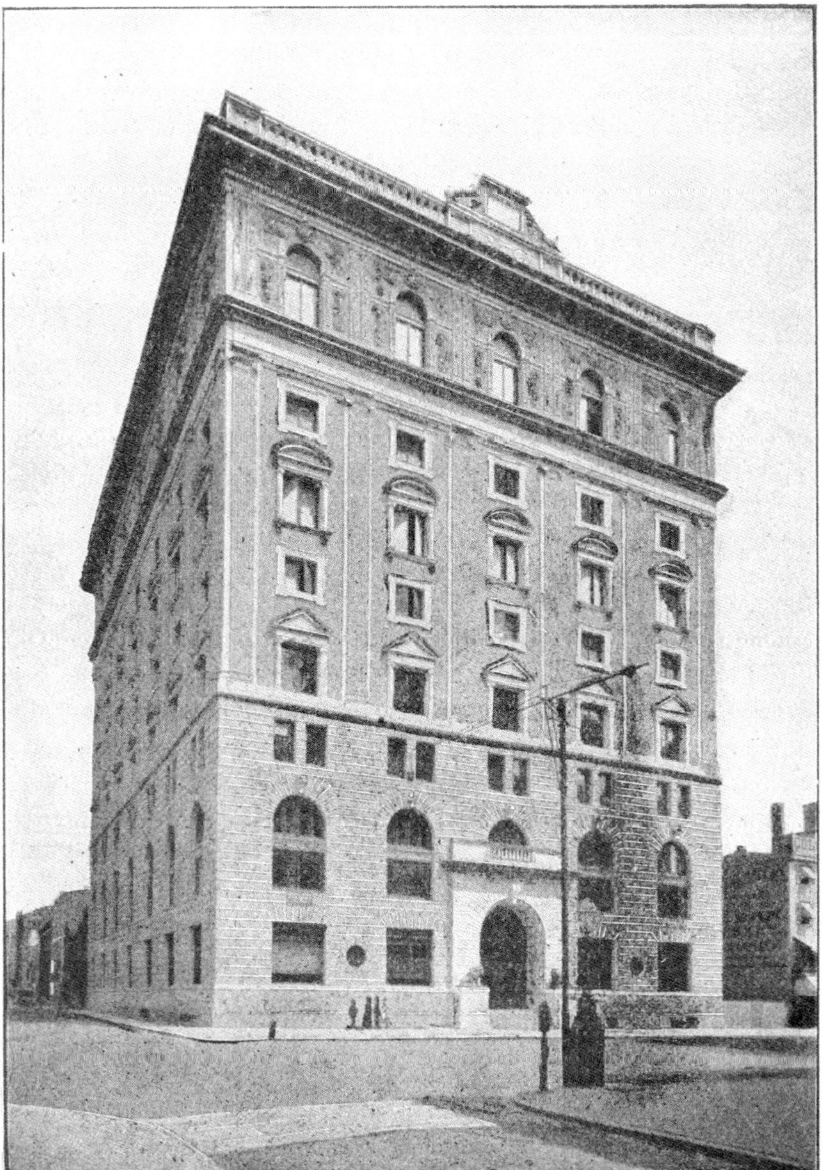

THE ODD FELLOWS' TEMPLE — Corner North Broad and Cherry Streets.

Athletic and Sporting Clubs.— Of these the leading interest lies in

Cricket.— Philadelphia is the home of American cricket. The great English game first gained a firm foothold in this country in this city, and its clubs speedily became the strongest in the land, so that they have frequently beaten crack teams from Great Britain and her colonies. These clubs are all socially influential and very exclusive in membership. The most famous is the *Germantown Cricket Club*, possessing the large Manheim grounds, near Queen Lane Station, on the Chestnut Hill Branch of the Pennsylvania Railroad. Here the members erected a number of club houses of the Colonial style of architecture, laid out a great cricket field, tennis courts, and grounds for other sports, and established a country club superior in some respects to the famous country club at Newport, R. I. Certain portions of the grounds are heavily shaded with rare old trees, and the whole space is handsome to the last degree. The *Philadelphia Cricket Club* owns grounds and houses on Wissahickon Heights, Chestnut Hill, where noted games with the Canadians have been played. The *Merion Club* has a highly ornamented park and field at Haverford, and the *Belmont* a field near the Forty-ninth Street station of the Pennsylvania Railroad, where some of the best-remembered matches with English elevens have been played.

Golf.— The recent widespread interest in golf has caused it to be extensively played upon the grounds of all the country clubs and in the parks; and during the playing season the newspapers contain frequent notices of games and matches open to the public, or able to be witnessed by them, and the railroads often offer and advertise special facilities for reaching the grounds. Persons interested in this sport can always tell, therefore, what is on foot.

Baseball.— The grounds of the local professional club, where the League games are played, are on North Broad Street, near Lehigh Avenue. Of the many amateur clubs, that of the University of Pennsylvania is probably the best.

Rowing.— There are twelve boat clubs on the Schuylkill River, within the precincts of Fairmount Park, and these are combined into the Schuylkill Navy, one of the most complete organizations in the United States. Each club owns its own club house, built from plans previously approved by the Fairmount Park Commissioners, and located on the east side of the river between the Green Street entrance of the park and Lemon Hill. The names of these clubs are the "Iona," "Malta," "College," "Vesper," "West Philadelphia," "Crescent," "Undine," "University," "Philadelphia," "Bachelors," "Quaker City," and "Pennsylvania." The aggregate value of the club houses is placed at $200,000, and the equipment at $50,000.

General Athletics.—Several notable clubs exist for the purpose of encouraging all branches of amateur sport. Prominent among these are the *Philadelphia Fencing and Sparring Club, Athletic Club, Schuylkill Navy, Caledonian Club, First Regiment Athletic Association, Third Regiment Athletic Association, State Fencibles Athletic Association*, and the *Athletic Association of the University of Pennsylvania*. The most important one is the Schuylkill Navy Athletic Club. This organization has a club house at 1626 and 1628 Arch Street, of graystone richly ornamented and elaborately equipped. The basement is given over to a bowling alley, Turkish baths, a swimming pool, bicycle-room, and the electric light plant; the first floor to parlors, reading-rooms, etc.; and the third floor to a gymnasium, in which there is a cinder running track. *Bicycle Clubs* are numerous, among the most prominent the Century Wheelmen, South End, Quaker City, Pennsylvania, Turner Cyclers, and the Wissahickon Wheelmen. The *Philadelphia Gun Club*, with grounds at Eddington, is the leading club of men devoted to shooting; while all anglers support the *Fish Protective Association*, at 1020 Arch Street.

Military Organizations.—There are in Philadelphia eight companies of the National Guards of Pennsylvania. The headquarters of the division commander and staff and of the first brigade commander and staff are in room 184, City Hall. The regiments and armories are named as follows:

Battery A.—Armory, North Forty-first Street and Mantua Avenue.

First City Troop.—Philadelphia City Cavalry armory, Twenty-first Street, near Market. This is considered the "swell" military organization in the State. Its members belong almost without exception to the most exclusive social circles in the city. The organization long antedates the Revolution.

Gray Invincibles.—This is a regiment composed exclusively of colored men. They wear showy uniforms, and their drilling is so good that they never fail to receive tumultuous applause whenever they appear on parade.

State Fencibles.—Armory, North Broad Street, below Race.

The State Fencibles Battalion is a widely-known military organization, and is esteemed to be the best drilled of any in the State.

First Regiment.—Armory, corner Broad and Callowhill streets.

Second Regiment.—Armory, Race Street, below Sixth.

First Battalion Naval State Militia.—This is generally known as the naval reserve, and, although only a few years old, has already received high praise from the Federal authorities for the excellence of its discipline and its effectiveness in the late war with Spain.

Third Regiment.—Armory, South Broad Street, near Wharton.

The United States Army Headquarters is at Fifteenth and Arch streets.

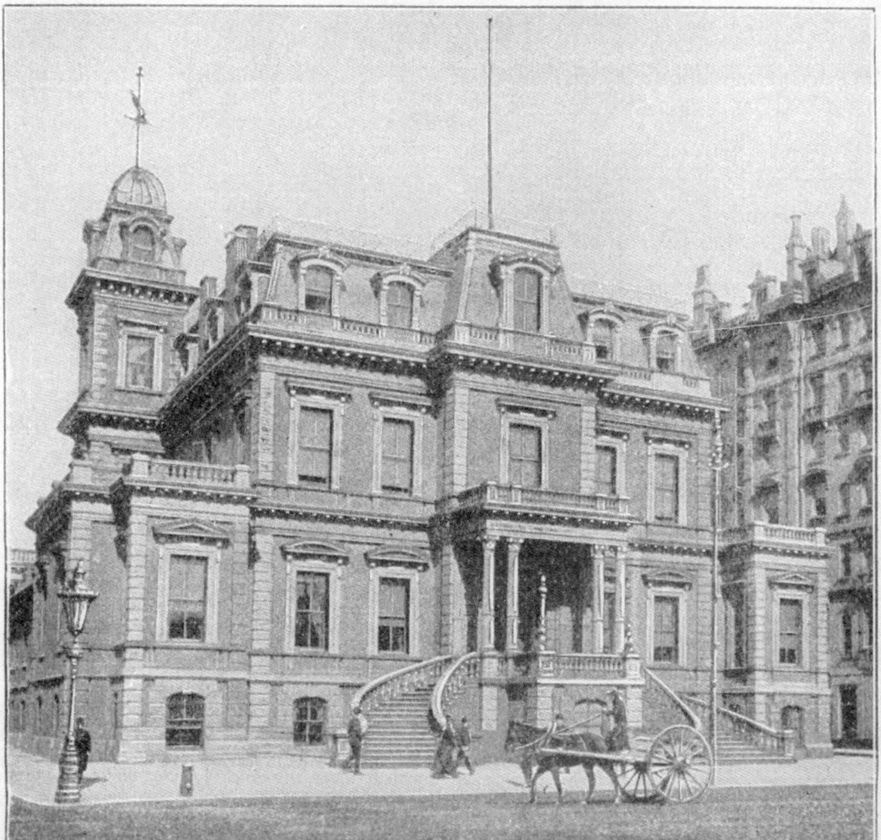

UNION LEAGUE CLUB—South Broad, from Sansom to Moravian Street.

XI.

THE SUBURBS AND SHORT TRIPS BY RAIL.

The Surrounding Country.—The topography of the country surrounding the heart of Philadelphia offers peculiar advantages for suburban settlement. It is all distinctly rolling, and in some parts almost mountainous. Thus many Philadelphia business men are enabled to live, within easy reach of their offices, in places which many towns would widely advertise as mountain or lovely summer resorts. These places have been fostered and built up largely by the direct efforts of the Pennsylvania, the Philadelphia & Reading, and the Baltimore & Ohio Railroad companies.

Germantown.

Of all the suburban sites the most famous is Germantown and its sub-sections, Mount Airy and Chestnut Hill. In the municipality of Philadelphia the district forms the Twenty-second Ward. It has some 60,000 inhabitants, and from the center of the city to the center of Germantown is about six miles. The Philadelphia & Reading Railway runs through it on the east, the Pennsylvania Railroad on the west, the People's Traction Company the center, and the Philadelphia Traction Company a little west of the center. The old part of the town is literally filled with historic houses, and to the east and west and at Chestnut Hill handsome and even palatial residences can be counted by the hundred. Indeed, a German baron, visiting the place a few years ago, designated Germantown as a "town of palaces." The place was founded in 1685 by a number of German "Pietists," who were persecuted in their mother country and were induced to settle in Pennsylvania, through the promise of William Penn that they should worship God without interference in the manner which seemed to them best. As a result many sects established themselves in

Germantown having peculiar beliefs and forms of worship in addition to the Dunkards and Mennonites, two sects which still flourish, particularly in Pennsylvania and Ohio. In the Colonial days Germantown was, with the banks of the Schuylkill, the favorite summer resort for the wealthy. Chief Justice Allen, who owned the first "landau" in the State, had a summer residence in Germantown, or that part of it now known as Mount Airy. James Logan, Chief Justice Chew, Christopher Saur (the famous printer), Francis Daniel Pastorius, all had homes in Germantown. In this village David Rittenhouse was born; and here, during the yellow-fever epidemic of 1793-'94, the seat of the National Government was located. Of all Philadelphia, there is no spot so replete with historic and interesting reminiscences.

David Rittenhouse's Birthplace.—Within the confines of Fairmount Park, on the line of Paper Mill Run, in Germantown, near where the little stream empties itself into the Wissahickon Creek, is a group of quaint old houses. Close beside an old bridge, and to its right, is one more picturesque and quaint than the others. In this ancient structure David Rittenhouse, astronomer, philosopher, and patriot, was born and spent his boyhood. His father managed the first paper mill in America, the machinery of which was operated by the sparkling waters of Paper Mill Run. The first structure was destroyed by a flood during David Rittenhouse's early manhood, but was rebuilt through the aid of the fellow townsmen of his father on an appeal from General Washington, in which the importance of the mill was strenuously urged. This old mill still stands on the banks of the stream, and the little settlement is still called "Rittenhouse Town."

Germantown Road.—It is on Germantown Road, or Germantown Avenue, as it is now called, that the most interesting historic places are to be found. They begin at Wayne Junction and extend to Mount Airy. At the corner of Fisher's Lane is *Hood's Cemetery*, originally known as the "Lower Burying Ground"; it was one of the two first public burial places in the town, "negroes" only being excluded. Here are buried many famous persons, including General Agnew, the British commander who was killed during the Battle of Germantown. Directly opposite the Soldiers' Monument is the house used as the *Executive Mansion* during the yellow-fever epidemic of 1793-'94, where President Washington carried on the business of the Government for a year.

One door above is a quaint structure occupied almost uninterruptedly for nearly two centuries by members of the Ashmead family, but for a short time used by *Count Zinzendorf* and his lovely daughters as a Moravian school, which was afterward removed to Bethlehem. At Lafayette Street is an open green, in the rear of which is a large brown structure surmounted by a high steeple. This is the old borough *Town Hall*, and in the tower is a clock whose bell is the one which replaced the old Liberty Bell of Independence Hall. In the rear of the hall are the police station and police-patrol house of the district.

The *oldest stone house* in Germantown is on Germantown Avenue, at the south side of West Walnut Lane. It is at present occupied by Miss Ann Haines, a descendant of the first builder. The house was built at three different periods, the first about 1690, by Hans Milan, a Hollander, who came to this country, presumably with Francis Daniel Pastorius, in 1685. His daughter married Dirk Jansen, and a daughter of this marriage wedded Reuben Haines in 1760. During the battle of Germantown, this house was used as a hospital for British officers and soldiers, and their blood still stains the floor of the second story, where they were laid when brought in from the battlefield. On July 25, 1825, General Lafayette gave a public reception here. Below, on the east side of Germantown Avenue, north of High Street, is the old *Pastorius house*, occupied by Francis Daniel Pastorius, the founder of Germantown, in 1685, a lawyer and poet of no mean skill, who, on account of his religious convictions, left his wealthy German home to dwell in the American wilderness. Just above Herman Street, on the east side of Germantown Avenue, is the *Mennonite Church*, the first in America. The present structure, which is a modest one-story affair, was built in 1774, and in front of it, behind a wall separating it from the street, lay the man who shot and mortally wounded General Agnew during the latter part of the battle of Germantown.

A low, dressed-stone house stands on the northwest corner of Germantown Avenue and Washington Lane, which was built close upon two centuries ago by a Janssen, who was an ancestor of the Johnson family which now own and occupy it. Here for a time dwelt *Peter Keyser*, a Mennonite preacher, who knew his Bible so thoroughly that he could repeat it from the first verse of the first chapter of Genesis to the last verse in Revelations without making a single mistake. During the battle of Germantown at this point, while the fog was heavy, Americans mistook Americans for foes, and many of them were killed before the mistake was discovered. An old board fence in this place was a shelter behind which several soldiers took refuge, and tradition says that the spot where four of them were killed is marked by four huge pear trees, planted soon after the battle was over.

On the east side, just above Washington Lane, is the *Concord* or *Old Ax Burying Ground*, in which Revolutionary and British soldiers are buried. The *Billmeyer house* stands at the northeast corner of Germantown Avenue and Upsal Street. On the steps of this mansion General Washington stood during the battle of Germantown and directed the course of the fight. On the same side, a few hundred yards north, just above Sharkneck Street, is the old *Dunkard* or *Brethren Church*. Here was established the first congregation of this faith in America, and because the first church, a log structure, was built by subscription, that section became known as Beggarstown. In the church building now standing were stored, during the Revolution, a large number of unbound copies of the edition of the Saur Bible, now so rare. These were seized by the British and used as wads for their guns and as bedding for their horses.

Pelham.—A few years ago a fine property in this section of the town, covering over one hundred acres, belonging formerly to the estate of George W. Carpenter, was purchased by a syndicate, and has now been covered by costly residences. The handsome character of the structures, the winding roads, and the general park-like appearance of this property make it well worth a visit.

Mount Airy—Beginning with the upper end of Pelham is that part of the Twenty-second Ward known as Mount Airy. On the left, after passing Carpenter Street, is the Lutheran Orphan's Home, and, nearly opposite it, the Memorial Free Library. The splendid mansion on the same side with the library, on the brow of the hill, belonged to the late Commodore Breeze, and many years ago the place was known as the Boat House, on account of its having been built by a retired sea captain, with all the peculiar recesses usually found on shipboard. About half a mile beyond, on the left, are the grounds and buildings of the Pennsylvania Institution for the Deaf and Dumb.

Chestnut Hill.—Chestnut Hill, the outlying district of the

Twenty-second Ward, is on the summit of a considerable elevation, one of a series which constitute the terminus of a spur of the Blue Ridge. It faces the picturesque White Marsh Valley with its ever-varying phases of loveliness, and contains some of the most magnificent residences in Philadelphia. To the west is *Wissahickon Heights*, a residence quarter of recent growth, containing the Wissahickon Inn, a picturesque Elizabethan structure frequented by wealthy summer boarders.

West Philadelphia and Beyond.

Some of the handsomest sections of northern West Philadelphia are comprised in Baring Street, Powelton Avenue, Springfield Avenue; and in the section bounded by Thirty-seventh and Forty-second streets and Chestnut and Spruce streets, including Chester Avenue.

All along the line of the Pennsylvania Railroad are dotted beautiful suburban towns; chief among them *Wayne* and *St. Davids*, which are about half an hour's ride from Broad Street. The ground is about 400 feet above the city, and the surrounding scenery is of a lovely character. Two more of these noted suburban towns are *Bryn Mawr* and *Devon*. At the latter is the Devon Inn, a hotel built on the plan of the Wissahickon Inn, at Chestnut Hill, and rivaling that house in popularity. Both places are connected with the city by a splendid driving road. Besides these there are Merion, Narbeth, Wynnewood, Ardmore, Haverford, Rosemont, Villa Nova, Radnor, Strafford, Berwyn, and Paoli, all thriving places devoted almost exclusively to homes of wealthy Philadelphia business men.

Camden.

While Camden can not be said to be a suburb of Philadelphia, in the strictest sense of the word, since it is in another State, its position opposite Philadelphia and its favorable situation in other ways, are causing Camden to become an industrial city of importance Prominent among its industries are chemical works, furniture factories, machine shops, soap works, and steel pen-making. All the railroads from the seaside resorts and from nearly all the New Jersey towns have their terminals in Camden, and a system of electric cars reaches all parts of the city, and extends to Woodbury and Gloucester. As to *Gloucester*, all that need be said at present is, that it is the resort of those who want amusements too "tough" to be tolerated in Philadelphia.

Along Reading's Main Line.

A ride, only second to an excursion, to Mauch Chunk and Wilkesbarre, in point of scenic beauty, is a day's trip along the main line of the Philadelphia & Reading Railway Company to Reading, or, if time permits, to West Milton, by way of the Catawissa branch, of which more will presently be said. Within twenty minutes after leaving the Reading Terminal Depot the train enters pretty scenery, which constantly increases in beauty to the end of the journey. Excluding for the present everything beyond Reading there are three notable places worth visiting. The first of these is Valley Forge.

Valley Forge. — This place is but twenty-three miles from Philadelphia, and an hour only is consumed in reaching it. Here were the winter quarters of the Continental army in 1777–'78 and the old breastworks, Washington's quarters, and other remains of the army's occupation are still to be seen. The State recently ordered the purchase of all the land on which are situated the most precious relics, for the purpose of preserving them, and converting the whole into a park. Valley Forge lies in a great basin on the banks of the Schuylkill. The rim is made up of high tree-clothed hills, almost high enough to be termed mountains. There are beautiful drives and picturesque nooks in plenty, and a little trout fishing in season, in one or two of the streams, and good black-bass fishing in the river offer inducements to the angler.

Pottstown. — A second place of great interest on the main line of the Reading is Pottstown, a thriving place forty miles distant, and one hour and a half's ride, from Philadelphia. The chief attraction here is a wonderful group of rocks a few miles outside of the town known as the Ringing Rocks. These boulders, which cover, like a moraine of a glacier, a large extent of ground, give out when struck sweet sounds like those of a chime of bells, and of their musical qualities a tragic but pretty Indian legend is told. It is too long to relate here, but according to it, the rocks first gave forth their sweet notes when an Indian warrior and his betrothed toppled from Signal Rock, the highest of the group, from the death wound received from vengeful foes who were watching their meeting. Recently a corporation has purchased the place, built an electric railway to the rocks, erected handsome pavilions and dancing floors, and arranged a lovely lake amid the abundant trees. It is becoming a favorite resort for Sunday School and other picnic parties.

Reading.—The trip to Reading is a source of constant delight. The winding Schuylkill, the rolling hills, the tree-crested and blue-tinted mountains all keep the eyes and senses delighted and unwearied. Reading, the county seat of Berks, was founded by the Penns, and named after their English homestead. Two mountains about a thousand feet high tower to the right of the river, one called Mount Penn and the other the Neversink.

Mount Penn.—Leaving the train, which departing from Philadelphia about 10 o'clock in the morning arrives about 11.40, the visitor takes, a square or two away, trolley cars for the foot of Mount Penn. Here at a quaint hostelry an excellent lunch may be had and the ascent of the mountain begun.

Penn Gravity Road.—This ascent is made by means of a gravity railroad, which starts close by the little hotel, and which is known as the Mount Penn Gravity Railroad. A "mountain climber" locomotive, with several open cars attached, then begins, with much puffing and blowing, to haul its load up the two-mile steep and winding incline, among thick trees and around steep rocks. Every now and then during the ascent open places are come upon, giving extended and glorious views of the valley for miles to the north and west. In fifteen minutes the summit is reached and the passengers disembark. Pen can not adequately describe the panorama. To the west there is a grand picture of Reading mapped out by nature; to the south-east is Birdsboro; and beyond, the silver thread-like Schuylkill winding toward Philadelphia. To the west, again beyond Reading, stretches the famous Lebanon Valley, bounded on the north by the Blue Mountains, with the South Mountains on the south. Embarking again, the train is found to be minus a locomotive, and the cars go rushing down the incline at a rapid pace, giving frequent glimpses of rare and lovely bits of scenery. A brief journey brings the visitor once more to the base of the mountain.

Neversink Mountain.—Returning by trolley cars the visitor alights at Ninth and Penn streets, and there takes the Neversink Electric road. Ten or fifteen minutes' ride brings him to the base of the Neversink Mountain, and as the ascent is made he is treated to a succession of delightful surprises. A few hundred feet of winding and twisting brings the car to the borders of a steep cliff, from which a charming panorama is unfolded. Spread out is a brave array of public buildings of various kinds. An amphitheater of hills bounds the horizon; Mount Penn, to the north, marshals the heights and serenely reviews Mounts Washington and Jefferson. Renewing the trip, the car passes a flourishing strip of woodland and emerges upon a spur looking upon Woodvale and the enchanting Antietam Valley. Poplar Neck Bend is in view with the winding Schuylkill and finally the famous Point Lookout. Soon after the summit is reached. Here is built a large and handsome hotel, called the Neversink Mountain House, where guests are received by the day or week, and from which magnificent views are obtained of the valleys and the encircling mountains. The journey down the Neversink is as full of delightful surprises as the ascent, not the least among which is Klapperthal Park, a place, as an enthusiastic Emerald Islander expressed it, "which is a charming sylvan retreat, surrounded by lofty forest-covered mountains, down which purling streams of clear spring water wind like silver threads." The journey from Philadelphia to Reading and return, including a visit to both Mounts Penn and Neversink, can easily be made in a day, allowing nearly six hours in which to make the two ascents.

A Four-Hundred-Mile Trip.—For those who are fond of beautiful scenery the following trip is recommended. It covers 400 miles and may be made in a single day by taking the newspaper train from 12th and Market streets in the morning, the time for arrival again in the city being about 10.30 P. M. By this trip a magnificent series of nature's pictures may be seen, the most glorious of which is compressed in some forty miles along the Catawissa road, in one part the train passing over seven immense trestle bridges, the largest about one mile in length and the highest about 300 feet. The whole route is over the Reading and its branches. Twelfth and Market to Reading; Reading to Lebanon; Lebanon to Pine Grove; Pine Grove to Auburn; Auburn to Pottsville, dinner at this point; Pottsville to Tamaqua; Tamaqua to East Mahony Junction; Catawissa road to West Milton; West Milton to Philadelphia. The waits between these different points are from five to twenty minutes, except at Pottsville, where there is an interval of about an hour and half between trains.

Gettysburg, Pa.—Unique among the great battlefields of history, Gettysburg, by reason of the vast forces engaged and the magnitude of the issues determined by its results, will ever be regarded as the most impressive tragedy the world has seen enacted in the theatre of war. Year after year, a constantly increasing throng of visitors pours into the little town of Gettysburg and scatters across its environing fields and slopes to look upon the various spots made ineffaceably historic by the events of those July days in 1863. The hundreds of monuments and memorial tablets which dot the field serve to make plain the story of the battle.

The highways around the town, and leading away in all directions, are much used by that enterprising element of our touring population, the wheelmen, who come here in large numbers by train, and make this the centre of a variety of pleasing excursions. The amateur photographer, too, finds along the winding streams of the valley a wealth of subjects, picturesque and historical, for his plates.

The most direct route is via the Philadelphia & Reading Railway. The traveler who has not much spare time, can have a good general view of the field by leaving the Reading Terminal, 8.36 A. M., and spending two and a half hours at Gettysburg, return to Philadelphia by 10.00 P. M. the same day.

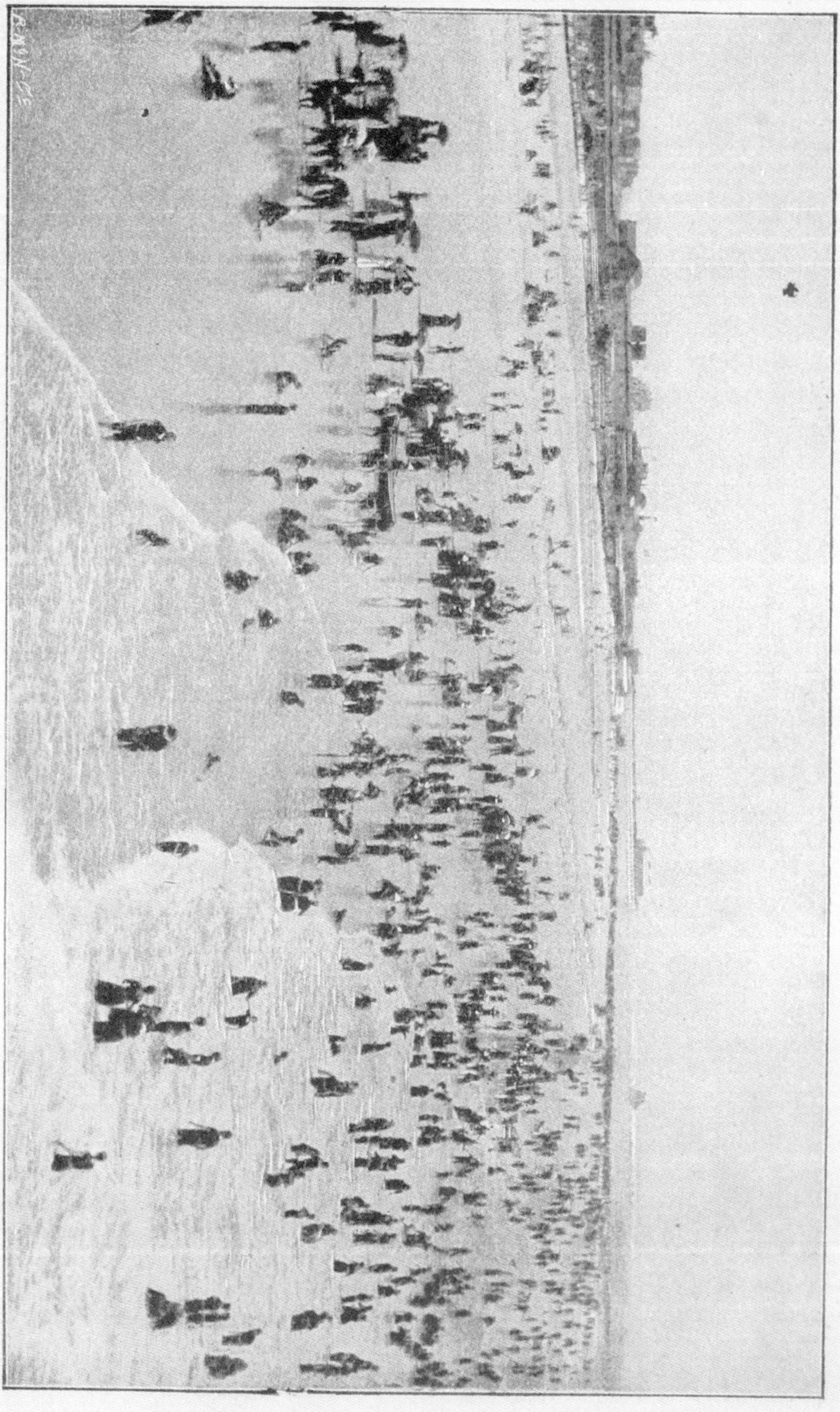

A BEACH SCENE — Atlantic City.

11

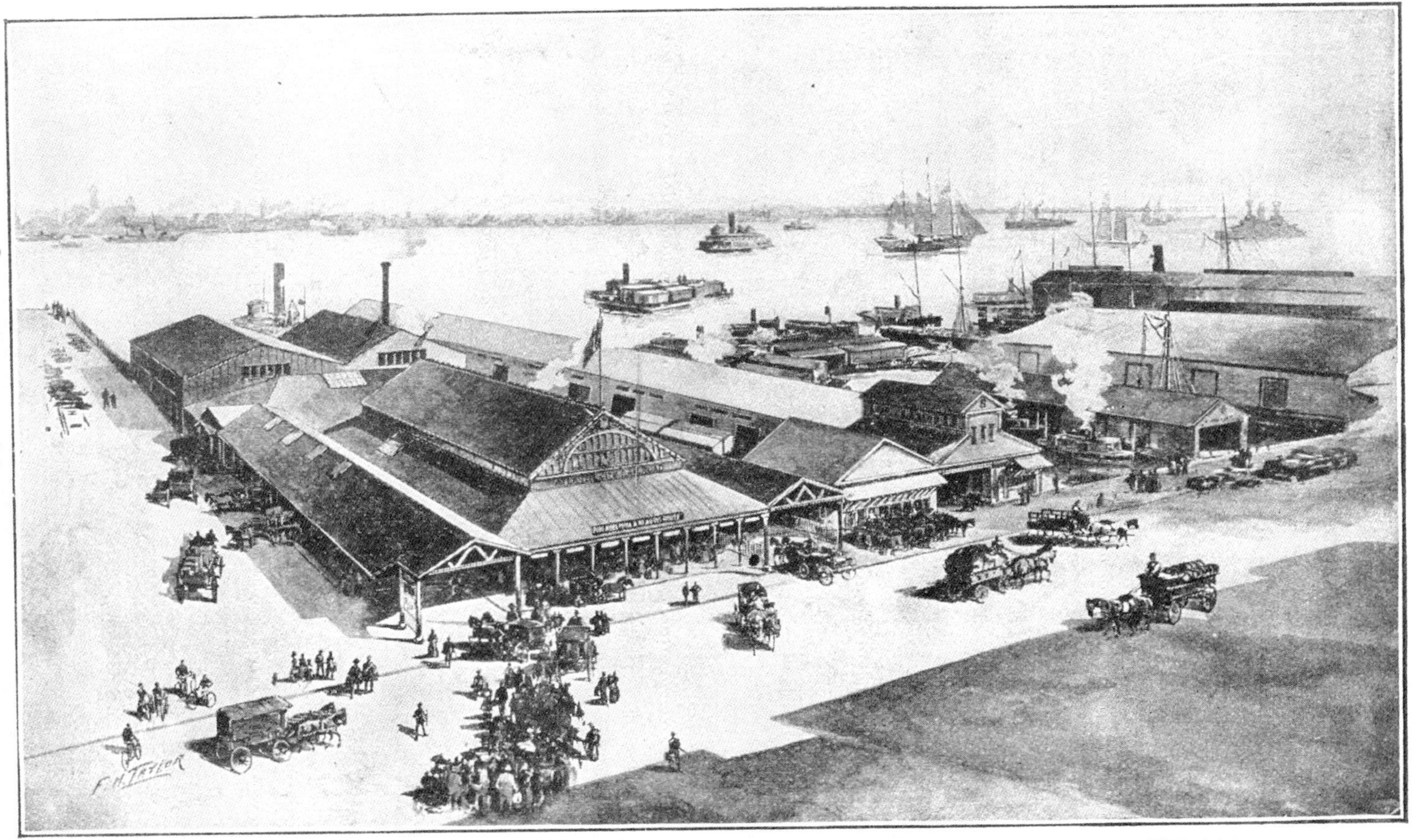

STATION OF PHILADELPHIA & READING ROUTE (ATLANTIC R R.)—Foot of Chestnut Street, Philadelphia.

XII.

SEASIDE RESORTS.

Atlantic City.

Although Atlantic City is on the ocean side of New Jersey, and is an independent city sixty miles from Philadelphia, it may, in many respects, be termed a suburb, from the fact that a majority of its floating population, and many of its semi-residents are Philadelphians. Atlantic City is a thoroughly democratic place, it being the pleasure resort of the poor man as well as of the millionaire. Orderly and innocent pleasure-loving people of all classes enjoy themselves in their several ways without caste prejudice. The permanent population is 21,000; in summer it occasionally reaches 150,000.

Atlantic City has arisen from nothing but sand-dunes within forty years, and has become wealthy and famous as a seaside resort from two causes—its magnificent shore-line and its wonderful board walk. The heavy surf which rolls in on the flat beach affords delightful bathing, perfectly safe to those who observe the cautions of the life savers. The beach is hard and nearly level, affording a splendid natural carriage drive, which is taken advantage of by pleasure parties by the thousand, both in summer and winter. The equable, healthful climate and admirable means of access and accommodation there have supplemented these natural attractions.

The city stands upon an island, separated from the mainland by a broad stretch of inlets and salt meadows. This island is low and level, the soil is pure sand, absorbing and draining away moisture quickly, and an admirable system of public sanitation is maintained. The water supply is obtained from artesian wells, and is ample for household uses and fire purposes. Effective police and fire departments exist; the city is lighted by gas and electricity, and has a system of electric street-cars connecting all important points.

The arrangement of streets is in straight lines, forming "squares." The main thoroughfares, running north and south, parallel with the seashore, are all named after oceans—first, nearest the shore, Pacific Avenue; then Atlantic (the Broadway of the town), and westward, in succession, Arctic, Baltic, Mediterranean, Adriatic, Caspian, etc. The streets running at right angles to these are named after various States, beginning with Maine at the north end of the island, along the shore of Absecon Inlet, and extending southward. These are divided into "East" and "West" by Atlantic Avenue. Both railway stations are in the center of town, on Atlantic Avenue, the Pennsylvania at Tennessee, and the Reading at Arkansas Avenue. Intermediate streets have also been cut through the large squares here and there.

The Board Walk.—The board walk, an avenue of planking along the ocean beach, on steel posts, is an invention of Atlantic City. When its popularity was assured, other seaside resorts followed, but none have equaled, much less surpassed, the famous waterfront promenade of the chief Atlantic Ocean pleasure town. Destroyed by the great storm of September, 1889, the original board walk was replaced by another nearly five miles long, forty feet wide, and twelve feet high, at a cost to the city of $150,000. During the summer season, the greater part of Atlantic City's population is to be found in the morning or the evening on this popular walk, which opens uninterruptedly to the sea, high tides almost reaching it; yet it never seems overcrowded, and the funny incidents constantly occurring there are sufficient to arouse the most blasé and to cure the most confirmed of misanthropes.

Atlantic City as a Place for Rest and Recuperation can advance many claims to the consideration of invalids. The southerly situation gives a short winter, and the neighborhood of the sea an equability of climate which inland places can not enjoy. The ocean breezes cool the air in the warm months, while the presence of this great mass of water modifies the winter temperature. Storms occur, of course; but against these is provided a sun-parlor in almost every hotel, and, on the whole, the winter weather is mild and sunny, yet invigorating. Thousands of persons take advantage of these favorable circumstances in winter, and, year by year, their numbers increase, and larger and better provision is made by the railroads and hotels for winter traffic. The comparative dryness of the air, prevailing at all seasons, and very beneficial to all persons troubled with weakness or diseases of the throat or lungs, is due to the fact that the prevailing winds are from the southwest, and hence come over many hundreds of miles of dry and sandy country, covered with pine forest, with whose balsamic strength the air is laden. Such a crowd of people amuse themselves in summer, as well as winter, so that no fear of dullness need keep any one away from Atlantic City at that season.

"The board walk is always in favor," writes Heston. "The air is so dry and mild, as a rule, that even convalescents, who are able to be about at all, may enjoy at least a brief walk on the great ocean promenade. Then, again, there are miles of drives, either upon the hard, smooth beach, or through the city, or across to the mainland. . . . Even the sight of so many new faces from all parts of the country—many of them those of distinguished people—is pleasant and refreshing, especially to those who are building up after an illness and have a horror of going to a dull place, and yet are not strong enough for more active pleasures."

Atlantic City is daily growing in public estimation as a sanitarium as well as a pleasure-place.

How to Get to Atlantic City.

Two lines of railway, one controlled by the Pennsylvania Company and the other by the Reading corporation, run from Camden to Atlantic City. Each varies little from sixty miles in length, the tracks of both are as straight, solid, smooth, and dustless as it is possible to make them; both companies run frequent trains of the finest cars, and both cover the distance in from sixty to eighty minutes, according to the train taken. *By the Pennsylvania Route* the traveler begins his journey at the handsome new station in Philadelphia at the foot of Market Street, and is ferried to Camden, where the station is upon the wharf. He gets a fair glimpse of Camden, but quickly passes beyond it into the flat, sandy, pine-covered plain of central New Jersey, broken by only small farming villages until Egg Harbor is reached, on the shore of the marshy lagoon between the island of Atlantic City and the mainland. The station of this company in Atlantic City is at Atlantic and Tennessee avenues, near the center of things.

The Pennsylvania Company also runs what it calls *bridge trains*, from the Broad Street Station, Philadelphia, which go via Frankford to and across the magnificent new Delaware bridge, reaching the main line at Haddonfield; it is by this bridge-connection that the many excursion trains reach the coast from interior cities.

By the Philadelphia & Reading Route, the passenger takes the railroad ferries from new station, foot of Chestnut or South Street, Philadelphia, to the station of the Philadelphia & Reading Route (Atlantic City R. R.) at Kaighn's Point, where he takes a train that swiftly delivers him at the station on Atlantic Avenue in Atlantic City, at the corner of Arkansas Avenue.

Excursion Tickets, good for fifteen days, are sold by both companies, at $1.75.

Hotels.—Atlantic City probably excels all other towns in the country in the number of its hotels, as well as in the variety of entertainment afforded by them. Good accommodations can be had at $6 a week, and from this the figures range upward gradually into the fifties. Following is a list of hotels, alphabetically arranged, with notes upon capacity, prices, situation, etc.:

Albemarle.—Virginia and Pacific avenues. $2 to $3 per day; $12.50 to $15 per week; 72 rooms.

Arlington.—Michigan Avenue, near the beach. $2.50 to $3.50 per day; $14 to $25 per week; 100 rooms; open all the year.

Berkeley.—Kentucky Avenue, near the beach. $2.50 to $3 per day, $14 to $18 per week; 86 rooms. Open February to October.

Boscobel.—Kentucky Avenue, below Pacific. $2.50 to $3 per day; $10 to $18 per week; 56 rooms. Open the year around.

Brighton.—Indiana Avenue, on the beach. $4 to $5 per day; $25 to $50 per week; 180 rooms. First-class; has a casino, band, large lawn, etc.

Cedarcroft.—South Carolina Avenue and the beach. $2.50 to $3 per day; $12 to $18 per week; 100 rooms. Spring and summer.

Central.—Tennessee Avenue. $2 to $3 per day, $12 to $18 per week; 70 rooms. Open June 1 to October 1.

Chalfonte.—North Carolina Avenue and beach. $3 to $4 per day; $15 to $25 per week; 95 rooms.

Chetwoode.—1709 Pacific Avenue. $2.50 to $3 per day; $12 to $18 per week; 60 rooms. Spring and summer.

Dennis.—Michigan Avenue and the beach. $3.50 to $5 per day; $18 to $30 per week; 250 rooms. Open all the year.

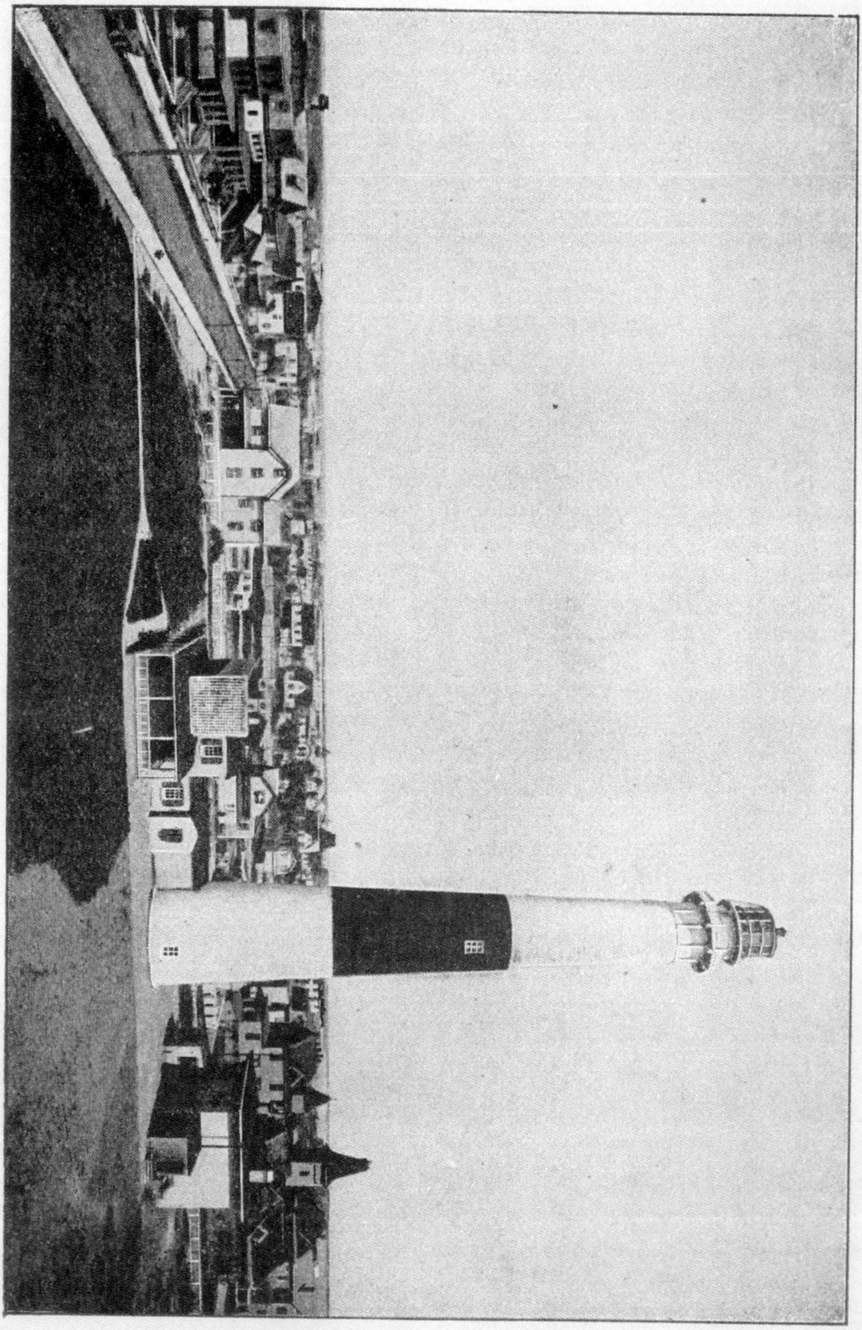

THE LIGHTHOUSE AT ATLANTIC CITY.

Dunlop.—Ocean Avenue and the beach. $3.50 to $5 per day; $21 to $40 per week; 200 rooms.

Garden.—Pacific and Illinois Avenue. $4 to $5 per day; $25 to $50 per week; 150 rooms. February to October.

Gladstone.—Brighton Avenue and the beach. $2.50 to $4 per day; $15 to $25 per week; 120 rooms.

Haddon Hall.—North Carolina Avenue and the beach. $3 to $5 per day; $18 to $30 per week; 86 rooms. Open all the year.

Holmhurst.—Pennsylvania Avenue. $3 to $3.50 per day; $16 to $18 per week; 60 rooms. Open all the year.

Islesworth.—Sea end of Virginia Avenue. $3 to $5 per day; $18 to $25 per week; 136 rooms. Open all the year.

Iroquois.—South Carolina Avenue. $3 to $4 per day; $15 to $25 per week; 90 rooms. February to October.

Irvington.—Virginia Avenue and beach. $2.50 to $3 per day; $15 to $25 per week; 70 rooms. Open all the year.

Kenilworth Inn.—South Kentucky Avenue. $3 to $3.50 per day; $10 to $15 per week; 90 rooms. Open all the year.

Koopman's.—New York Avenue. $3 to $4 per day; $15 to $25 per week; 85 rooms. Open all the year.

Lehman.—Pennsylvania Avenue, below Pacific. $2.50 to $3 per day; $13 to $18 per week; 80 rooms. Open all the year.

Loraine.—St. Charles Place. $3 to $3.50 per day; $18 to $25 per week; 80 rooms. February to October.

Luray.—Kentucky Avenue and beach. $3 to $4 per day; $16 to $25 per week; 150 rooms. Open all the year.

Majestic.—Virginia Avenue, near the beach. $2.50 to $3 per day; $12 to $20 per week; 100 rooms. February to October.

Morton.—Virginia Avenue. $2.50 to $3 per day; $15 to $20 per week; accommodates 200. Open all the year.

Ponce de Leon.—Virginia Avenue, near the beach. $2.50 to $3.50 per day; $12 to $18 per week; 100 rooms. Open all the year.

Pennhurst.—Michigan Avenue, near the beach. $2.50 to $3 per day; $12 to $18 per week; 100 rooms. Open all the year.

Raleigh.—St. Charles Place. $3 to $4 per day; $16 to $30 per week; 90 rooms.

Revere.—Park Place, near the beach. $2.50 per day; $12 to $18 per week; 40 rooms. Open all the year.

Royal Palace.—North end of Pacific Avenue, on the beach. $4 to $5 per day; $18 to $40 per week; 250 rooms. February to October.

Rudolph.—New Jersey Avenue and beach. $3 to $4 per day; $18 to $30 per week; 400 rooms. February to October.

St. Charles.—St. Charles Place. $4 to $5 per day; $20 to $30 per week; 150 rooms.

St. George by the Sea. — Montpelier Avenue and the beach (Chelsea). $2.50 to $4 per day; $16 to $25 per week; 125 rooms. February to October.

Seaside.—Pennsylvania Avenue and the beach. $3 to $4 per day; $16 to $30 per week; 150 rooms. This house has a fine situation at the edge of the sea, and is open all the year.

Senate.—Rhode Island Avenue, $3 to $3.50 per day; $14 to $18 per week; 125 rooms. February to October.

Shelburne.—Michigan Avenue and beach. $4 to $5 per day; $18 to $30 per week; 150 rooms. The situation is admirable, and the management and furnishing of the house are highly recommended. It is open the year through.

Strand.—Pennsylvania Avenue and the beach. $3 to $4 per day; $15 to $25 per week; 125 rooms. This hotel is new and fireproof; open all the year.

Sterling.—Ocean end of Kentucky Avenue. $3.50 per day; $15 to $25 per week; 100 rooms. Built of brick, and fireproof; open all the year.

Traymore.—Illinois Avenue and the beach. $3.50 to $5 per day; $18 to $25 per week; 175 rooms. A large hotel overlooking the ocean. Open at all seasons.

Wellington.—Kentucky Avenue. $2.50 to $3 per day; $10 to $18 per week; 100 rooms. Open all the year.

Westminster.—Kentucky Avenue. $2 to $3 per day; $10 to $15 per week; 60 rooms. Open all the year.

Wiltshire.—Virginia Avenue. $3 to $4 per day; $14 to $20 per week; 100 rooms; February to October.

Windsor.— Illinois Avenue and the beach. $3.50 to $5 per day; $18 to $25 per week; 150 rooms. Open all the year.

Amusements.

Life along the Board Walk.—The Board Walk is bordered for more than a mile by restaurants, bathing "pavilions," shops for the sale of fancy articles and knickknacks, candy and ice-cream counters, and shows of every inoffensive description one can think of, several of which give continuous variety performances from noon to midnight. There are merry-go-rounds and mechanical bicycles that spin you horizontally, and Ferris wheels that whirl you vertically, an electric railway that runs far out to sea and back, and nickel-in-the slot attractions for eyes and ears, each more gaudy or noisier than the last.

"In fact," remarks a recent and enthusiastic observer, "it is here that the life of the resort centers. On one side lies the beach, with its white sand and its caressing waves, and beyond stretches away the illimitable sea with its rolling billows, its lights and shadows, its whitecaps and its sails. Here and there, along the board walk, pavilions have been erected where one may sit with the ocean breeze in his face and watch the bathers' sport, the breaking waves, the distant ships, the nearer yachts, or the undulations of the sea. Turning, there is another scene, a constant stream of ever-varying but always joyous life. This scene during the early hours of a summer's evening is one worthy to behold and to be held in remembrance. The life, the light, the color are wonderful. The animation, the laughter, and the overflowing good humor are irresistible. To take this promenade on a summer's evening is a supreme pleasure. The endless but orderly throng, with its bright colors, the electric lights and illuminated shop windows, the rolling chairs, the splashing waves, the soft air, the iridescent sea, the full moon over the sea, and over all the beautiful heavens, inspires a sweet ecstasy seldom experienced. Without this grand esplanade Atlantic City would be lost to itself and to the world.

"Three great piers extend from the board walk out into the ocean. One of these is of wood, one of iron, and one of steel. Each affords an excellent view from its farther end, and they have become quite popular with fishing folk. Here one secures all the benefits of a sea voyage. The new steel pier is a staunch structure at a popular point, extending a thousand feet into the sea. It has an immense auditorium, a theater, and an assembly hall, all brilliantly lighted at night by electricity. A number of pavilions have also been built upon it, in which, protected from the sun, one obtains a delightful air and an enviable view of the strand. Many of the larger hops are held upon these piers. . . .

"There is much free social gaiety at Atlantic City. Most of the larger hotels have their own orchestras for the season, and hops are given every evening. These are often brilliant affairs, and are participated in by many of the leading society people of the country. Concerts are frequent, and amateur theatricals, private parties, and progressive euchers are in constant vogue. First-class performances by some of the best musical and dramatic talent are also given in the Grand Opera House and the Academy of Music."

Bathing.— The facilities for bathing at Atlantic City are of the best. The beach is smooth, the slope gentle, and the conditions are as safe as possible; in addition to which a patrol of life-savers is in constant attendance. Bathing-houses are numerous and well arranged, passages to and from all of them leading to the water under the board walk, adding to the convenience and privacy of bathers. The ordinary price for excellent bathing-suits is 25 cents. At several places tub-baths in hot or cold sea-water may be taken.

At the Inlet — Sailing, Fishing, Gunning. — The Inlet is the broad opening north of the Island, admitting the sea-water to the inland tidal bays and reaches. It is a mile or more from the center of the city, and the northern terminus of the board walk and the electric-car line. At the Inlet sailboats are for hire from early morning until night, either by the trip, the hour, or the day, at $5 to $8 per day. Frequently owners of large sailboats form parties, charging from 25 to 50 cents a head. In addition to the sailboats, there are at the Inlet small steamboats and tugs for the purpose of taking persons on short trips to adjacent islands or out to sea, for small sums, according to the distance covered. The thoroughfares which divide the island from the mainland are broad, deep, and placid; even the most timid, or those who are subject easily to seasickness, may enjoy a sail over the waters of the thoroughfare without fear of unpleasant consequences. Those who are fond of heavier water may indulge their liking to their heart's content, for from the wharf to the wide ocean is but a few minutes' sail.

Fishing is one of the principal occupations for many visitors here, and may be practiced continually. All the fish usually found along the New Jersey coast are abundant, and plenty of boats, both oar and sail, may be had at the Inlet or at the railroad bridge for small sums.

Gunning.—The meadows surrounding Atlantic City are a hunter's paradise, where wild geese, brant, black ducks, broadbills, redheads, snipe, willets, plover, and many other wild fowl abound in season. The laws provided for the proper protection of these birds are severe and strictly enforced.

Excursions of great interest are possible. A steam ferry at the Inlet carries one across the channel to *Brigantine Beach*, the next beach north, and there a trolley car is waiting for a nine-mile ride along the ocean strand to the hotels and cottages of Brigantine Beach, which have many attractions of their own. The cost of this round trip is 60 cents.

The Trolley Ride to Longport is another very attractive excursion. Taking the car on Atlantic Avenue, you reach at the lower end of the city the *Seaview House*, which is the resort of almost daily excursion parties brought by the railroads in special trains, where refreshments, bathing, and varied amusements may be had in a pleasant place by themselves. From here to Longport, at the southern end of the island, is a delightful run along the beach through Chelsea, Ventnor, and South Atlantic—beautiful suburbs. "This nine-mile ride is one of the most exhilarating imaginable. The clean white strand, the booming billows, the fresh salt breeze, and the ocean itself are all glorious and make the blood tingle with exquisite pleasure. At Longport a staunch little steamer is taken for a ride across Great Egg Harbor Bay to Somers Point or to Ocean City. The trip to Ocean City occupies about seventeen minutes, and is a delightful ride. At Ocean City the open cars of the motor line are taken, which run through to Stone Harbor and complete the trip. The trip from Longport to Somers Point occupies about twenty-five minutes. Here another motor line may be taken for the return by rail via Pleasantville and the meadows.

Ocean City is a resort rapidly growing in favor. Its beach is of peculiar hardness, giving a famous seven-mile drive; and Great Egg Harbor Bay affords the best of opportunity for sailing, boating, fishing, and gunning. It is a well-ordered town, having electric lights, trolley cars, etc. The largest hotel is the Brighton, but many smaller ones exist, and boarding-houses are numerous. The town is accessible via electric cars and the Longport ferry from Atlantic City as above described; or by rail via Sea Isle City and the Cape May rail routes from Camden, and by through express trains via Philadelphia & Reading Route.

Sea Isle City, on the next beach south, contains good hotels, has a "board walk," and the other appurtenances of a beach resort, and is connected with the world by a branch railway of the Reading's Cape May Line. The fishing is especially fine in its neighborhood, especially for the drum.

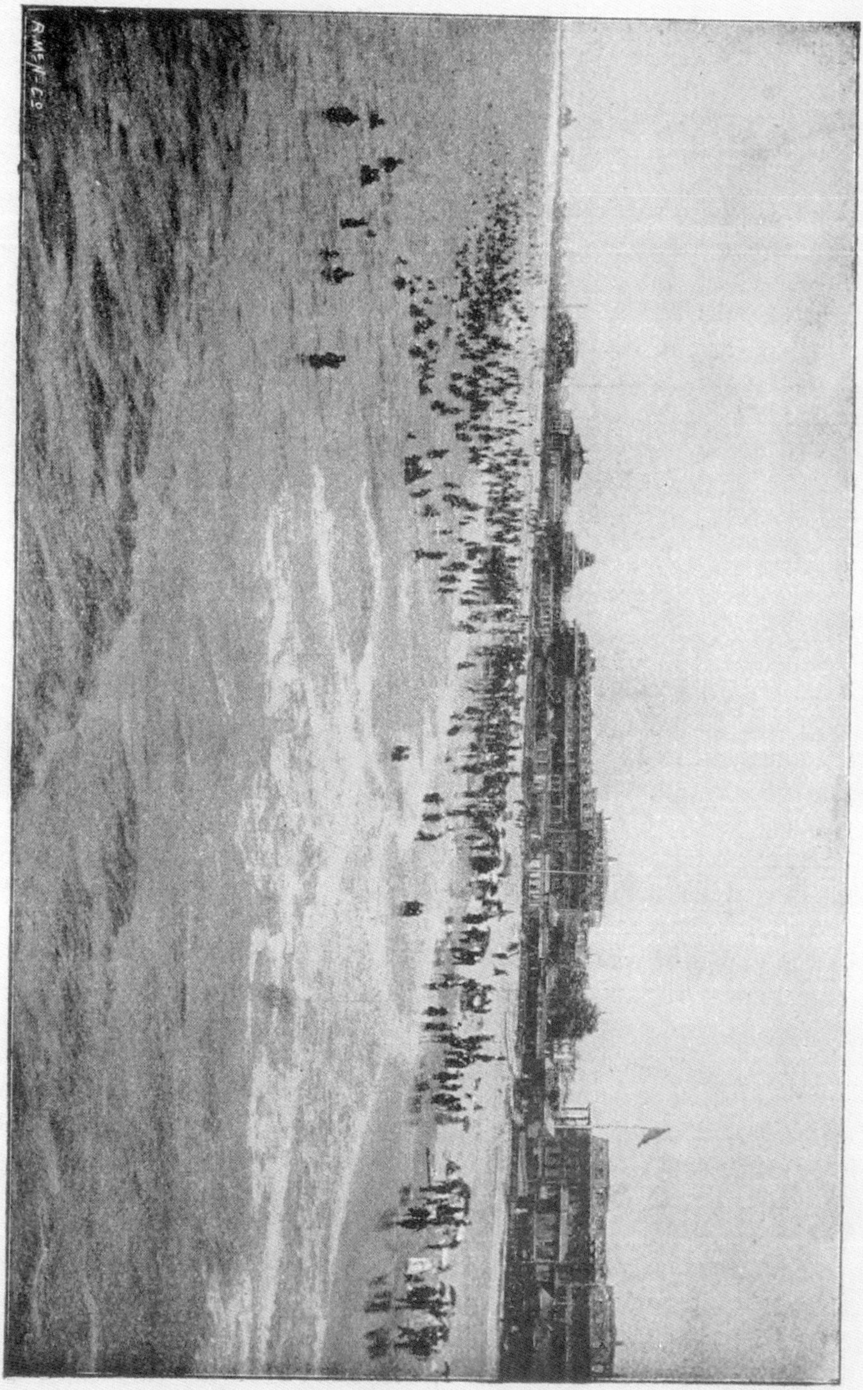

CAPE MAY.

Cape May.

Within easy reach of Philadelphia is CAPE MAY, one of the most delightful seaside resorts in the country, readily accessible at all times, and thoroughly enjoyable at every season of the year. The town, as substantial in appearance as a thrifty New England village, is located at the southern extremity of New Jersey, and is built on an upland island on the ocean side of the extreme point of the cape, facing southeast. Both shores of the lower peninsula of New Jersey are exceedingly picturesque, the great sand-dunes and gnarled cedars on the bay side forming a strange yet interesting picture; and the wonderful phenomena noticeable in the growth of the rich holly woods, cedars, persimmons, and sassafras trees, at Wildwood and Holly Beach, are extremely interesting to all students of nature.

"There is but a single town on the whole coast of the United States,' says an excellent authority, "that can compare with it in respect to climate, and that one is Key West, at the very southern extremity of the Florida reef. The frosts of winter and the heats of summer are tempered by her proximity to bay and ocean. Snow and ice speedily disappear under the influence of the south wind, and the same breezes bring to her shores in summer, cooling zephyrs for thousands who yearly take advantage of them for health or pleasure. The climate of Cape May is semi-tropical in character. Cotton and cane will mature, and fruits and plants of the southern zone flourish if properly cultivated."

Routes to Cape May.—*The Philadelphia & Reading Route* (Atlantic City Railroad) is by the Chestnut Street or South Street ferry to Camden, and thence over the former South Jersey line, which has lately been thoroughly rebuilt and provided with a first-class service of trains, run several times a day and connecting with branch trains to Ocean City and Sea Isle City. Round-trip tickets cost $2.

The Pennsylvania Railroad's Route is over the former West Jersey tracks, from Camden, and is a little longer. It has an equally good service of trains, which pass through Vineland and other interesting towns. The round-trip fare is $2.00.

The Beach and Bathing Facilities.—The whole length of the

beach, from Cape May Point to Sewall's Point, is five miles. That portion of it used for bathing purposes is about a mile in extent. The shore is broad and smooth. Its firmness renders it useful and quite comfortable for driving as well as for pedestrian exercise. Bathing facilities are ample, and indoor sea baths, hot or cold, may be had by those who do not like surf-bathing.

The boulevard, with promenade and drive, extends from Cape May Point to the Stockton Hotel, about three miles. Along this route the ocean is in clear view, the waves, at high tide, rolling to within a few feet of the carriage-way. What is known as the Turnpike Drive has become a favorite carriage route for visitors, enabling them to enjoy the ocean view for a considerable distance, then taking them through pleasant roads and avenues in the district around Cape May City.

At the foot of Decatur Street is the iron *Ocean Pier*, now about eight hundred feet long. It is a favorite promenade. On one part an amphitheater, to seat several hundred people, has been constructed. Summer opera is given in the inclosure at intervals by select traveling companies. At the farther end of the pier is a lower deck for the accommodation of fishermen. Adequate provision is also made for boating and yachting. Cat-rigged and schooner-rigged boats are for hire. The naphtha packet *Wildwood* runs several times a day to the resorts on Five-Mile Beach, taking the inside route. The headquarters for yachting is at Sewell's Point. Water fowl shooting can be indulged in during the season. There are athletic grounds and a baseball park. For the children and such others as enjoy the sport, a large carousel, with music and modern appliances, has been erected near the beach.

Places to Visit.—Some of the most interesting places in the Cape May district are within convenient driving distance of the city, and form pleasant morning or afternoon outings for visitors.

Cape May Lighthouse, with revolving light, 145 feet high, is at Cape May Point; it was first built in 1800, and rebuilt in 1859. Near the Point also is *Lake Lily*, about three and one-half acres in circumference. Rowing is allowed on this body of water. A favorite beach drive is to *Diamond Beach*, on Delaware Bay, where Cape May diamonds are found. Three miles above Cape May is *Cold Spring*, where clear, bubbling, fresh spring water may be seen issuing from the salt meadows. Near this place is a Presbyterian church, established nearly two hundred years ago. There are *Life-Saving Stations* at Cold Spring and Cape May Point. An *electric road*, about six miles long, extends from Cape May Point to Sewell's Point, along the beach.

Historical Data.—According to old chronicles, Henry Hudson, an English mariner, in a third voyage to this country in 1609, landed at Cape May after narrowly escaping shipwreck. In 1623, Cornelius Jacobsen May, of the Dutch East India Company's fleet, rounded the south point of New Jersey, and, recognizing its geographical importance, named it after himself. The first European proprietors were Goodwyer and Bloemart, who purchased in 1629 what is now Cape May County, from nine Indian chiefs, Cape Island being included in the acquisition. In 1689 Doctor Cox, who obtained possession from the original proprietors, sold the island to William Jacocks and Humphrey Hughes; the latter person leaving a large posterity which still clings to the proprietary soil. These individuals held the title till 1700, tilling the land down to the water's edge. It is noted from the records that Cape May was a whaling colony two centuries ago, the period of greatest activity in this industry being from 1680 to 1715. Settlers came originally from Long Island. It is also recorded that British troops landed during the War of 1812. The town was bombarded by the British in 1814. Within the last thirty-five years Cape May has suffered much loss from fire, the last serious fire being that of 1878. Such disasters can not now occur, there being a first-rate fire department and a plentiful water supply.

Henry Clay visited Cape May in 1847, Franklin Pierce in 1855, Buchanan in 1866, Grant and his cabinet in 1873, Arthur in 1883, and Harrison in 1892. Other distinguished men who have lived there, or remained during parts of one or several seasons, were Horace Greeley, James A. Bayard of Delaware, Hannibal Hamlin, Governor Hendricks of Indiana, and James G. Blaine. Cardinal Gibbons visits Cape May every summer when in the United States.

Hotels.—Cape May can boast of having some of the finest and best hotels on the New Jersey coast. The reputation of the Stockton and of Congress Hall, in the matter of capacity and of first-rate accommodation for a large number of guests, is an enviable one throughout the United States, and that of the Windsor for coziness and comfort, is almost too well known to need repetition. As these three are without doubt or question among the best hotels of the first class, at any really select ocean resort from Maine to California, they are worthy of special mention.

Congress Hall is the only brick and practically fire-proof hotel on the Atlantic coast. It stands on the site of the original Congress

Hall, which was built nearly a century ago. The rooms are large, light, well equipped, and well ventilated. Several improvements have recently been introduced, including a new hydraulic passenger elevator and better sanitary arrangements. An electric light plant and furniture costing $40,000 have recently been put in. Concerts by a well-trained orchestra under Professor Hassler, and dancing in the capacious out-door pavilion, are prominent attractive features.

The Stockton, accommodating easily more than one thousand guests, is situated directly upon the beach front, with an extensive lawn running to the water's edge. It has been completely reorganized and re-decorated, and is now under the management of Mr. Horace M. Cake, of the Hotel Normandie, Washington, D. C., whose family has been long and favorably known to residents of and visitors to Cape May, in connection with hotels at this resort. Special features are the billiard room, bowling alley, ball-room, and orchestral music. Every department is under expert management, to insure good service. The Stockton is announced as being distinctly a family resort.

The Windsor, about one hundred feet from the beach, fronts on Beach Avenue. The location is excellent, and the method of construction so admirable that every guest receives the full benefit of good light, pure air, and an interesting view. The hotel is delightfully homelike in its furnishings and general equipment. Its patrons are quiet, cultivated people who desire rest, courteous treatment, the comforts of a well-served table, occasional music, and congenial companionship. All modern facilities are available. This house is open in spring, summer and autumn. There are several lofty sun-parlors. Steam-heat appliances have been perfected. The baths accommodate 200 persons.

Marine Villa, situated on the beach, is noted for its cuisine, which is of the finest. It is patronized by many leading railroad officials, representatives of foreign countries, public men, and their families. It has been under the same management for twenty-six years.

INDEX.

HOTEL MARLBOROUGH

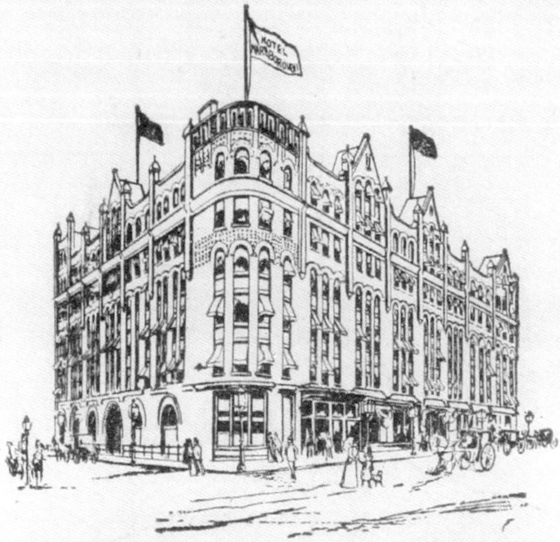

Broadway,
36th and 37th Sts.,
Herald Square,
New York.

UNDER
NEW MANAGEMENT.

Completely renovated and refurnished throughout.

The largest and most attractive LOBBY and ROTUNDA in New York has been newly opened up.

Special inducements to COMMERCIAL MEN with samples. Thirty large and well lighted SAMPLE ROOMS, with or without bath. Forty large front suites, with parlor, two bedrooms, and private bath; suitable for families or parties traveling together.

THE OLD ENGLISH GRILL ROOM

is an innovation. Unique and original.

THE GERMAN RATHSKELLER

is Broadway's greatest attraction for special food dishes and popular music.

EUROPEAN PLAN—Rates:

Single room, without bath, $1.50, $2.00, $2.50.

Single room, with bath, $2.00, $2.50, $3.00.

SUITES:

Parlor, bedroom, and bath, $3.00, $4.00, $5.00 per day.

Parlor, two bedrooms, and bath, private hall, $5.00, $6.00, $8.00 per day.

$1.00 extra where two persons occupy a single room.

Not a dark room in the house.

The hotel is of fireproof construction and the sanitation is first-class, as the building is modern and up-to-date.

SWEENEY-TIERNEY HOTEL COMPANY,

E. M. TIERNEY, Manager.

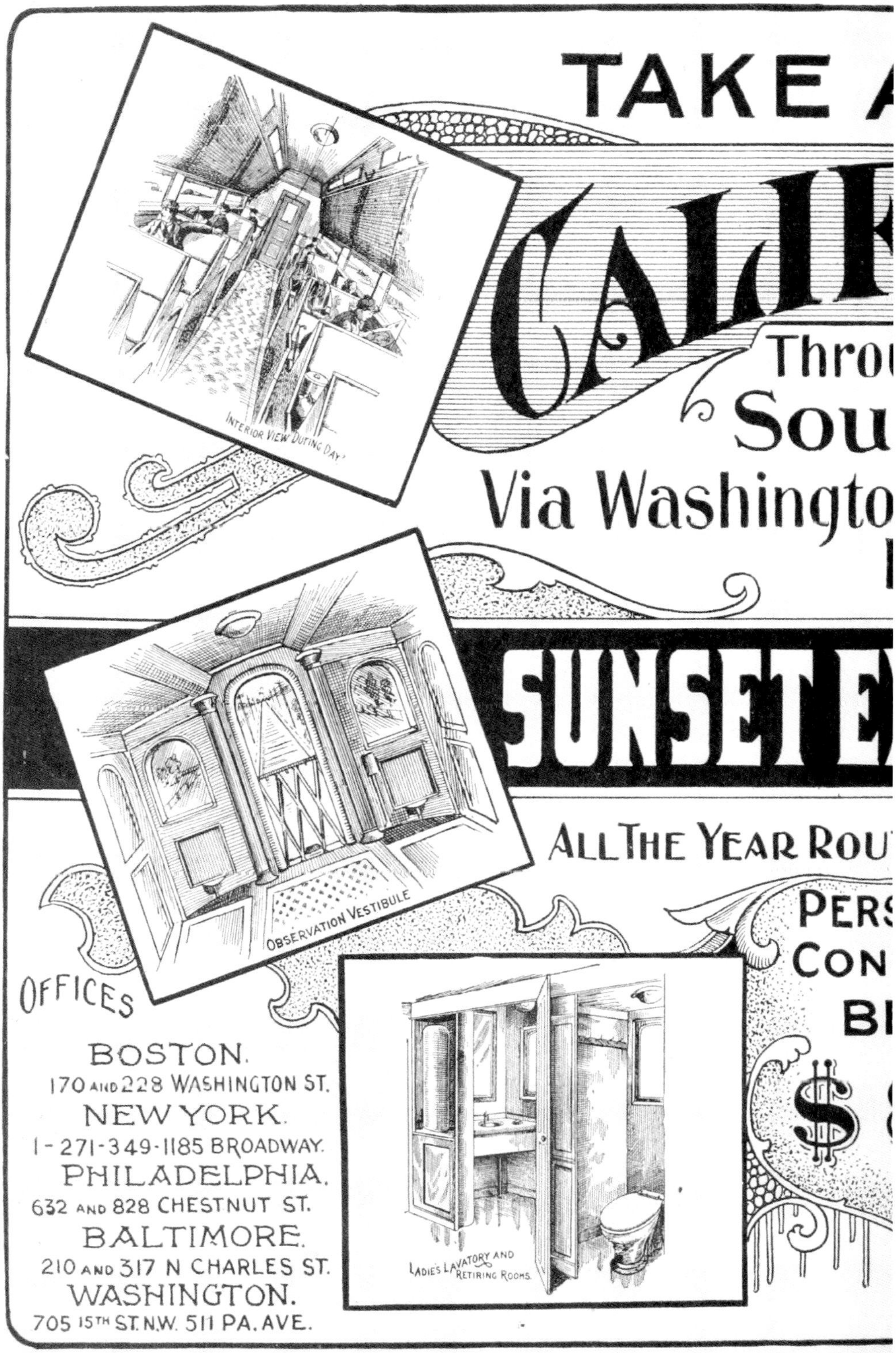
TAKE A
CALIF
Throu
Sou
Via Washingto
SUNSET E
ALL THE YEAR ROU
PERS
CON
BI
$ 8
INTERIOR VIEW DURING DAY
OBSERVATION VESTIBULE
LADIES' LAVATORY AND RETIRING ROOMS
OFFICES
BOSTON.
170 AND 228 WASHINGTON ST.
NEW YORK.
1-271-349-1185 BROADWAY.
PHILADELPHIA.
632 AND 828 CHESTNUT ST.
BALTIMORE.
210 AND 317 N CHARLES ST.
WASHINGTON.
705 15TH ST. N.W. 511 PA. AVE.

TRIP TO

ORNIA

n the

nland

San Francisco

ne.

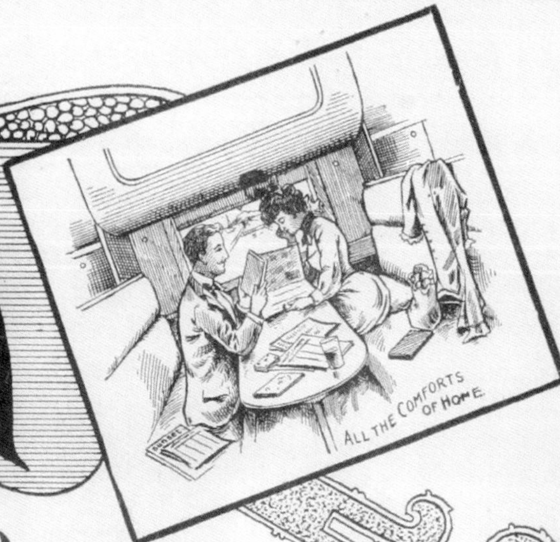

ALL THE COMFORTS OF HOME

CURSIONS

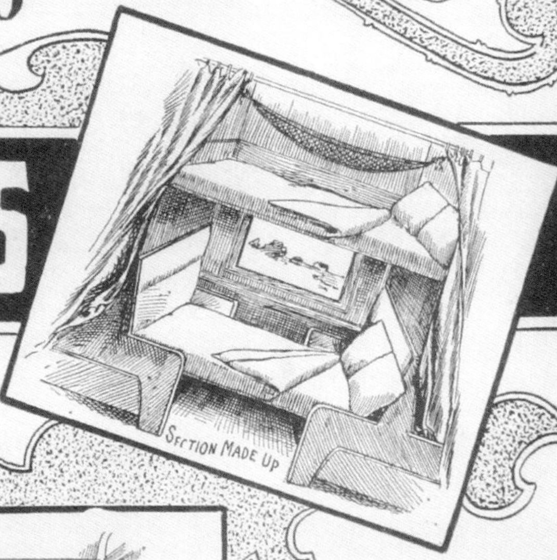

SECTION MADE UP

WITHOUT CHANGE.

ALLY

CTED

TH

50

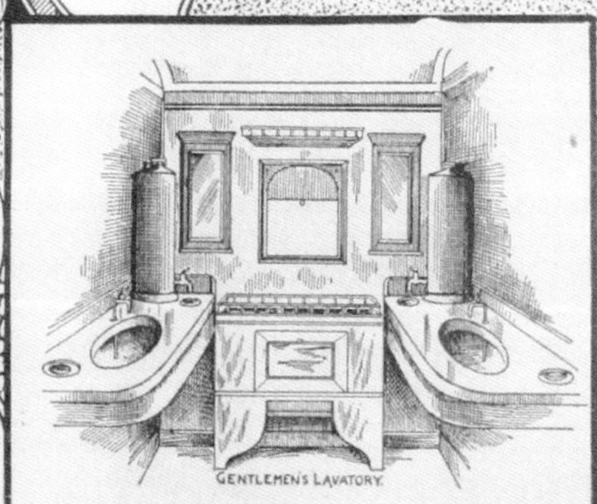

GENTLEMEN'S LAVATORY

L.H.NUTTING.
G.E.P.A. 349 BROADWAY
NEW YORK.

A.J.POSTON.
GENERAL AGENT
511 PENNA. AVE.
WASHINGTON, D.C.

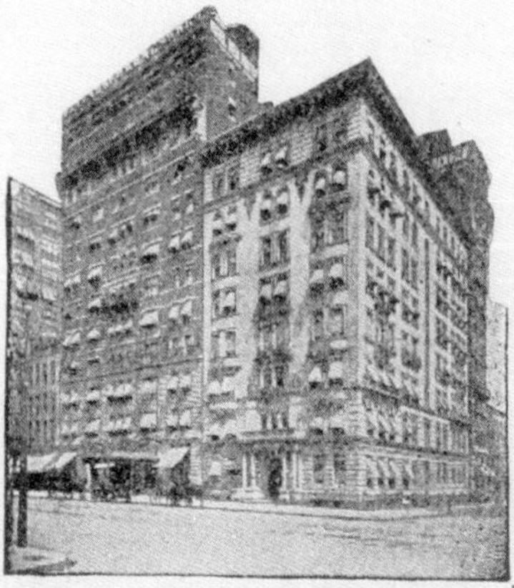

THE

WELLINGTON

7th Ave. and 55th St., NEW YORK

New, modern, fireproof. Shower baths. Long distance telephone in each room.

Room with bath, $2.00 per day. Room without bath, $1.50 per day.

RESTAURANT A LA CARTE

All Broadway cars pass the door.

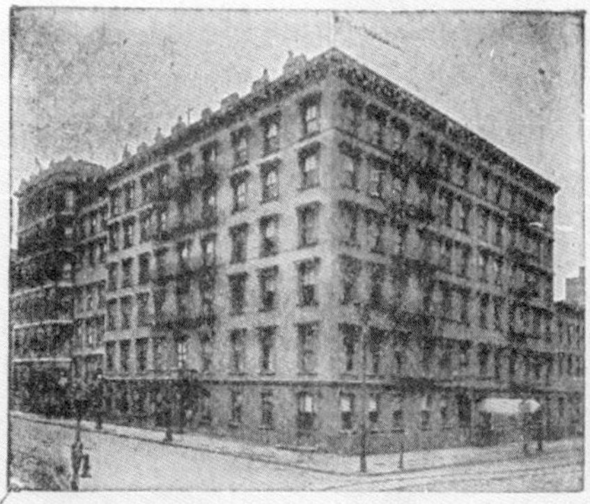

THE

WESTMINSTER

16th Street and Irving Place, NEW YORK

Entirely remodeled. New bathrooms and new plumbing throughout, telephone, steam heat, electric lights, open fires in every room.

Rates $1.00 per day and upward.

RESTAURANT A LA CARTE

MUSIC

A. W. EAGER

WRIGHT'S HOTEL

Corner Plain and Richardson Streets,

COLUMBIA, S. C.

A NEW HOTEL, with all modern conveniences, steam heat, and open fireplaces. Rooms en suite, with bath and toilet. Public baths and toilets on each floor. Large sample rooms.

CUISINE AND SERVICE FIRST CLASS

Rates: $2.50 to $4.00 per day Special rates by week

LETTERS OF INQUIRY PROMPTLY ANSWERED

W. C. WRIGHT, Proprietor

HOTEL HIGHLANDS

(NEW)

Ninety-first Street Near Lexington Ave. **New York**

Near Central Park Telephone 3131 79th

HIGH-CLASS HOUSE AT MODERATE RATES

Room, Bath, $1.00 per day, up; $5.00 per week, up Suites with Bath, $9.00 to $17.50 per week. Transients with board, $2.00 to $5.00 per day.

SPECIAL RATES WEEKLY OR SEASON

400 ROOMS
100 BATHROOMS
100 TELEPHONES

DELIGHTFUL ROOF GARDEN

To reach Hotel Highlands from Depots, Docks, Theatres, Shopping District, etc take Broadway-Lexington Ave. Trolley (free transfers from Crosstown Lines), or Third Ave. Trolley (similar transfers), or Third Ave. Elevated to 89th Street Station, (free transfer at Battery from Sixth and Ninth Ave. Elevated.)

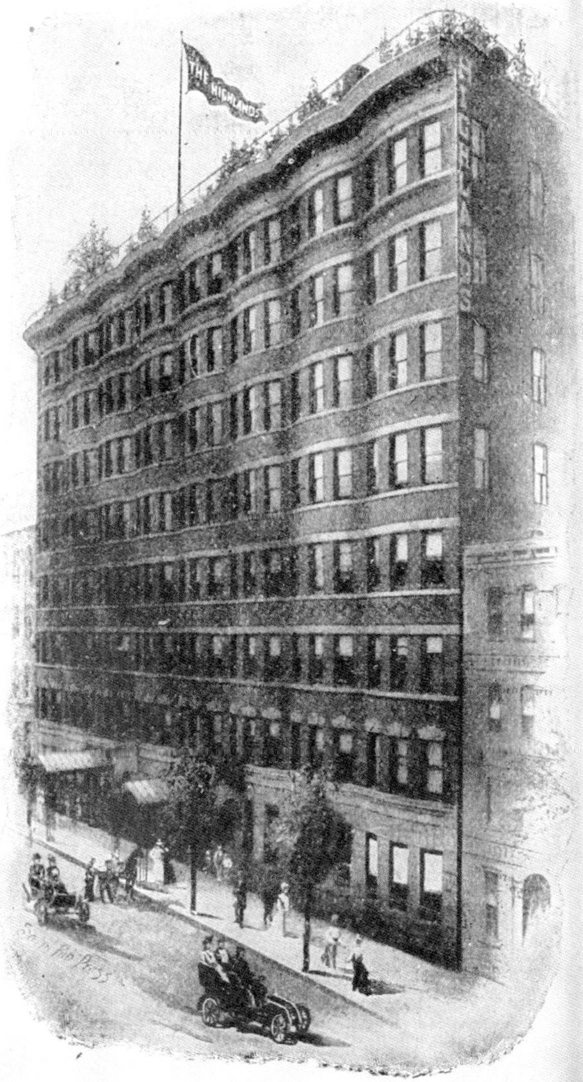

RIGGS HOUSE
WASHINGTON, D.C.

American Plan . . . .
$3.00
per day . .
and . . . . .
upwards .

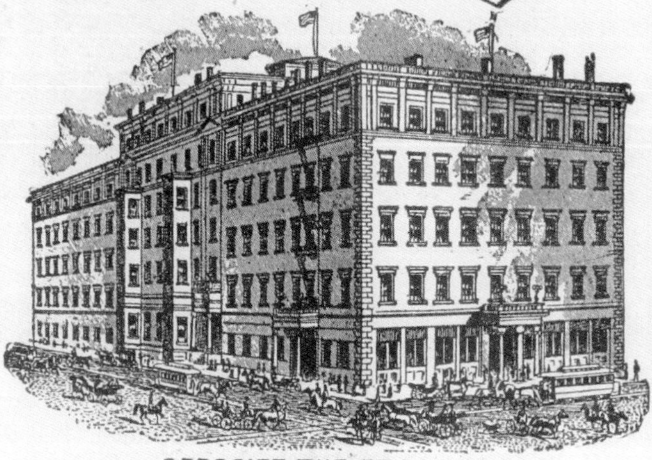

OPPOSITE THE TREASURY
ONE BLOCK FROM THE WHITE HOUSE

THE HOTEL PAR EXCELLENCE OF THE NATIONAL CAPITAL

Electric Cars pass the door to all parts of the city.
The most centrally located of any hotel in the city.

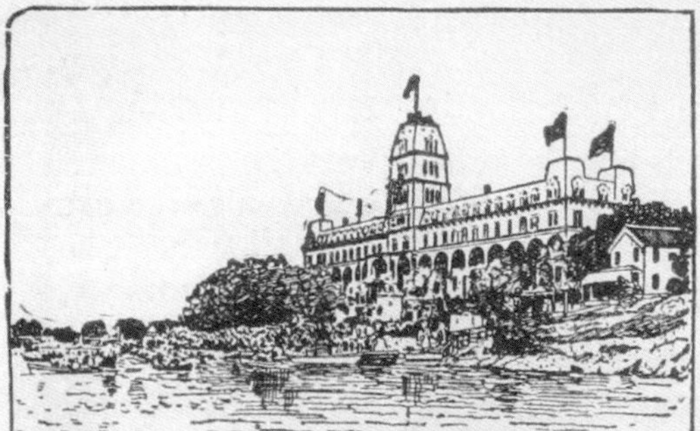

ALSO

Thousand Island House

ALEXANDRIA BAY,
N. Y.

AMERICA'S MOST BEAUTIFUL RESORT.

Send two 2-cent stamps for beautiful illustrated guide, to

O. G. STAPLES, Proprietor and Owner.

NATIONAL HOTEL

WASHINGTON, D. C.
Opposite Pennsylvania Railroad.

O. G. STAPLES, = = Proprieto

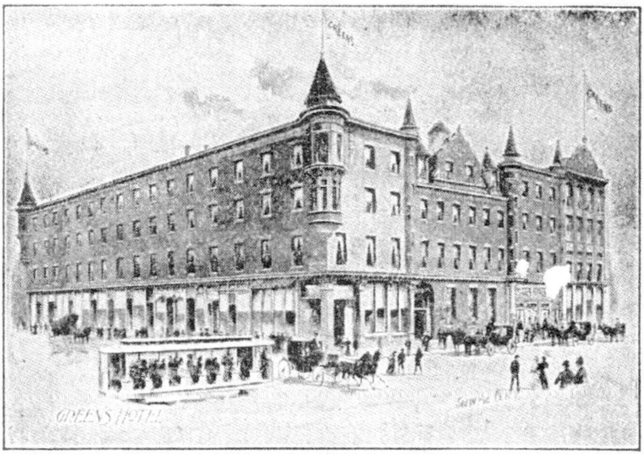

GREEN'S HOTEL

Corner Eighth and Chestnut Sts.,

PHILADELPHIA, PA.

FOR LADIES AND GENTLEMEN. **EUROPEAN PLAN.**

315 Rooms at $1.00 and $1.50 per Day and Upwards.

60 New Rooms with Bath Attached at $2.00 per Day.

FINEST RESTAURANT IN PHILADELPHIA.

ALL MODERN CONVENIENCES TELEPHONE IN ROOMS.

Table d'Hote Dinner 50 cents, from 12 m. to 8 p. m.

MUSIC BY PROFESSOR MEYER'S ORCHESTRA.

Eighth and Chestnut Street Trolley Cars pass the Hotel at the Rate of Three per Minute to all Parts of the City.

This hotel is centrally located, and in the very heart of the city, being but one square from the Postoffice, Strawbridge & Clothier's, Lit Brothers, and opposite Gimbel Brothers, and Partridge & Richardson, and easy of access to all Theaters, Railway Stations, Public Buildings, and Points of Interest.

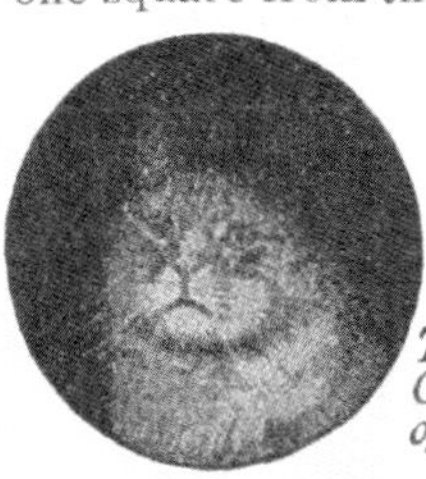

Tix,
Celebrated Angora Cat
of Green's Hotel

MAHLON W. NEWTON,
Proprietor.

POPULATION ON THESE MAPS GIVEN ACCORDING TO OFFICIAL CENSUS OF 1900.

Rand, McNally & Co.'s

LIST OF

INDEXED POCKET MAPS

Price, 25 Cents Each.

	Inches.
Alabama	21 x 28
Arizona Territory	14 x 21
Arkansas	21 x 28
British Columbia	21 x 14
California	21 x 28
Colorado	28 x 21
Connecticut	21 x 14
Delaware	21 x 14
Florida	28 x 21
Georgia	21 x 28
Idaho	14 x 21
Illinois	21 x 28
Indiana	21 x 28
Indian and Oklahoma Territories	28 x 21
Iowa	28 x 21
Kansas	28 x 21
Kentucky	36 x 18
Louisiana	28 x 21
Maine	14 x 21
Manitoba	21 x 14
Maryland	21 x 14
Massachusetts	28 x 21
Michigan	21 x 28
Minnesota	21 x 28
Mississippi	21 x 28
Missouri	28 x 21
Montana	21 x 14
Nebraska	28 x 21
Nevada	14 x 21
New Hampshire	14 x 21
New Jersey	14 x 21
New Mexico Territory	14 x 21
New York	42 x 28
North Carolina	28 x 21
North Dakota	21 x 14
Nova Scotia, N. Bruns. and Pr. Ed. Is.	21 x 14
Ohio	28 x 21
Ontario	28 x 21
Oregon	28 x 21
Pennsylvania	42 x 28
Quebec	28 x 21
Rhode Island	21 x 14
South Carolina	28 x 21
South Dakota	21 x 14
Tennessee	40 x 14
Texas	42 x 28
Utah	14 x 21
Vermont	14 x 21
Virginia	28 x 21
Washington	28 x 21
West Virginia	28 x 21
Wisconsin	21 x 28
Wyoming	21 x 14

VEST POCKET MAPS

Price, 15 Cents Each.

	Inches.
Alabama	21 x 28
Arizona Territory	14 x 21
Arkansas	21 x 28
British Columbia	21 x 14
California	21 x 28
Colorado	28 x 21
Connecticut and Rhode Island	21 x 14
Florida	28 x 21
Georgia	21 x 28
Idaho	14 x 21
Illinois	21 x 28
Indiana	21 x 28
Indian and Oklahoma Territories	28 x 21
Iowa	28 x 21
Kansas	28 x 21
Kentucky	36 x 18
Louisiana	28 x 21
Maine	14 x 21
Manitoba	21 x 14
Maryland and Delaware, in one book	21 x 14
Massachusetts	28 x 21
Michigan, Northern	28 x 21
" Southern	21 x 28
Minnesota	21 x 28
Mississippi	21 x 28
Missouri	28 x 21
Montana	21 x 14
Nebraska	28 x 21
Nevada	14 x 21
New Hampshire	14 x 21
New Jersey	14 x 21
New Mexico Territory	14 x 21
New York	42 x 28
North Carolina	28 x 21
North Dakota	21 x 14
Nova Scotia, N. Bruns., and Pr. Ed. Is.	21 x 14
Ohio	28 x 21
Ontario, Province of, Canada	28 x 21
Oregon	28 x 21
Pennsylvania	42 x 28
Quebec	28 x 21
South Carolina	28 x 21
South Dakota	21 x 14
Tennessee	40 x 14
Texas	42 x 28
Utah	14 x 21
Vermont	14 x 21
Virginia	28 x 21
Washington	28 x 21
West Virginia	28 x 21
Wisconsin	21 x 28
Wyoming	21 x 14
United States	28 x 21

CHICAGO and NEW YORK.

DRINK

DELICIOUS!

REFRESHING!

Coca-Cola

ALL SODA FOUNTAINS 5 CENTS PER GLASS

SPENCERIAN·STEEL·PENS ·ARE·THE·BEST·

DA·LOCUM·MELIORIBUS

TRADE·MARK

The Standard American Brand

(Established 1860)

THEY cost a trifle more than the common makes, but you get a Pen that will last longer and write better. A complete sample card—**42 Pens for 25 cents** or a card with selected numbers—**12 Pens for 10 cents** will be sent postpaid on receipt of price.

Spencerian Pen Co., 349 Broadway, New York City

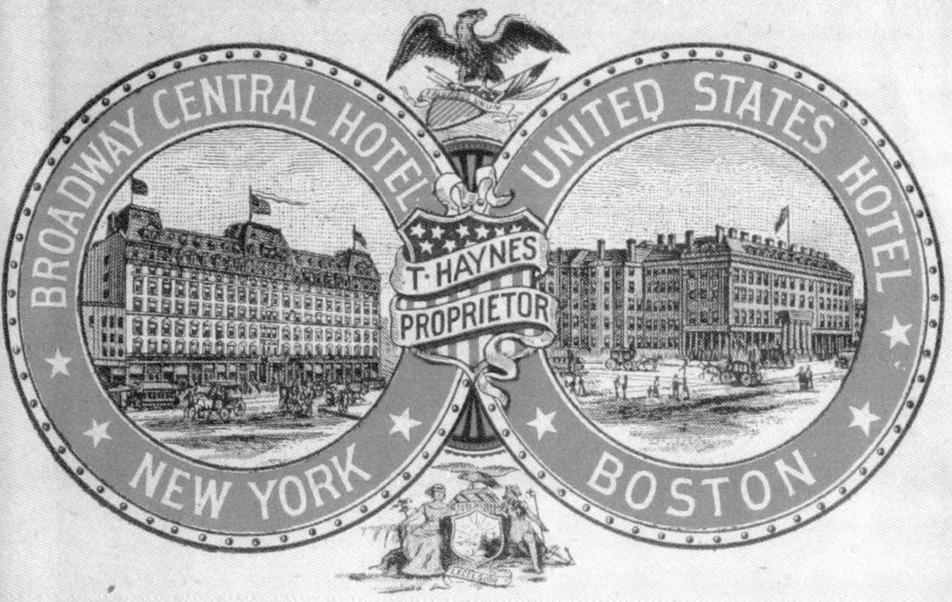

BROADWAY CENTRAL HOTEL

NOS. 667 TO 677 CORNER THIRD STREET. } **NEW YORK** { MIDWAY BETWEEN BATTERY AND CENTRAL PARK.

Has during the past five years been thoroughly rebuilt and completely reorganized at an expense of over a quarter of a million dollars, and is perfect in detail and unsurpassed in comfort and convenience. Recommends itself for its thoroughly careful management, its clean, well-kept rooms, admirable table and service, and reasonable charges.

LOCATION ABSOLUTELY UNEQUALED FOR BUSINESS, SIGHT-SEEING, AND PLEASURE.

All the New Rapid Transit Electric Lines passing the doors, run the entire length of Broadway from the Battery to Central Park, Grand Central R. R. Station, Lenox Avenue, Harlem River, High Bridge, and Grant's Tomb, passing all the fashionable stores, theatres, and principal attractions of the city.

GRAND CENTRAL DEPOT PASSENGERS CAN TAKE SUBWAY TRAINS TO BLEECKER STREET, one block from hotel, or **LEXINGTON AVENUE ELECTRIC CARS** one block east of the station, direct to or from the hotel to 42d Street, or Fourth Avenue cars direct to Astor Place or Bond Street, one block in front.

TWO LINES OF ELEVATED RAILROADS: Sixth Avenue Station, Bleecker Street, one block in the rear. Third Avenue Station, Houston Street, two blocks in front.

All cross-town cars transfer at Broadway with the electric lines, taking guests direct to the hotel.

Passengers arriving by any of the ferries, or either foreign or coastwise steamers, can take any cross-town car, or walk to Broadway and take electric cars direct to the hotel or via the Sixth or Third Avenue Elevated, stopping at Bleecker on Sixth Avenue, and Houston Street Station on Third Avenue line, three minutes from hotel.

THE CENTRAL WILL BE RUN ON BOTH THE AMERICAN AND EUROPEAN PLAN.

The Regular Tariff of Charges for each person will be

For Room only, - - - - - $1.00, $1.50, and $2.00
For Room and Board, - - - - $2.50, $3.00, and $3.50
For Single Meals, - - - - - - - - - - 75 cents
Meals, when taken with rooms, for full day, 50 cents each
Rooms with parlor or bath, extra
According to size, location, and convenience, and whether occupied by one or more persons.

SPECIAL RATES FOR FAMILIES OR PERMANENT GUESTS.

FOR FULL PARTICULARS, SEND FOR LARGE COLORED MAPS AND OTHER INFORMATION TO

UNITED STATES HOTEL, BOSTON.	**TILLY HAYNES,** PROPRIETOR. CABLE ADDRESS "TILLY."	BROADWAY CENTRAL HOTEL, NEW YORK.

PENN MUTUAL LIFE INSURANCE COMPANY

OF PHILADELPHIA

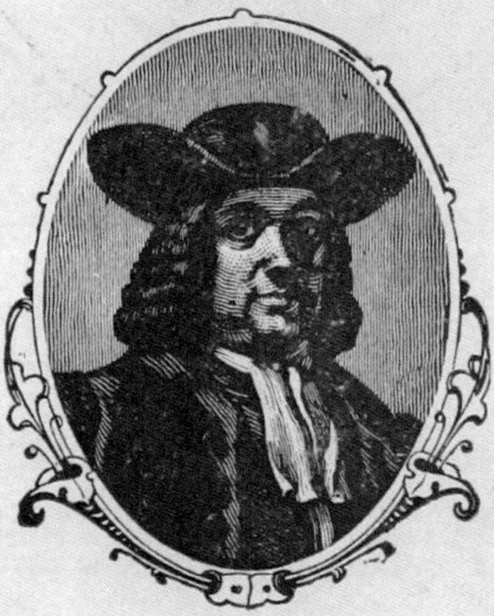

Your insurance should be adapted to your circumstances, age, and occupation.

If you need to emphasize protection you will buy a life policy.

If you wish to combine Saving and Investment with Insurance you will buy an Endowment Policy.

If you are advanced in years and wish to be relieved from financial care you will buy an Annuity Contract assuring you an annual income for life.

If you are undecided as to the kind of Policy, or if you do not now feel able to carry the kind you think you want, THE PENN MUTUAL has a low premium Policy well suited to your case. This contract enables you to start your insurance now, and to have your payments credited on any other policy you may wish to select later—the premium rate of the new Policy to be that of your present age.

FOR PARTICULARS, CALL UPON OR ADDRESS

PENN MUTUAL LIFE

921=3=5 Chestnut Street, PHILADELPHIA